# The Revolutionary Internationals, 1864-1943

Hoover Institution Publications

Edited by Milorad M. Drachkovitch

# The Revolutionary Internationals, 1864-1943

*Contributors*

Milorad M. Drachkovitch
Jacques Freymond
Carl Landauer
Branko Lazitch
Miklós Molnár
Boris I. Nicolaevsky
Gerhart Niemeyer
Max Nomad
Stefan T. Possony

*Published for the*
Hoover Institution on War, Revolution, and Peace
*by Stanford University Press, Stanford, California 1966*

The Hoover Institution on War, Revolution, and Peace, founded at Stanford University in 1919 by Herbert Hoover, is a center for advanced study and research on public and international affairs in the twentieth century. The views expressed in its publications are entirely those of the authors, and do not necessarily reflect the views of the Hoover Institution.

Stanford University Press, Stanford, California


Printed in the United States of America
L.C. 66-15299

# Preface

The essays collected in this volume are revised and expanded versions of papers and comments offered on the first day of an international scholarly gathering, a conference on "One Hundred Years of Revolutionary Internationals," organized by the Hoover Institution on War, Revolution, and Peace, and held on October 5, 6, and 7, 1964, at Stanford University. Papers presented on the second day of the conference have been published by Stanford University Press in a volume called *Marxism in the Modern World.* Papers from the third day of the conference will appear simultaneously with this volume in *Marxist Ideology in the Contemporary World: Its Appeals and Paradoxes,* published by Frederick A. Praeger, Inc.

The seven essays presented in this book are comparative historical studies of the three formally Marxist revolutionary Internationals and their onetime arch-competitor, the international anarchist movement. It is hoped that in their divergent approaches—and in the case of the Second International, their sharp disagreement—the authors of the present volume will introduce both the layman and the professional historian to new facets of an extremely complex historical phenomenon.

It is my sad duty to report that on the very day his essay was set in type, one contributor, Boris Nicolaevsky, suddenly died. In its originality and thoroughness, his article on "Secret Societies and the First International" stands with the best of his many contributions to the world of scholarship.

Finally, I should like to acknowledge the valuable assistance of Mrs. Muriel Davison of Stanford University Press in giving the volume its final form.

M. M. D.

March 15, 1966

# Contents

# Contributors

MILORAD M. DRACHKOVITCH is a Senior Staff Member of the Hoover Institution on War, Revolution, and Peace, and Lecturer in the Department of Political Science at Stanford University. He previously served as Director of Studies at the College of Europe in Bruges. He is the author of *Les Socialismes français et allemand et le problème de la guerre, 1870–1914* (1953), *De Karl Marx à Léon Blum* (1954), and *U.S. Aid to Yugoslavia and Poland* (1964), and the editor of *Marxism in the Modern World* (1965).

JACQUES FREYMOND is Professor of International History at the University of Geneva and Director of the Graduate Institute of International Studies in Geneva. He is the author of *Lénine et l'impérialisme* (1951), *Le Conflit sarrois, 1945–1955* (1959), *La Première Internationale* (1962), and *Western Europe Since the War* (1964), and editor of *Etudes et documents sur la Première Internationale en Suisse* (1964).

CARL LANDAUER was born and educated in Germany, and taught at the School of Business Administration in Berlin from 1926 to 1933. For a time he was active in the German Social Democratic Party. A Professor of Economics at the University of California at Berkeley since 1936, he became emeritus in 1959 but continues to teach. His writings include *Theory of National Economic Planning* (1947), *European Socialism* (1959), and *Contemporary Economic Systems* (1964).

BRANKO LAZITCH, a French scholar of Serbian origin, is a graduate of the University of Geneva. He is an editor of the Paris review *Est & Ouest* and lectures occasionally at various European universities. He is the author of *Lénine et la Troisième Internationale* (1951), *Les Partis communistes d'Europe, 1919–1955* (1956), and *Tito et la révolution yougoslave, 1937–1956* (1957).

MIKLÓS MOLNÁR was a journalist, a literary critic, and editor of the *Literary Gazette* in Budapest until the 1956 uprising. He is now Associate Professor of History at the Graduate Institute of International Studies in Geneva. He is the author of *Jozef Katona* (1952) and *Le Déclin de la Première Internationale* (1963) and co-author (with László Nagy) of *Imre Nagy: Réformateur ou révolutionnaire?* (1959).

BORIS I. NICOLAEVSKY was Curator of the Menshevik collection at the Hoover Institution. An active member of the Russian Social Democratic Party, he became Director of the Moscow Marx-Engels Institute after the revolution of 1917. Deported from Russia in 1922, he later became Director of the International Institute of Social History in Amsterdam. He is the author of *Aseff, the Spy, Russian Terrorist, and Police Stool* (1934) and *Power and the Soviet Elite* (1965), and co-author (with Otto Maenchen-Helfen) of *Karl Marx: Man and Fighter* (1936).

GERHART NIEMEYER is Professor of Government at the University of Notre Dame. He has taught at Princeton and Yale Universities, and has served on the faculty of the National War College. He is the author of *An Inquiry into Soviet Mentality* (1956) and *Facts on Communism, Volume I: The Communist Ideology* (1959), and co-editor of *Handbook on Communism* (1962).

MAX NOMAD, a political exile from his native Austria since 1904, has been in turn a smuggler, typesetter, metalworker, underground propagandist, journalist, and lecturer at New York University and the New School for Social Research. His most recent books are *Aspects of Revolt* (1961), *Apostles of Revolution* (rev. ed., 1961), *Political Heretics from Plato to Mao* (1963), and *Dreamers, Dynamiters, and Demagogues* (1964).

STEFAN T. POSSONY is Director of the International Political Studies program at the Hoover Institution. He was Professor of International Politics at Georgetown University from 1946 to 1961, and has been a visiting professor at the Universities of Pennsylvania and Cologne. His books include *Strategic Air Power* (1949), *A Century of Conflict* (1953), and *Lenin, the Compulsive Revolutionary* (1964).

Milorad M. Drachkovitch

# Introduction

"Socialism is a word the connotation of which varies, not only from generation to generation, but from decade to decade." This observation of R. H. Tawney is particularly applicable to the three nominally Marxist Internationals whose divergent destinies are described and analyzed in the essays that follow.

Marxist revolutionary internationalism, which took organizational form with the creation of the International Workingmen's Association in 1864, was at once the heir to an old historical tradition and the begetter of a new political movement. Its roots can be traced to the revolutionary messianism of medieval and Reformation Europe, and, closer to our time, to the message of 1789 and the effects of the industrial revolution. The words of the Babouvist *Manifeste des égaux,* written in 1796, "The French Revolution is the precursor of another, more magnificent revolution, which will be the last," found an eager echo in many quarters half a century later, when another *Manifesto* re-issued the same battle cry, more meaningful now because of the transformation of Western Europe by the growth of industry.

The First International began its militant life with a twofold aim, which was the only real link between the First International and the Second and Third: to unite the proletariat of all countries under a single banner, and to destroy the system of private property. But if the three Internationals could invoke the same precursors and pursue the same ends, everything else was there to make the history of each of them distinct. Their divergence may be attributed to the following three factors: the basically dissimilar national and international conditions in which each International was born and had to act; fundamental disagreements on the problems of organization and tactics; and differences of personality and temperament among the leaders of the different Internationals. One might say that the First International was dominated by the ideas of one *man,* Karl Marx; the Second by the experience of one *party,* German Social Democracy; and the Third by the existence of one *state,* Bolshevik Russia. Marx's own ideas, or more precisely their fundamental ambiguity, contributed to both the rise and the collapse of the First International; they were interpreted in radically different ways by the German Social Democrats, led by August Bebel, and by the Russian Bolsheviks, under the iron guidance of Lenin.

Probably the most arresting findings of this book relate to the First International, whose internal history weighed heavily on its successors. Marx's vacillation between flexible decentralization and rigid centralism ultimately contributed not only to the downfall of the International Workingmen's Association (IWA), but also to the espousal of different roads by the Second and Third Internationals. Let us outline briefly the historical consequences of these shifts. According to Boris Nicolaevsky, the novelty of the IWA lay in the fact that it was "born out of the struggle against the old methods of political conspiracy and secret organizations." If Marx and Engels agreed to join the IWA, it was because they thought it represented the "real forces of the workers," and so wanted to join and ultimately to lead "the real representatives of the working class." The slogan Marx took over from Proudhon, "the emancipation of the working class should be the work of the working class itself," meant in concrete terms that the workers should build mass political parties and organize labor unions. Open workers' organizations were to replace the small groups of revolutionary conspirators. The essay by Jacques Freymond and Miklós Molnár shows the diversity of the IWA's origins and the heterogeneity of its composition, which Marx and Engels consciously tolerated during the first seven years of the IWA's existence. Similarly, Nicolaevsky opens his essay with the statement that the inner life of the First International in its early years consisted essentially of the "struggle between the members and allies of [secret] societies on the one hand, and Karl Marx and his working-class supporters on the other." And Max Nomad demonstrates that Bakunin's document *Organization,* the 1866 charter of his secret "International Brotherhood," was the organizational antithesis of the IWA.

This was, however, only a half of the story. Freymond and Molnár show that in 1871, at a conference of the IWA's General Council in London, Marx suddenly abandoned his earlier flexibility and pragmatism and had adopted "resolutions of hitherto unthinkable rigidity" on organizational, political, and ideological questions. The powers of the General Council were extended, and the toleration of the autonomy of the IWA's individual sections ended. But the attempt to make the First International "monolithic" by purging Bakunin and his followers, although superficially successful, was one of the key factors in the IWA's demise.

The two faces of Marx's leadership of the First International can easily be detected in its successors. While they disagree on many points in their interpretation of the historical role of the Second International, Gerhart Niemeyer and Carl Landauer agree that one of its basic characteristics was its desire to represent the entire working class. The "unity principle" of the International meant, as Niemeyer argues, that the revisionists and reformists remained in the same party as the "orthodox" or revolutionary Marxists. Thus the Second International came to resemble the First in its early years, when so many non-Marxist tendencies flourished in a body led by Marx himself.

And yet, just at the time—around the turn of the century—when the Second International was losing, as Landauer remarks, its Marxist "elitism," one of its members, Lenin, came to the conclusion that the revolution could be achieved only if an elite corps of professional revolutionaries (intellectuals of bourgeois origin, alienated from their social milieu and masters of Socialist theory) led the proletariat to the barricades. This central idea, formulated in 1902 in Lenin's pamphlet *What Is To Be Done?* was the ideological birth certificate of the Third International, which came to life officially 17 years later. But the most interesting aspect of this paradoxical process was that Lenin's concept of the International bore a striking resemblance to Bakunin's design for the International Brothers. As Nomad points out, Bakunin's key document, *Organization,* distinguished between the "International Family," a central, policy-making organ, and the "National Families," the local sections in each country that would be subject to "absolute and exclusive control" of the International family. "*Organization,*" writes Nomad, "was an anticipation of Lenin's and Stalin's methods under an anarchist guise," while Leninism represented "a hybrid of Bakuninist activism and Marxist terminology."

Each International had a life of its own, and was to a large extent conditioned by the historical and socio-political environment in which it was born and within which it had to struggle to survive. Freymond and Molnár note that the whole period of the First International was one of prosperity in Europe, which explains why the labor movement as such was evolutionary in outlook, and not revolutionary, a fact that Marx himself alluded to in his Inaugural Address to the IWA. The same was even truer of the period of the Second International. In both cases Marxist revolutionary dialectics had a hard time adapting to the political and socio-economic order of pre-1914 Europe, which the Socialist parties at once participated in and rebelled against. The official pronouncements of the Second International corresponded neither to the real feelings and situation of the working class, nor to the International's ability to carry out the radical injunctions of its resolutions. Bebel's angry reply at the 1911 congress of the German Social Democrats to the French and English Socialists, who wanted to impose on the unwilling Germans the decisions of the Stuttgart and Copenhagen congresses of the International, indicates better than anything else that the International was essentially a consultative political body, without either the means or the collective will to put its theories into practice: "Well, it is your business to decide and you may decide whatever you want, but we, the Germans, will not be a part of it!"

Lenin's Third International was established as a complete departure from the Second International and a protest against its practices. But before the Third International could become what it became, the cataclysm of World War I had to shatter every foundation of the pre-1914 European order, including the Second International. Lenin's creation was one of the typical consequences of the totally new postwar world; particularly in its earliest phase, it reflected the turbulent political and social realities as faithfully as the Second International had the Victorian and Bismarckian world and its afterglow. Still, if Lenin execrated the Second International for its failures and its betrayal of the world revolution, his own International did not fare much better, and its destiny was no less different from the intentions of its founders. As the two essays of this book on the Comintern demonstrate, the Third International failed in its central mission—to revolutionize the world—and in the process became the sorry tool of Stalin's foreign policy. Lenin's most trusted revolutionary offspring died strangled at the hands of Lenin's heir.

Still, the nominally Marxist revolutionary movement continued after 1943; it was at a time when no formal International existed that the Communists achieved two of their most significant successes: the seizure of power in China, and the adoption of "Marxism-Leninism" by the leader of the Cuban revolution, Fidel Castro. Moreover, as if to confirm R. H. Tawney's words quoted earlier, the recent emergence of polycentric Communism points to a new historical phase for the protean movement that began its official life a hundred years ago. What lies ahead may be better assessed if we reflect on the portraits of its historical antecedents presented in the essays that follow.

# The First International

Jacques Freymond and Miklós Molnár

# The Rise and Fall of the First International

In the general social and intellectual history of the last century, the First International occupies only a modest place. Its history can be described in terms of a few sporadically active local sections, of congresses and conferences with faint repercussions, of quickly forgotten manifestos and tracts and short-lived newspapers. Still, the First International created quite a stir. It aroused the anxieties of both factory owners and heads of states when strikes, which at times reached epidemic proportions, were organized under its banner. The Paris Commune—in which the International was mistakenly considered to have had a decisive influence—caused not only the French bourgeoisie but all of Europe to shake in its boots. At the Gastein, Salzburg, and Berlin meetings, where a system of alliances between the emperors of Russia, Austria-Hungary, and Germany was being consolidated, Gortshakov, Andrassy, and even Bismarck discussed the dangers created by the International and considered taking radical measures against it. The name of a certain Dr. Marx, hitherto unknown outside the small circles of militant revolutionaries and political police, was beginning to arouse their interest.

This interest was somewhat belated. The formidable Dr. Marx had withdrawn to his study by 1872 to conclude *Das Kapital.* At the close of the Hague Congress of the First International in 1872, its General Council had transferred its headquarters to New York. The local sections, after a period of great activity, were losing members. The divided, strife-torn International was dying. A few sparks flickered here and there, in Italy, in Spain. The first systematic attempt to unite the proletariat of all countries under a single banner had failed to build on its early successes.

Nevertheless, the experiment yielded much information, the value of which those who claim to be its heirs may not fully appreciate. There is an underlying continuity in the history of the international workers' movement that is concealed by superficial discontinuity. The changes wrought in the structure of international society over the last century have not affected the basic problems facing leaders of the international socialist movement. Today, as before, powerful figures compete for worldwide pre-eminence, conflicts arise from differences in national character and national circumstances, tactics and methods are disputed. The conflict between reformists and revolutionaries, between British trade unionists, Proudhonists, Mazzinists, and Blanquists, which culminated in the clash between the titanic figures of Marx and Bakunin, contained the seeds of the great battles of the twentieth century among the standard-bearers of international Socialism. The fate of the First International, like those of the Second and the Third, was affected by the social setting in which it tried to exert its influence, and by the changes taking place on both the national and the international scene. As an example, take the controversy aroused by the relations of some of the founders of the International with the French government, the consequences of the Franco-Prussian War, or the shock produced by the Commune.

It is just this contemporary character of the First International that makes its history both fascinating and difficult to narrate. Everyone is tempted to interpret it according to a particular concept of Socialism. For some, Marx is the incarnation of the International. Others, less numerous, see it in the light of Bakunin's influence or Proudhon's ideas. Though one hundred years have elapsed since the St. Martin's Hall meeting at which the International Workingmen's Association was founded, feelings about it are still so intense that the historian may find himself caught up in an unwelcome controversy, denounced by some and cheered by others. Another difficulty is that both public and private archives have been scattered. Worse yet, the study of the First International involves not only the history of social ideas and social facts, but also the history of states and of international relations. Since we do not yet have at our disposal all the necessary elements for a synthesis, we will have to content ourselves with a state-of-the-art report on the question. This study aims to add to the published documents and studies the partial results of research in progress; it does not claim to present definitive answers, but rather to sketch the most promising lines of approach.[1]

### *The Complex Origins of the First International*

The circumstances surrounding the creation of the International Workingmen's Association (IWA) are fairly well known. Nevertheless, as soon as we look into them closely, we find conflicting evidence to be taken into account. In the eyes of the French participants in the St. Martin's Hall meeting, on September 28, 1864, the initiative came from Paris. They consider the starting point of the undertaking the impression made on them by their 1862 visit to the London world's fair and their meetings with the British trade unionists.[2] George Howell's opinion was diametrically opposed to theirs. "The Exhibition of 1862 had nothing whatever to do with its inception," he wrote. " 'The brat was [not] born in Paris,' as a very pretentious writer has declared."[3] Others claimed that the IWA was Marx's personal creation, although Marx himself denied this. Indeed, however influential Marx may have been from the very start of the Association, at the time of its constituent assembly, his role was, as he himself said, that of a silent spectator. And even if some London trade unions did exchange letters with the Neapolitan General Workers' Association, even if Mazzini was represented at the September 1864 meeting, the initiative still belonged to a handful of Frenchmen and Englishmen. After preliminary contacts were made in 1862, a meeting in support of Polish independence was organized on July 22, 1863. This meeting served as a point of departure for an exchange of views between the French delegation, which included Henri Tolain, a metal cutter, a mechanic named André Murat, and a bronze worker named Joseph-Etienne Perrachon, and the British trade unionists, among them George Potter and George Odger. The discussion, which covered ways in which the workers of different countries could join forces, was followed by the publication of an appeal by British workers to French workers. Tolain then proposed, through the intermediary

[1] Numbered notes will be found at the back of the book, pp. 225–47.—Editor.

of Victor Le Lubez, a Frenchman living in London, the convening of an international congress. A republican named Henri Lefort, who was planning a trip to London at the time of Garibaldi's highly acclaimed visit, shortly thereafter offered his services, and they were accepted.

What took place during the five months between Lefort's trip and the meeting of September 28? In truth, we know little about it. Lefort and Le Lubez apparently were conducting the negotiations with the British trade unionists without reporting back to Tolain. Their attitudes are at the bottom of a long quarrel with Tolain, from which Tolain emerged victorious thanks to the support of the General Council. The ups and downs of this affair were recounted by Max Nettlau, in his "Zur Vorgeschichte der Internationale."[4] If we return to the sources, notably the correspondence between Lefort, Le Lubez, Pierre Vésinier, and others in the archives of the International Institute for Social History in Amsterdam, we find considerable evidence that Lefort and his friends were acting not out of personal vanity, but out of as much disinterested enthusiasm as Tolain. Lefort, in an unpublished 17-page letter, undated but presumably written in 1865, appealed to the London Committee, accused E. E. Fribourg (a friend of Tolain's who had attacked him) of jealousy, and declared his willingness to go to London whenever his going would serve the International, his offspring, for which he felt a purely disinterested love. He wished only to save the honor of the International from those who were threatening it.

Was the group around Tolain justified in accusing its opponents of vanity, lies, and intrigues? Or were Lefort, Le Lubez, and their somewhat obscure ally Vésinier right to question Tolain's sincerity and accuse him of conniving with certain circles at the court of Napoleon III?

The present state of our knowledge does not permit a definite answer to this question. Vésinier's often-reiterated accusations against Tolain are based primarily on the undeniable fact that Armand Lévy, the editor of *Espérance,* a newspaper published in Geneva, and of a series of "workers' pamphlets," between 1860 and 1862 tried to arrange a rapprochement between the liberal circles at court—mainly Prince Napoleon—and representatives of the labor movement. In particular Vésinier claimed that around 1861, Lévy contacted him (Vésinier) and his friends, to seek their support for Napoleon III's government on the basis of its sympathy for the workers. Vésinier claimed that he and his friends turned down the offer with the statement that they distrusted the government and were determined to attack it.[5] Yet in 1862 Tolain accepted the government's offer to finance the workers' trip to the London Exhibition!

To jump from these few facts to the farfetched conclusion that the midwife—even by indirection—of the International was no other than Armand Lévy, seconded by Jérôme Bonaparte and the Emperor himself, would mean following too circuitous a path over too uncertain a territory. As for Lévy, David Riazanov proved that his relationship with Tolain was no more permanent than was his influence with the authorities.[6] In fact, Lévy vainly asked for permission to transfer the paper *Espérance* from Geneva to Paris, as we learn from the very interesting documents published by Edmund Silberner in the Amsterdam *International Review for Social History*.[7] It seems to us equally farfetched to trace the origins of the International to the 1860 trade agreement between France and Great Britain, a pact that was hailed by the Neo-Saint-Simonians, among them Arlès Dufour. It seems more reasonable to us to attribute the birth of the International to the convergence of a number of factors and circumstances than to any particular intrigue, person, trade agreement, or trade-union claim.

The special interest of the Tolain-Lefort affair does not lie in trying to determine which of the two groups might more justly claim to have fathered the International. What does interest the historian is the emergence, behind the façade of personal disagreements, of two rival tendencies—one is almost tempted to say two pressure groups. In a study on the founding of the IWA published 16 years ago,[8] we said it was impossible to know whether Freemasonry had had a hand in it. Subsequent research has not resolved the question. However, on the basis of the unpublished correspondence of Vésinier and Le Lubez, it is reasonable to assume that a group of masons took an interest in the IWA, and that they may have tried to supplant Tolain's group.

In any event, some members of the IWA, among them Emile

Holtorp and probably also Le Lubez, belonged to the Concorde Masonic Lodge, a branch of the Universal Rite founded in London in 1857. In August 1865, Vésinier was invited to undergo the Lodge's initiation rituals.[9] An undated and illegibly signed letter implies that Vésinier was also invited to a meeting convened in order to set up, once and for all, as the letter expresses it, "the communalist revolutionary lodge." Further research is necessary to clarify the role of the French refugees in London who were organized as early as 1852 in a group called La Commune Révolutionnaire. Under several different names, this organization was to play an important role in the IWA's affairs.* It now seems clear that this group of French émigrés, particularly the masons among them, must be reckoned among the precursors of the International.

However, it is as difficult for the historian to measure the influence of this or that "precursor" as it is for him to disentangle the web of special interests and intrigues that led certain businessmen and politicians in France and England to support the international workers' organizations. The detailed study of various public and secret societies acting on an international scale makes a valuable contribution to our understanding of the IWA's origins. We must mention here the study by Theodor Rothstein, of the Association of Fraternal Democrats; by Arthur Mueller-Lehning on "The International Association"; and, above all, the enlightening studies of David Riazanov.[10] Riazanov would have one believe that the true precursor of the International was the Communist League, the first Communist organization, which, in his words, "coined the battle-cry of the international union of the working class: 'Workers of the world, unite!' "[11] Rothstein goes back even further, to 1845, the year in which the association of Fraternal Democrats was founded: "It was the first international organization of the working class, in a sense the precursor of the International."[12] Mueller-Lehning believes that "the International Association, which existed in London from 1855 to 1859 . . . is to be regarded as the first international organization of a proletarian and socialist character."[13] There are as many precursors of the International as there are authors in the field.

* For a detailed discussion of the role of masonic sects in the founding of the First International—with which we are not in complete agreement—see the essay by Boris I. Nicolaevsky, "Secret Societies and the First International," pp. 36–56 below.

The same holds true for the different theories of the IWA's ideological ancestry. Marxist historians and theoreticians take as their starting point the undeniable fact that Marx gradually won out over all his opponents—the followers of Mazzini, Proudhon, and Blanqui, as well as the anarchists—and from this they deduce that the International Workingmen's Association was the legitimate child of the author of *Das Kapital*. But is not this thesis at least partially invalidated by the fact that the followers of Mazzini and Proudhon, later removed from the General Council under Marx's leadership, were much more active in the founding of the International than Marx himself? What is more, all these factions, from Proudhonism to Bakunin's anarchism, maintained their influence over a large number of sections even in the face of successive defeats. Far from descending from an isolated precursor, far from being the spiritual child of a single intellectual current, the International from the very start was "characterized by the diversity of its origins and of the preoccupations and temperaments of the men who founded it."[14]

The place of the International in history was the result of a temporary convergence of different interests. The "New Model" British trade unionists, conscious of the strength and prestige their recent successes had earned them but at the same time anxious not to compromise themselves by any risky undertaking, were in close touch with political developments. They supported the efforts of the Reform League. They kept close watch over events on the Continent. But they were mainly preoccupied with economic issues, and their ambitions were limited to their profession. In their eyes, the usefulness of the International Workingmen's Association was measured by its ability to prevent the importation of strikebreakers to England.

The French workers who looked beyond the borders of their country could not claim to be as well-organized or experienced as their British counterparts. Though granted the right to strike in 1864, they were to wait another twenty years for the right of association. But they had a revolutionary tradition to draw on, and a stock of ideas accumulated by social theorists in the first half of the nineteenth century. Some were followers of Blanqui. Others, particularly those who were active in the founding of the International, were consciously or unconsciously guided by Proudhon, who was at that very moment proclaiming his faith in the political potential of the working class. Everything encouraged the French working class to act: the social tensions created by rapid structural transformations in the economy; the vacillations of the government between authoritarianism and the desire to reach out to the people; the incoherent policy of the employer class, urged on by the profit motive and the threat of competition from England resulting from the 1860 trade agreement and incapable of adopting a conciliatory position toward labor. But what form should this action take? Should one venture into the political arena? Side with the republicans against the imperial regime? Concentrate instead on the improvement of the working-class lot? The workers were uncertain. Mutualism, the expression of their naïve belief in the innate goodness of man, was too vague to serve as a basis for the effective transformation of social structures. The creation of an international association offered them both an escape from the political and social crises resulting from the industrial revolution and the weakening of the Second Empire and an opportunity to find outside France the models and support they needed.

And yet, the International cannot be viewed simply as a Franco-British dialogue. The appeal sent in 1861 by Neapolitan workers to their English comrades demonstrates the development of working-class consciousness among Italian workers, too. It is true that for the Italians, political objectives—unity and liberty for Italy—were the primary goals. But they also requested support for "the organization of work." The International was thus carried along by a ground swell that was felt in all of Europe, a product of the combined impact of two revolutions, the French revolution and the industrial revolution. Under the impetus of continuing technological change, the International took up the unfinished business of 1848, extending it to reflect the new balance of revolutionary forces. The questioning of the social order had become more specific, more imperious. The "democratic" bourgeois who took part in the launching of the IWA could not ignore for long the fact that beyond the demands for political rights lay an attack on the whole system of private property and that the International was asserting its working-class and Socialist character.

The technological revolution that promoted the emancipation of the toiling masses also made it possible to coordinate action on an international scale. The convergence of interests alone cannot explain the fact that hitherto scattered and even divergent forces managed for a decade to take their lead from a single center and to merge their differences in it. The marked progress after 1848 in transportation and communications should not be overlooked as a contributing factor. Although this is a well-established fact, it must be taken into account at a time when historians are seeking to understand why and how the first international workers' organization was created and organized. It is noteworthy that on September 4, 1870, Edouard Vaillant and Charles Longuet, heading for the Corderie du Temple, stopped at a post office to send Marx and others telegrams with this terse message: "Republic proclaimed, act!" And it is well known that Marx, residing in London, was able to make his influence felt only through the ceaseless efforts of emissaries of the General Council, to maintain contact with the sections.

The International was the child of a period in which technical progress and the growth of industry expanded both the economic and the political horizon. However, such generalizations tend to be misleading, and it must be remembered that in 1872 some men who had contributed to launching the undertaking condemned it as premature. We agree with Georges Duveau, who took issue with the argument of Albert Thomas and others that "The Socialist movement of the Second Empire was an outgrowth of economic developments." Duveau held that while the workers' state of mind did depend to a large extent on their material situation, it does not follow that "the industrial situation determines the moral and ideological climate." "The industrial climate of the Second Empire," as Duveau put it, "contributed a certain tension to the lives of the workers, but . . . it did not generate a new light."[15]

## *The Establishment of the International in Europe*

The International, the outgrowth of a revolutionary century, was born amidst confusion. The men who gathered in London for the most part had only a very hazy notion about the "international organization" of which they spoke. Of course they had no trouble agreeing on the need for such an organization, but that was as far as they could go. If this was true of the handful of men constituting the original leadership of the IWA, it was still more true of the different societies and groups that formed the body of the International. If the men gathered in London were shaped by different influences and traditions, if they had only a vague notion of what their international association should be, this was true to an even greater extent of the national and local groups that joined the International. Their heterogeneity was even more striking, their ideas even vaguer.

These groups, the future sections of the International, multiplied in some countries with surprising speed. Despite the uncertain relations between the heads of the Paris bureaus and the government, seven months after the London meeting, the International had won adherents not only in Paris but also in the provinces. It made its influence felt in workers' associations, particularly in cooperative societies, which were permitted by the government and which therefore had become one of the most widespread forms of organization. In the spring of 1865, propaganda centers attached to the International were set up in a number of cities: Rouen, Le Havre, Caen, Condé, Lille, Amiens, Lyon, Nantes, Lisieux, Roubaix, St.-Etienne. In all these cities, a correspondence bureau was set up, headed by a provisional council. The members came primarily from middle-class and artisan circles. "Nearly all the remnants of the republican groups dissolved by the Empire came to join the [Rue des] Gravilliers section," according to Fribourg. "Doctors, journalists, businessmen, and army officers supported the undertaking."[16] Their interest was welcomed, and they were often given responsibility for propaganda in the provinces. The instructions they received shed light on why Frenchmen took an interest in the International. What mattered, Fribourg noted, was "to recruit most heavily among republicans, to emphasize that the International was a Socialist organization, a foreign association without formal status in France." "Membership cards printed in English were to be used to prove that the correspondents were only intermediaries whose function it was to facilitate the implementation of Articles 5 and 7 of the General Statutes [of the IWA]." It was suggested, moreover, to each newly established group, that "it cease at once all correspondence with Paris, which could not give it orders, and that it apply to the General Council in London for all information on internal organization."[17]

The creation of the International thus allowed Frenchmen to circumvent the regulation banning associations of more than 20 persons. By linking their organization to an association established outside France, they could take full advantage of "the silence of the laws on this new phenomenon."[18] The initial success of the International in France can be explained by the fact that it seemed to allow a regrouping of anti-government forces and to offer a way to exploit the government's recent concession of the right to strike.

In England, the progress of the International was less spectacular. Although political meetings on Poland or electoral reform, the great political problem of the day, attracted many people, the unions were reluctant to take a stand. Some did join in 1865. But though it was difficult to penetrate the labor movement in depth, the leaders of the movement still recognized the Association and joined in some of its efforts, and some of them even sat in the General Council and participated in its activities.

Another link was established in Italy, where the creation of the IWA was announced at the congress of Italian workers' organizations held in Naples from October 25 to 27, 1864. (F. B. Savi, an eminent comrade of Mazzini's, rather than Major Luigi Wolff, Mazzini's secretary, was the man who reported to the congress, in reply to a question from the representatives of the Trani workers.) It was decided to have the Italian workers represented at the international congress that was due to be held. But there was no great enthusiasm for participation. What lay behind this hesitancy? A slowdown in joint undertakings of the Italian workers' groups, which would not hold another congress until 1871? The fact that everyone was preoccupied with the search for unification? Mazzini's reservations about an International conceived in a different spirit from the movements briefly rallied under the banner of "Young Europe"?* Mikhail Bakunin's arrival in Italy? Only fur-

* The attitude of Mazzini is not easy to define. It ought not to be viewed solely in the light of statements made by those who supposedly represent it. See, for example, the following account from the unpublished minutes of the General Council for the meeting of December 4, 1866:

"*Orsini,* who had just entered the room, desired to state the substance of an interview of several hours' duration which he had that morning with Joseph Mazzini. The whole of that time had been devoted to conversation concerning the Association. Mazzini acknowledged that he had been deceived by the reports of Wolff, Lama, and others. Mazzini claimed that for 35 years he had preached the

ther research will throw new light on events during these early years.[19]

We know just as little about the beginnings of the International in Spain, in Austria, and in Prussia, where, according to a note by Marx[20] and a report by Wilhelm Liebknecht, [21] the founding of the International Workingmen's Association was greeted with an enthusiasm that was tempered only by the law restricting association and by the reservations of Lassalle's followers.

Belgium and French Switzerland, on the contrary, were much more receptive to the International's propaganda. Geneva became a very active center. One section of the International was founded there by a French refugee, Jean-Baptiste Dupleix, in March 1865. Shortly thereafter, Johann-Philipp Becker created a German section. Soon other cities followed suit. Lausanne, Montreux, La Chaux-de-Fonds, Sonvilier. German Switzerland became active too. At the Geneva Congress of 1866, fifteen Swiss sections were represented, as against four French sections and three German.

One might see evidence of the historic necessity of the International in the fact that during the two years' time between the St. Martin's Hall meeting and the Geneva Congress, the International was able to rally under its banner over a hundred organizations and groups as different from one another as British trade unions, French mutual aid societies, clockmakers from Geneva and the Juras, Belgian freethinkers, the first German Marxists, and republican and democratic bourgeois. But the diversity of motives out of which these different groups joined the International and the range of objectives the sections set out to reach persisted in the face of the unifying force of common aspirations, and in the end proved more powerful. Every group jealously guarded its independence of the others. Not just the General Council in London but even the federal committees failed to establish their authority over the sec-

---

abolition of wage-slavery and the right of the workman to participate in the profits of his work. That, for all that, he did not concur in every sentiment given utterance to in the original Address of the Association. That he was ready to enter into a debate concerning the principles of our Association; that he would be happy to receive a deputation from the General Council to talk the matter over with him at his private house; that he could not attend Bouverie Street on account of the infirmity of his health, and that he disavowed any responsibility for anything that might have been said by Wolff or others concerning himself."

tions. Liège and Ghent were as vigilant against the "dictatorship" of Brussels as Brussels was against London's, and nobody missed an opportunity to assert his independence. In Switzerland, the Juras crusaded against Geneva; even in Geneva the building-trades workers rebelled against the clockmakers, long before and irrespective of the Marx-Bakunin conflict, which finally split the International into two hostile camps.

In France, no national federation was ever established. In Spain, with its communal traditions that excluded almost a priori any outside interference in the sections' activities, there was a federation. It organized and was active everywhere, but as soon as London tried to intervene and force the sections to accept its decisions, the whole IWA in Spain rebelled, broke away from the General Council, and continued as before, nearly indifferent to the concerns of others. This jealous independence, this spirit of autonomy that came close to indifference (except when strikes or other obvious class conflicts called forth demonstrations of solidarity) plagued the International throughout its entire history from its founding to its collapse. It showed up in the remote origins of the sections, most of them offshoots of former local societies or groups.

Let us take, for example, the little Swiss town of La Chaux-de-Fonds. After 1865, this peaceful watchmaking center became one of the first strongholds of the International, thanks to a certain Pierre Coullery, a doctor and friend of the poor, who, at least at first, did not see any incompatibility between his own ideas of Christian philanthropy and the Statutes of the International drafted by Marx. He founded the La Chaux-de-Fonds section, and it reflected his influence for many years. We recently came across the handwritten minutes of this section,[22] and, moved by an interest in Coullery, a worthy and colorful figure as well as one of the founders of the International, we considered publishing them. Having deciphered the minutes—they were taken in the phonetic spelling so dear to the Swiss internationalists of the day—we had to abandon the project because the records lacked general historical interest. Nonetheless, they accurately reflect the state of mind and the preoccupations of the region's inhabitants. For weeks at a time the section discussed such local matters as the admission of the local brass band, the "Persévérante," to the International, or the appointment of a food-purchasing commission with the special task of buying winter vegetables wholesale.

The section certainly sent its delegates to the general congresses, where they submitted motions on such issues as the settlement of the discount question and spelling reforms. It would be unfair to say that the members of this section in the Juras, cut off from the world as they were, did not share the preoccupations of their comrades in Paris, London, and Brussels. The section's newspaper, *La Voix de l'Avenir,* reported regularly on political news and proclaimed the solidarity of the internationalists from the mountains with their striking and persecuted comrades. Even a small weekly newspaper from the provinces is an authentic indicator of the public opinion and political behavior of a group or region, though the reality it depicts may differ from that of documents giving a detailed account of daily life. Thus, whereas the newspaper focuses on events of general interest, the section was more concerned about the 12 watches manufactured cooperatively by and for the Association, which worked so badly that they did not meet the standards of the comrade watchmakers responsible for checking them.

But let us leave behind the history of the dozen watches of La Chaux-de-Fonds, lest we create the impression that the internationalists of the Juras were indifferent to the great ideas that gave birth to the First International. The region of the Juras, indeed, was destined to play a key part at the time of the conflict between Bakuninists and Marxists. Although the Swiss workers from the Juras were formed by their local traditions, they still were imbued with the ideas of universal working-class solidarity and the emancipation of the working class by its own hands. And their loyalty to the IWA would not falter even when the German and British sections, though from much more advanced countries, had turned inward and abandoned the International. Thus one may conclude that a provincial movement might have been very limited by local preoccupations and at the same time very responsive to the appeal of international solidarity, so long as its independence was not threatened. It is a fact that the brass band La Persévérante still perseveres today, though not one of the players may realize that his predecessors belonged to the International Workingmen's Association inspired by Karl Marx.

While the formation of sections in French Switzerland is often linked to the influence of such figures as the poor man's doctor or Father Constant Meuron of Neuchâtel, in Belgium, to take a different example, the International was grafted onto former rationalist, freethinking, and mutualist movements, all of which kept to their own paths and defended their independence as jealously as their Swiss comrades.

On the very first page of the unpublished minutes of the Brussels federation,[23] we are confronted with problems that characterized the entire history of the IWA. On July 17, 1865, Laurent Verrycken, Martin James Boon, César De Paepe, and others, all of them members of a group called Le Peuple, gathered at the "Union Hall" in Brussels to found a Belgian section of the IWA. One week later, it appears from the minutes, the section was formally established. We quote verbatim:

Citizen Fontaine, claiming to be the delegate from the London Committee, asserted that the workers must get their cards from him in order to found a Belgian group. He himself had received these cards from London. Citizens [Désiré] Brismée, De Paepe, Verrycken, and others contested this procedure, and said that Belgian workers must form an independent group, and not submit to the decisions of any other section. They wished the Belgian section to be founded first, and then it would address itself to London. The Belgian section had to take its place alongside the other national sections, with its own program and statutes, its own administration—in short, its complete rights.

Citizen Fontaine replied that this procedure would not be tolerated in London, and that, in fact, if we did turn directly to London, we would be referred right back to Fontaine.

Several members said that if Fontaine's alleged rights were upheld, they would be forced to abandon the idea of founding a Belgian section. It was decided to write to London and find out for certain what steps we should take.

We happen to know the sequel to this story. The minutes of the September 5, 1865, session of the General Council contain the following account:

Citizens Duthy and Cheval attended as delegates from Belgium to ask if there was any objection to the Belgians' electing their own officers.

Citizen Carter proposed, Eccarius seconded, "That branches have the power to elect their own officers subject to the approval of the Central Council." Carried unanimously.[24]

After this business had been settled, tempers cooled and the Belgian section proceeded to organize as it pleased, reassured that its independence had been acknowledged. It would not be accurate to say that the democratic organization, the most important of which was the group Le Peuple, and the freethinking and rationalist groups were merged with the International. Rather, the Belgian International became, on De Paepe's motion, "a section of the organization Le Peuple, though granting the members of the abovementioned International section the greatest independence in the management of their section."

But that was not all. At that same session, Esselens, who was as authentic a representative of the Belgian movement as De Paepe, expressed the hope that all the little Belgian democratic groups would join forces soon. For two years, unification with the most varied democratic and republican organizations remained the principal goal of the Belgian members of the International, who continued to be influenced by these organizations and by traditions that can be traced back to medieval journeymen's guilds.[25]

The distinctiveness and independence of the Spanish branch was no less marked, and can also be traced to old traditions, notably the "instinctive" federalism that led the mayor of the village of Mostoles personally to declare war on Napoleon. Although the influence of the *comuneros* and the *comarcales* had been lessened by the failure of the revolutionary movements of the 1820's, the nullifying of liberal legislation, and the execution of guerilla leaders, their traditions remained very much alive in the Spanish workers movement at least as late as the Spanish Civil War of 1936–39, if not later.[26] As for the First International, it only penetrated Spain in 1868, four years after its founding. Although the General Council at its November 22, 1864, session, had authorized a certain L. Otto* "to correspond in the name of this Association with the friends of progress in Spain,"[27] little is known about the ties he established there. The first workers' congress was held in Barcelona, December 24–26, 1865; it decided on a federation of the forty corporations represented at the congress and launched the paper *El Obrero*. The Gen-

* According to a manuscript by Max Nettlau on the International in Spain, to be published under the direction of Renée Lamberet, the real name of L. Otto, a native of Stuttgart, was Otto von Breidtschwerdt.

eral Council in London learned the news "from the bulletin of the Paris journal '*L'Association*,' and . . . citizen Dupont was requested to begin corresponding with the president of the Barcelona Congress."[28] A few weeks later, Paul Lafargue took over Eugène Dupont's post as secretary for Spain, but the only outcome of his efforts was an article in *El Obrero* on March 18, 1866, devoted to the IWA's steps to operate mutual credit associations on an international scale.

Studies of the Spanish labor movement, such as *El Proletariado militante* by Anselmo Lorenzo, do not contradict these accounts. Before Giuseppe Fanelli's trip as Bakunin's delegate, in 1868, the IWA was not represented in Spain, and the founding of its first sections coincided with the founding of the Bakuninist Alliance, and some sections even belonged to both groups. In the minutes of the Alliance, which include Fanelli's report on his return to Geneva in February 1869, it is not clear whether he was referring to the Alliance or the IWA.[29] One important fact is frequently neglected by historians who are more concerned with the repercussions of the struggle between Marx and Bakunin in Spain than with the special national characteristics of the labor movement in that country: all or nearly all the early leaders of the International were under the influence of the great republican Francisco Pi y Margall, whose political thought, though inspired by Comte and Proudhon, was profoundly affected by the special conditions of Spain.

Of course, the influence of a Pi y Margall or of Belgian thinkers like Jean Guillaume Hippolyte Colins cannot be put on an equal footing with that of a Proudhon or a Lassalle, of a Mazzini or a Marx. The workers' growing consciousness of their international solidarity must be considered in the context of a general intellectual trend toward Socialism and a universal concept of human destiny. This growing awareness, like the organizing of the International itself, was the offspring of neither a fleeting enthusiasm nor a chance encounter. It was the product of over half a century's evolution. Without going back as far as Tcherkessov does, to Thomas Morus, Thomas Münzer, and the Anabaptist movement,[30] let us recall the steadfastness, the persistence through the entire nineteenth century, of the ideal of brotherhood, brotherhood that could not be confined within the narrow framework of the nation. It would be foolish to neglect the influence that Christianity still had on the working class, particularly in Great Britain, where the Methodist revolution had had a profound impact. In France, the Revolution of 1789 had a similar impact, with its appeals for reconciliation between peoples separated from one another by their tyrannical rulers and with its confidence in an understanding between men once they had been enlightened. Only recall Isnard's speech of November 29, 1791:

> Let us tell Europe . . . that all battles peoples wage by order of their despotic rulers are like the blows two friends exchange in the dark, egged on by a perfidious instigator; as soon as the light of day penetrates, they throw down their arms, kiss, and punish the deceiver. In the same way, if the light of philosophy should strike the eyes of the enemy armies locked in combat with ours, the peoples will fall into each others' arms under the very eyes of the overthrown tyrants, the comforted earth, and the rejoicing heavens.

"The peoples will fall into each other's arms." This theme recurred repeatedly in political literature. It was a hope inspiring most of the social reformers of the nineteenth century. Saint-Simon and his disciples came back to it several times, envisioned a unified "European society," and proclaimed that their new form of Christianity was destined to "establish a permanent state of peace among all peoples"; they perceived a "tendency toward universal association in the human mind" once man's exploitation of man had been eliminated. And Félicité Robert de Lamennais, Charles Fourier, Robert Owen, Victor Considerant, Etienne Cabet—all these men shared the same faith in a reconciliation of all peoples through the reorganization of society. All of them, in their own way, worked toward the application of their doctrine. Fourier believed the phalanx to be the most effective means. Owen tried the New Harmony experiment, Cabet his Republic of Icaria. Saint-Simon was more specific, and visualized a European government; he was followed in this direction by Considerant and Constantin Pecqueur. Mazzini, in turn, carried this idea even further in his "Young Europe," which both prefigured and served as an instrument of European federation, and whose realization hinged on the triumph of Socialist-oriented republicanism.

But despite the favorable climate of the century, it cannot be denied that the International of 1864 was, above all, the end product of an evolution in the ranks of the laboring masses, a stage in the history of the labor movement. The first paragraph of its Statutes is certainly significant. It begins with these words: "Considering that the emancipation of the working classes must be conquered by the working classes themselves." Accordingly, one must look for the origins of the International in the labor movement, investigate its theorists and even more carefully its leaders, and peer into the life of the sections, which has so far been inadequately studied. That is why we have complemented the history of the formation of the International by a few details drawn from two or three countries by way of illustration. To repeat, narrating the history of the First International entails retracing the economic, social, and intellectual evolution of half a century. We have presented this survey, which makes no claim to being exhaustive, in the hope that it will at least give an inkling of the deep roots of the International and the many and often contradictory elements that contributed to its formation.

*The Collapse of the First International*

Half a century in the making, founded in 1864, the International reached its zenith between 1869 and 1871. Sections proliferated throughout Europe and the United States, and during the large strikes of 1868 and 1870 and the Paris Commune of 1871, several hundred thousand workers proclaimed their allegiance to the IWA. Decline set in immediately thereafter. The Fifth General Congress, which was held at The Hague in 1872, confirmed the split into two factions, that is, between the "Anti-Authoritarians" and the General Council, which by then had moved from London to New York. Of course, the history of the IWA was not yet over; the anti-authoritarian branch continued its activities for another five years, organizing four more general congresses and maintaining vigorous sections in Italy, Spain, Belgium, and Switzerland. The so-called Marxist branch did not expire all at once either. The General Council in New York, headed by the diligent Friedrich Albert Sorge, tried to breathe new life into the loyal sections, and only announced the dissolution of the International at the Philadelphia Congress of 1876.

However, the last four years were a mere epilogue, even if they had some interesting and noteworthy aspects; the International was an altogether different thing from what it was before the Hague Congress. There were now two simultaneous and competing Internationals. Two Internationals do not equal a double International but rather half a unified one, even if both of them still enjoy a certain amount of prestige. The Hague Congress was at least a turning point, if not the concluding chapter. Just as the meeting of St. Martin's Hall, for all its importance, cannot explain the founding of the IWA by itself, the Hague Congress, taken in isolation, did not contain all the elements of its disintegration. This is so not only because the Hague Congress was *followed* by a confused postscript, but also because it was *preceded* by a decline that began two years earlier. That is not all. Bold as this claim may seem, we believe that the First International bore from its inception the seeds of the final crisis. As a result, its existence was always precarious: cohesion barely won out over the centrifugal forces. "We always knew that the bubble *was bound* to burst" as Engels stated (his emphasis) in reference to the "huge success" registered by the International after the Commune.[31]

We do not hesitate to subscribe to Engels' opinion, for there is no doubt that the International was never defeated by the attacks made upon it. It is true that the failure of the Commune led to a breakdown of the IWA's organization in France, but this failure was largely offset by successes elsewhere, notably in Italy and Belgium.[32] Engels was correct to speak of a "huge success," a success that was due, in part, to the indignation and feelings of solidarity aroused by the bloody week in which the Commune was destroyed, and the persecution of the Communards.

But what was this bubble that was bound to burst? Was it the bubble of *success,* or the bubble of *unity*? In his letter to Sorge of September 12–17, 1874—a very revealing letter—Engels implied that he was referring to unity. It is worth quoting the entire passage of the letter:

Your withdrawal marks the final winding up of the old International. That is as it should be. It belonged to the period of the Second Empire, in which the oppression prevailing in all of Europe made unity and the avoidance of all internal polemics essential to the reviving labor movement. It was the moment when the common cosmopolitan interests of the proletariat could come to the fore; Germany, Spain, Italy, Denmark, had just joined the movement or were in the process of joining it. In 1864, the theoretical character of the movement was still very poorly defined in all of Europe, so far as the masses were concerned, that is. German Communism was still nonexistent in terms of a labor party; Proudhonism lacked the strength to ride its hobbyhorse; Bakunin's newest whims had not yet taken shape even in his own head; even the English trade-union leaders believed that they could join the movement on the basis of the program laid down in the *Considérants* of the statutes. It was inevitable that the first substantial success would disrupt this naïve collaboration of all factions. This success was the Commune, which was beyond doubt the intellectual child of the International, even though the International did not lift a finger to bring it about, so that it was perfectly fair to make the International responsible for it. When, on the strength of the Commune, the International turned into a moral power in Europe, the bickering erupted at once. Every faction wanted to exploit this success for itself. Collapse followed inevitably. Jealousy of the growing power of those men who were really resolute enough to continue to work for the old comprehensive program—the German Communists—drove the Belgian followers of Proudhon into the fold of Bakuninist adventurers. The Hague Congress was a true death knell—and for both sides. America was the only country in which the name of the International still had some luster, and through a lucky intuition the top administration was transferred there. Now its luster has been tarnished even there, and any further effort to galvanize it back to life would be folly and wasted effort. For ten years, the International channeled European history in one direction—the direction of the future—and it can look back proudly on its achievement.[33]

The lucidness of this clever application of historical materialism is all the more admirable in a man who not only originated the theory, but also played a leading role in the events he analyzed so moderately and dispassionately. No doubt he made a few unflattering remarks about "Bakuninist adventurers," but all personal animosity gave way to a perceptive analysis of the underlying causes of the IWA's failure. In a way the letter was the rough outline of a thesis; if its antithesis is spelled out, a synthesis emerges. The entire history of the International bears out his view that the 1860's were the time when the "cosmopolitan interests of the proletariat" and the consequent need to join forces against "the oppression prevailing in all of Europe" won out over all other considerations. The recognition of this need represented in some way the lesson learned from the failure of the isolated revolutions of 1848 fifteen years later, when economic and political conditions permitted the "re-awakening of the labor movement" that culminated in the First International.

Engels' statement that the working masses had no grasp of the "theoretical character of the movement" in which they joined was also borne out by events. We have tried to prove how great a distance separated the Juras watchmaker, a loyal follower of Coullery, from the Parisian worker, a disciple of Proudhon, the London trade unionist from the Genevan bricklayer, and the Barcelona weaver from the Milanese follower of Mazzini. And an abyss separated all these workers from revolutionary Communists such as Marx and Engels.

Therein lay the root of the problem; the heterogeneous sections of the International, notwithstanding their diversity and even their divergences, could still agree on the general principles proclaimed by the IWA at the time of its founding and its first congresses. True enough, at the Geneva, Lausanne, and Brussels congresses, and particularly at the Basel Congress of 1869, the debate between the different groups was very heated, and the collectivist revolutionary "Montagne" finally won out over the followers of Proudhon and other moderates. But it was a far cry from these disputes to the inevitable disintegration of the whole Association. This is where a link is missing in Engels' chain of arguments. Neither for him nor for Marx did the "theoretical character of the movement" have the same meaning as it did for the "working masses" mentioned earlier in Engels' letter.

This is such an obvious fact that there is no point in multiplying examples. Marx and Engels certainly were fully aware of the distance that separated the "class consciousness" of the revolutionary leaders—most of them intellectuals—from the class consciousness of the masses that they led. It is true that Marx and Engels were pronouncing a-posteriori truths in explaining that the "bubble" had to burst out of "historic necessity." But at the outbreak of the crisis, neither Marx nor Engels believed that all was lost, because they failed to realize that the IWA "belonged to the period of the Second Empire," and that, consequently, it had no hope of outliving it; nor did they suspect that "the first substantial success was bound to disrupt this naïve association." On the contrary, they never emphasized the need for reorganizing the Association on the basis of a doctrine and political program binding on all members as much as they did in 1871. At the 1871 Conference in London, they counted on the success of this policy; only after this conference, when the rebellion of the sections wrecked their hopes, did they begin to view matters in a new light. We will come back later to this reversal, but let us first look at the other side of the coin. It would be a mistake to assume that Marx, brilliant tactician that he was, was misled by his own theory, or that he was indulging in wishful thinking.

Let us return once more to the founding of the International to summarize briefly Marx's role in it and the spirit that motivated him. We know that the initiative did not come from him. As the head of the Communist League and the author of the *Communist Manifesto,* he could surely claim an ideological share in the formation of the IWA. However, he found the organizers of the first meeting, as well as the semi-unionist, semi-bourgeois-democratic spirit animating the meeting, more alien than congenial. He was invited at the very last minute, and did not take the floor. His hour came later, at the meetings of the subcommittee responsible for drafting the Statutes of the new Association. Here Marx could act, and wanted to. The way in which he blocked the proposals of John Weston, a disciple of Owen, and those of the Mazzinist Luigi Wolff, and won acceptance instead for his own texts, embodied in the provisional Statutes and the so-called Inaugural Address of the Association—all this is too well known to require comment here.[34]

Marx's motives, however, about which little is known, arouse our curiosity: Why did he expend so much effort in a cause with which he did not fully identify? "I accepted *this time* because it involved a matter where it is possible to do some important work," he explained to Joseph Weydemeyer in a letter dated November 29, 1864.[35] The wording of the German original, "diesmal bedeutend zu wirken" (to act in a significant way this time), shows even more clearly that Marx, long isolated from the "real forces" (wirkliche Kräfte) of the labor movement, eagerly seized this opportunity to become part of it again because the IWA happened to represent its "real forces" and thus gave him the opportunity to "act in a significant way." Engels realized this at once. In reply to Marx's long letter of November 4, 1864, in which he gave a full report on the first sessions of the Association, Engels congratulated him on the Inaugural Address, which under the circumstances "must have been a real sleight of hand" (muss ein wahres Kunststück sein), and he added, "But it is all to the good that we are once more in contact with people who are at least representative of their class."*

Another equally important consideration is brought out in two letters Marx wrote on the same day as the Weydemeyer letter—the first to his friend Ludwig Kugelmann, and the second to his uncle Lion Philips. In both of them Marx went so far as to claim that the founding of the IWA was what decided Palmerston "to avoid war with the United States."[36]

It is true that Marx sometimes misjudged the weight of the labor movement in the balance of political forces.[37] But this makes it all the more understandable why Marx hoped in "compensation" for his "ideological concessions," to reap the benefit of the new "power" (Macht) that the IWA was beginning to be on the international scene. He was well aware—which is why we said earlier that he was not led astray by his own theory—that these ideological concessions were the price that had to be paid to secure this power. He was aware that it would take time "before the revived movement [was] in a position to use the bold language of yore," and that the IWA, as the meeting ground of diverse movements and "sects," was still far from "ripe" for the revolutionary doctrine and policy of the veteran members of the Communist League.

A certain flexibility, a little pragmatism, were thus a sine qua non of equilibrium among the divergent forces within the International. For that very reason, though Marx and Engels hoped that "exchanges of ideas and discussion . . . will gradually produce a com-

* This was in reply to Marx's statement that it had been "very difficult for him to phrase it in such a way that our own opinions would be in a form acceptable to the present point of view of the labor movement. In a few weeks these same people will hold meetings with Bright and Cobden to obtain the right to vote. It will take some time before the reawakened movement will be in a position to use the bold language of yore. What is needed here is *fortiter in re, suaviter in modo*. You will get the thing as soon as it is printed." Marx and Engels, *Letters to Americans, 1848–1895: A Selection* (New York, 1953), pp. 238, 240.

mon theoretical program,"[38] they carefully refrained, until 1871, from making this "theoretical program" binding on the sections. This program was there all along, as early as 1864. It lay concealed behind the subtle phrases of the Statutes and the Inaugural Address written by Marx. The General Council, as Marx put it, waged a ceaseless battle "against the sects and the attempts of amateurs, who try to keep a toehold in the International at the expense of the real movement of the working class";[39] but until the outbreak of open warfare with Bakunin, this ideological ammunition was never fired.

What, then, did happen in 1871? As we know, the General Council convened a private conference in London, where resolutions of a hitherto unthinkable rigidity were adopted, not only with respect to Bakunin's supporters but also with respect to organizational, political, and ideological questions. In the words of one resolution, political action, which had been viewed as a *subordinate* instrument for economic emancipation, was now linked "indissolubly" to it. The proletariat's transformation into a political party would henceforth be considered "indispensable for assuring the triumph of the social revolution aiming ultimately at the abolition of all classes."[40] Moreover, the powers of the General Council were extended, at the expense of the independence of the national federations and the local sections.

The "common theoretical program," which two years earlier the General Council had hoped to see emerge "gradually" through "exchanges of ideas," became law from one day to the next. The earlier flexibility and pragmatism disappeared, giving way to a leadership of a centralist or "authoritarian"—as Bakunin's supporters called it—bent. But no matter what it was called, it was an undeniable fact; the change was clear-cut and its repercussions serious.

What happened after the 1871 Conference? Let us summarize in a few sentences the eventful twelve months that elapsed between this conference and the Hague Congress, which signaled the end of the IWA as a unified organization, and the closing of its London headquarters. The London Conference was a pyrrhic victory for Marx. The majority of the sections, notably the Spanish, Italian, Belgian, and the French Swiss sections, and the section of French émigrés, rebelled against the General Council. The same phenomenon occurred, although gradually and for rather special reasons, in the United States, where the new General Council maintained its influence only over the German émigrés. In England the break was only completed in 1872, but it started in 1871, if not in 1868. The rebellion did not always occur spontaneously; it was fed and cleverly guided by Bakunin and his friends. The General Council, for its part, did not remain a passive onlooker during the debacle. It mobilized its supporters everywhere, and succeeded in keeping a few sections in its orbit, in both the Anglo-Saxon and the Latin countries, if one counts what Engels called its "toehold" in Spain.

At the Hague Congress, Marx and Engels thus succeeded in rallying a majority—a majority their opponents considered fictitious—behind the so-called authoritarian policy. As a result of this clever maneuver and the support of the followers of Blanqui, the Hague Congress not only approved the London resolutions but voted in favor of expelling Bakunin and his friends. The transfer of the General Council to New York was also approved, despite the opposition of Blanqui's followers, who tried to seize power within the weakened General Council. It may well be that it was to thwart them that Marx decided to relegate the center of the Association to the other side of the Atlantic, where it would be sheltered from Continental influences that might have proved too dangerous.

The resolutions of the Hague Congress were not sufficient to consolidate the so-called Marxist position. On the contrary. The break they made finally cost the General Council some of its already decimated allies in England, the Latin countries, and even Holland. The Italian, Spanish, Belgian, and Juras sections, with the support of the English federation under the leadership of the IWA's former General Secretary, John Hales, together with a few French émigré groups, founded an "Anti-Authoritarian" International. Other sections, including the sections of Blanquist leanings and the Geneva section, which so far had remained loyal to Marx, also broke loose, although they condemned the anarchists.

The "old International," to use Engels' term, was dead. Those who claimed to keep faith with its ideas became part of the anarchist group, whereas the last attempted regrouping of so-called Marxist forces resulted in a fiasco. The tireless Johann-Philipp

Becker managed "to produce out of thin air 13 delegates, in order to give greater luster to the congress by virtue of a larger membership and to assure the proper faction of a majority."[41] There was nothing impossible about pulling 13 delegates out of a hat. But the hope of reviving the real movement around the program of the General Council had become illusory, even in Germany, Austria, and Holland, where the Bakuninists had not won any following. The German labor movement, to which we shall return shortly, confined itself to vague expressions of a purely platonic sympathy with the International.

What lay behind this sudden collapse? One cause of the fall of the International was surely Marx's political reversal at the London Conference, which brought in its wake the disastrous revolt outlined above, of the majority of the sections. An explanation of this reversal is called for.

It is puzzling in the face of Marx's full awareness, when he joined the International, that the "class-consciousness" of the members was weak. For him as for Engels, the International represented a "real movement" and an important one, which they tried to direct and influence, but which they never considered *their* party in the same way as they had the defunct Communist League.

Why this sudden change of tactics, which proved fatal for the International? Was it simply to prevent Bakunin from gaining control of the Association? This factor, which has been subjected to careful scrutiny by several historians, undoubtedly had some influence on Marx's decision. But it does not explain everything, because it was not necessary to introduce such radical structural changes just to thwart Bakunin. Two hypotheses seem plausible: either Marx thought that the time had come to put forth his political doctrine by imposing it on all the sections; or—and this hypothesis seems to us less likely than the first—Marx thought only of eliminating the influence of his main adversary, Bakunin. In the first case, the "Bakunin question" must be viewed from a wider perspective, as part of a "strategic" operation carefully prepared by Marx. In line with the second hypothesis, "operation London" was no more than a clever indirect maneuver to fight Bakunin. We use the word "indirect" because the resolutions do not specifically name Bakunin. The strategy then would have been to win the political battle first, and once the sections had accepted Marx's policy, Bakunin would be eliminated.

Which of the two hypotheses comes closest to the mark? We do not know. But irrespective of Marx's secret motives, he did not confine the battle to the personal plane, but extended it to the political and organizational spheres—at the risk of overturning the entire Association. This was a real challenge. But unless suicide is contemplated, a challenge implies the will to win. Even the slightest hope of victory had to rest on the support of the majority of the sections and their approval of the theses and the cause of the General Council. Marx and Engels did cherish this hope. In the light of the discussions at the London Conference and of their correspondence, it is clear not only that they relied on the support of the sections but that they were confident of victory. That is why they were deeply and cruelly disappointed, when during the whole following year, news of one defection after another overwhelmed the Council in London.

A mistake in calculation? Unquestionably. But not simply the mistake of a tactician who overestimated his own influence and underestimated that of his adversary. For the adversary Marx misjudged; his real adversary was not Bakunin or any other leader, but the nearly physical resistance of the environment. Much has been made of the increasingly revolutionary "radicalism" of the International. That this was a factor in the collapse cannot be denied. The discussions and resolutions of the general congresses, the more and more strident tone of their demands, do bespeak a certain radicalization and a retreat of the moderates. However, this radicalization was more superficial than one might think. In other words, revolutionary collectivism did gain ground, but this headway was not in the least indicative of a profound change either in the consciousness of the masses or in the economic and social structures which, according to Marxist theory, condition or determine that consciousness.

What had changed on that level since the founding of the International? Except for a passing depression in 1866, this whole period was characterized by a high level of prosperity, which continued until the great crisis of 1873. General prosperity meant improved living conditions for the workers. Although their position remained precarious, especially when inflation is taken into account, the rise in wages more than offset the increased cost of living in Western Europe. In such a period of sustained advances, without either great leaps forward or great crises that shake the whole world economy, society in general also remains safe from upheavals. Thus the Paris Commune of 1871 was not so much an insurrection provoked by general social unrest as an outgrowth of the frenzied state of a besieged and starving Paris; as a result, it was doomed to isolation from the start. The frequently mentioned but rarely analyzed fact that the International had little responsibility for the Commune only substantiates our hypothesis. In our opinion, the social struggles, the many strikes, and the mounting demands of the workers notwithstanding, the whole period of the First International was an *evolutionary,* and not a revolutionary, phase in the history of the labor movement. Revolutionary ideas were certainly making themselves felt and workers were learning to organize more effectively than before, but the society in which they lived had not changed enough to foster a new "class consciousness" that was likely to produce the "common theoretical program" to which Marx aspired, and which he sought to impose in 1871.

Still, it would be simplifying things to conclude that the failure of the International can be ascribed to a miscalculation on the part of Marx, a miscalculation that he and particularly Engels were later to recognize, if only implicitly. This would amount to saying: "If the General Council had not insisted on resolutions that were binding on sections eager to preserve their independence, the IWA would not have gone under, and today it might still be the only worldwide organization of the proletariat." This opinion would be as misguided as its opposite, namely that Marx and Engels, thanks to the "scientific foresight" of their theory, recognized the "historic necessity" of putting an end to the obsolete International. For even if their alleged foresight was nothing but "hindsight,"* it was still true, as Engels says, that the International collapsed at practically the same time as the Second Empire. The historian is certainly free to postulate what would have happened if the General Council had not hardened its line on the sections, for this harden-

* Even in 1872, the decision of the Hague Congress "to transplant" the IWA to America was dictated by considerations of tactics, not theory.

ing undoubtedly hastened the end. It is quite possible that flexible tactics would have postponed the demise of the IWA. But the end was unavoidable; the "old International" was doomed to disappear sooner or later.

We have seen why on both social and tactical grounds. We have shown how Marx's tactics, based on a "new consciousness," proved to be mistaken because the foundations of society had not changed. However, this only serves to explain the speed with which the inevitable split between the so-called anti-authoritarians and the General Council materialized. The "backward" Italian and Spanish workers, the isolated Swiss workers from the Juras, the Belgian workers with a very low standard of living, all of them tied to their own communalist or federalist traditions, declined to submit to a policy they considered authoritarian, centralist, and even bourgeois. But what about the English, and especially the Germans? If the "common political theory" foreseen and then imposed by the General Council was beyond the grasp of the "backward" regions of Europe, surely it suited the most advanced countries? According to this hypothesis, the "advanced" branch of the IWA should have emerged stronger and more coherent than before from the crisis of the years 1871–72. But this did not happen. Not only did the French, who were dispersed in exile, and the English, who were still dominated by their trade-union interests, desert the International, but even the Germans abandoned ship. And yet, the IWA's beginnings in Germany had been rather hopeful. In spite of various legal obstacles confronting the German Socialists, the two rival Socialist parties both proclaimed their ties with the International. The loyalty of August Bebel and Wilhelm Liebknecht to Marx and the International was never in doubt. The Eisenach party's program, which stated that "the Social Democratic Labor Party . . . considers itself a branch of the International Workingmen's Association" only consecrated, basically, the political line traced out and followed by these two men. By 1868, even the Lassalleans, in spite of their opposition to Marx and particularly to the Bebel and Liebknecht group, tried to exploit the growing popularity of the International. Johann Baptist von Schweitzer, the president of the Allgemeiner Deutscher Arbeiterverein, made overtures to Marx, who showed some interest in them, especially when Schweitzer published a review consisting of no fewer than 12 articles on Marx's *Kapital* in his *Sozial-Demokrat*. In October of the same year the *Sozial-Demokrat* announced in an editorial presumably written by Schweitzer that:

The organization [the Allgemeiner Deutscher Arbeiterverein] would not perhaps be formally obliged to collaborate with the International Association if it declared itself in complete agreement with its objectives, but it would surely have the moral obligation to keep step with it as far as possible.

In any case, there is no incompatibility between membership in the Allgemeiner Deutscher Arbeiterverein and in the International Association. To be a member of the Allgemeiner Deutscher Arbeiterverein is already equivalent to participating in the efforts of the International Association, to the limits of the law. One does not exclude the other, as being a French or a Russian citizen; it is rather like one person saying: I am from Canton Uri, and another one saying: I am from Switzerland. Canton Uri is part of Switzerland.

At the same time, we believe we must strive for: 1. Elimination of all laws preventing workers from uniting in any way they choose in pursuit of their just demands. 2. Gradually strengthening the central leadership of the International Association to the point where it can assume, to a greater extent than it does at present, the role of the national centers of the labor movement.

The last paragraph of the editorial deserves special attention, inasmuch as it expresses a point of view shared by all German Socialists but unknown in the Latin countries:

In any case, our goal must be centralization, greater and tighter centralization. Only when the forces of the laboring masses are thus tightly bound centrally, nationally as well as on a world-wide scale, the working class can unleash all its might. Democratic centralization—that is the key to the victory of the working class.[42]

However, the Lassalleans' contact with Marx and the International soon came to an end. As Ernst Schräpfer demonstrates with ample documentation in the *Archiv für Sozialgeschichte*,[43] after Schweitzer retired, attacks against Liebknecht and then Marx resumed with renewed intensity, and the International finally became a target, too.

The break between the Lassallean Allgemeiner Deutscher Arbeiterverein and the "Marxist" General Council was less startling, however, than the attitude of the leaders of the Eisenach party, an orthodox Marxist group. While Bebel and Liebknecht never disavowed the International, and continued to express their devotion to Marx and Engels, the affiliation of the German Social Democratic Party with the International took on an increasingly platonic character after 1871. The correspondence between Marx and Engels and their German comrades, particularly Liebknecht, is revealing in this respect. Let us limit ourselves to quoting the following telling letter:

Your opinion that the German members of the International should not pay dues, and that in any case it makes no difference whether the International has many or few members in Germany is the opposite of our own. If you did not collect the annual dues of one Silbergroschen per person per year, or used them up yourselves you will have to settle this with your own conscience. I fail to understand how you can imagine that other nations should bear your share of the costs, while you are with them, like Jesus Christ, "in the spirit," and keep your flesh and your money all to yourselves. This platonic relation must certainly come to an end, and the German workers must either *belong* to the International or *not* belong. The French are under much greater pressure, and our organization there is better than ever. If you have no interest in this matter personally, we will have to rely on other people, but you can be sure that this business will be clarified, one way or the other.[44]

In one of Engels' letters to Liebknecht of May 1872, one comes across the following passage:

2. Does the Social Democratic Labor Party intend to be represented at the congress, and if so, how does it plan to be in good standing with the General Council so that its mandate cannot be challenged at the congress? For this purpose, it must (a) expressly and not just *figuratively* declare itself as the German federation of the International, and (b) pay up its dues *in that capacity* before the congress. This matter is getting serious, and we have to know where we stand, or else you will compel us to go ahead on our own and consider the Social Democratic Labor Party an alien body, indifferent to the International. We cannot allow, out of motives which are unknown to us but which are surely petty, the mandates of the German workers to be squandered or frittered away. We ask for a prompt and clear-cut answer.[45]

As we mentioned earlier, Liebknecht remained loyal to the International, but he, too, in his own way, spoke up for the independence of his party. He never turned his back on Marx, but the affairs and interests of the International concerned him less and less. The German Social Democratic Party followed its own path, and waged its fight in the context of the difficult and yet promising conditions of the Bismarckian Empire.

The International, which was not born out of the enthusiasm of a single day, did not plunge to its grave in the disarray of a single congress. From the very start, it bore within itself the seeds of its dissolution: diversity aggravated by the adoption of a centralist strategy. Alongside this internal conflict, the International also suffered from the consequences of a reversal of forces in Europe. The attainment of Italian and German unity, in particular, made the collapse of the old International coincide with the end of the old Europe. It still knew a few successes, notably in Italy and Belgium, but this extension of its history ushered in a new era, the era of Social Democracy and the Second International. In Germany, France, Belgium, Switzerland, and Austria, everywhere the veterans of the International, the Liebknechts, the Greulichs, the Guesdes, were the men who headed the new labor parties in their respective countries, while in Italy and in Spain, and in a powerful segment of the French labor movement, the anarchist branch turned into revolutionary anarcho-syndicalism.

"The International," Engels wrote in his letter-epitaph, "channeled ten years of European history in one direction—in the direction of the future—and it can look back proudly on its achievements. . . . I believe that the next International will be . . . Communist outright, and will re-establish our very principles." To what extent did this "scientific prediction" coincide with the development of the "real movement"? To what extent did the diversity of social structures and national interests allow the emergence of a "truly common theoretical program"? We must leave these questions to be answered by the authors of Parts II and III of this volume.

Boris I. Nicolaevsky

# Secret Societies and the First International

Secret societies, outwardly of masonic form, played a decisive role in the forming of the First International. The struggle between the members and allies of these societies on the one hand, and Karl Marx and his working-class supporters on the other, constituted the inner life of the International in its early years, and in the end was responsible for its demise. Because of the importance and the complexity of the problem, and because it has been unexplored to date, I shall limit my essay to this rather narrow subject. Furthermore, I shall deal primarily with secret societies having their roots in France, a country of special interest to the historian of the First International. Therefore this essay should be regarded as a preliminary report, which aims not to exhaust the subject but to draw attention to it and to demonstrate its importance.

### *Official and Underground Masonry*

Freemasonry was never a unified movement, even within a particular country. This is even truer if we speak of the political role of masonry, and particularly in France in the period that interests us—that is, the period in which the First International was formed. After the defeat of the revolutions of 1848 in all the countries of Western Europe, leadership of the official masonic organizations passed into rightist hands. Of course, there were various shades of rightist leadership, but they were merely shades. In France Napoleon III established an undisguised dictatorship over masonry, placing men he had personally selected at the head of its official organizations—first Prince Lucien Murat, later Marshal Magnan. These appointees carried out the policy laid down by the government;

they maintained a strict surveillance of the lodges, suppressing the slightest hints of opposition to the regime. This kind of masonry, of course, played no part at all in the formation of the First International, and could not have played any.

True, after 1865, with the death of Marshal Magnan and the adoption of a new and more liberal masonic constitution, the situation changed. The lodges began to open their doors to free discussion of social and political questions, and were thus gradually transformed into recruiting centers for members of various revolutionary organizations, the sections of the International among them. It is precisely through these doors that many students entered the International—young people such as Charles Longuet and Paul Lafargue who later played a prominent part in the Socialist movement. But even for this period one cannot speak of official masonry as a factor in the formation of the International. Young people used the premises of the lodges for their political self-education, but they did not accept masonic ideology; their attitude toward masonry was critical, to say the least.[1]

Official masonry in France was never a factor in the formation and development of the First International. But in the France of the Second Empire there existed not only the official masonry recognized by the government, but also an underground masonic movement, persecuted by the government because it sought the revolutionary overthrow of the Empire. The role of these undercover, government-persecuted masons in the forming and developing of the First International was enormous. It has hardly been studied by historians, although quite a bit of relevant material has come to light. Some of the most interesting documents on the subject were preserved in the archives of Pierre Vésinier and published some sixty years ago by Max Nettlau.[2] (Vésinier himself played only a minor role in the revolutionary masonry now under discussion, joining a lodge for the first time in 1865.) In recent years some very important material on these revolutionary masons has been published.[3] We now know the names of approximately 100 members of their principal lodges; these lodges operated in England, and brought together primarily, but not exclusively, French émigrés. These materials, together with the émigré publications of the period, make it possible for us to begin to understand the history of these masons, the political activities of their leaders, and their relation to the First International. It is important to determine the nature of these groups, which for the sake of brevity we are calling revolutionary masonry.

Outwardly, these groups had the form of a masonic organization and bore a masonic name, the Lodge of the Philadelphians (Loge des Philadelphes). Some of the members may in fact have considered themselves masons. But veteran masons, those who headed the lodges, must have realized that their lodges had little in common with real masonry.

The Lodge of the Philadelphians was formally part of an association that, at the beginning of the 1850's, bore the name of the Order of Memphis.[4] The history of this order is obscure. Historians of masonry do not accord it much attention or sympathy, and as a matter of fact, much of its history is contradictory and incomprehensible. An odd mixture of pseudo-Eastern mysticism and obvious leftist political sympathies on the part of the leaders of the order leaves a strange impression. As a rule, the left wing of Freemasonry tried to lead the movement away from mysticism in the name of rationalism and free thought, and insisted on simplification of the statutes. The Philadelphians had a completely different outlook. Not only did they trace their forebears to ancient Egyptian priests and to the legendary Chaldean magi who went to Bethlehem to pay tribute to the Christ child, but they preserved the 96 grades of initiation and the post of Le Grand Hiérophante at their head. At the same time, almost from the moment the Philadelphians appeared on the scene during the July Monarchy, they tended to draw support from left-wing, even extreme-left-wing, elements. The historian is faced with the paradox that whereas Jean-Etienne Marconi, founder and head of the order for many years, was utterly indifferent to politics, the Supreme Council of the order for 1855 was composed entirely of Republicans and Socialists who sat with the extreme left in the National Assembly of 1848–49.[5]

We are not concerned here with explaining these contradictions, but there is no doubt that after 1848, in any case, the Lodge of the Philadelphians and all organizations related to it, especially those in London, brought together exclusively leftist elements, and that all their activity was leftist in direction. They did not maintain organizational ties with official masonry either in France or in England. Among the English masons there was a small and uninfluential radical wing, but it was dedicated primarily to anti-religious propaganda. The organs of this group were *The Free Thinker, The Reasoner,* and *National Reformer.* With this group, the Philadelphians soon established intimate ties, but official English Freemasonry never recognized the Philadelphians, and its publications maintained that they were not masons but an ordinary secret society with revolutionary goals.[6]

The first Lodge of the Philadelphians in England was established at the end of 1850. Its constitution was ratified by the Supreme Council of the Order (Conseil Suprême de l'Ordre Maçonnique de Memphis) on January 31, 1851.[7] It became the center of the Philadelphians' activity among the French émigrés, though in general anybody who spoke French was admitted. The Lodge's work was successful. In addition to the names of roughly 100 persons who at one time or another were members, Jean Bossu lists ten lodges that were connected with it;[8] for some of them the Lodge of the Philadelphians was the "mother lodge." The Lodge was distinguished by its stability: it functioned at least until the end of the 1870's.

Who precisely were the founders of the Lodge is unknown. Yet if we juxtapose the names on Bossu's list with those of known political activists among the French émigrés, we find a close connection between early members of the Lodge and a political grouping known as La Commune Révolutionnaire, which emerged soon afterward. All the outstanding leaders of the Commune were apparently members of the Lodge, whereas other groups were represented by few if any leaders, but only by minor figures. The connection, of course, was not fortuitous. There is no reason to assume that the Commune group founded the Lodge, since the Commune was organized a year and a half later.[9] The relationship was no doubt the reverse: acting behind the scenes, the Philadelphians helped to found and organize the Commune.

The close relationship between the Commune Révolutionnaire and the Lodge of the Philadelphians undoubtedly persisted through the years. We can therefore assess the political activities of the

Lodge with reasonable accuracy by studying the publications of the Commune. It seems clear that the Lodge of the Philadelphians (soon after its formation, though we do not know when exactly, it began to call itself La Grande Loge des Philadelphes)[10] was, by its very nature, one of those secret societies which outwardly imitated the masons but which were essentially conspiratorial political organizations. The Lodge itself did not openly engage in political activities, unless one regards the banquets it organized as such activities. For political occasions it created special organizations, which formally led an independent existence but in fact were under the complete control of the Lodge, which used them as political instruments.

### *Conspiratorial Organizations and Political Terrorism*

Similar combinations of old forms of organizational structures and political activity were widespread in France during the Restoration and the July Monarchy, when revolutionaries generally belonged either to the Carbonari, Young Europe, and similar groups, or to groups of latter-day Babouvists; all these organizations were, to a greater or lesser extent, essentially conspiratorial in nature. It was only during the years immediately preceding the Revolution of 1848, principally under the influence of the English Chartist movement, that new forms of organizational structures as well as social and political activities began to emerge. The new organizations shifted their attention to the open propagation of Socialist and Communist ideas and to the building of mass organizations of laborers in the city and on the land. Throughout Western Europe, the general trend was away from relatively small groups of active revolutionary conspirators who were isolated from their environment, and toward mass political parties, political clubs, and labor unions. On the eve of the revolution of 1848, the new-style organizations increasingly tended to supplant the old, conspiratorial groups, which were under the influence of masonic principles of organization. The new-style organizations were thrown back two or three decades by the defeat of the 1848–49 revolution, and the old type of organization came once again to the fore. This trend was particularly marked among the French refugees from the Second Empire.

The Commune Révolutionnaire, organized, as we have seen, in

1852, is one of the best examples of the revival of these old conspiratorial organizations. In general works on the history of the period, it is all too frequently bracketed with the Blanquists. This is a mistake. True, a number of Blanquists took part in the Commune Révolutionnaire. Some of them, such as Jean-Baptiste Rougé and Théophile Thoré, were close companions-in-arms of Blanqui; but none of them were prominent political leaders, and within the Commune Révolutionnaire they were indistinguishable from the mainstream. It was the so-called Montagnards (sometimes called Jacobins) who became the literary and political leaders of the years 1848–49, and almost all of them were veterans of conspiratorial organizations of the 1830's.

It is necessary to point out that in the course of the great debates on Socialism that precipitated the first major split among the French émigrés in England, in the early 1850's, the members of the Commune Révolutionnaire were, without exception, Socialists. Not one of them would have joined the groups of open opponents of Socialism like Alexandre Ledru-Rollin and Giuseppe Mazzini. But the theoretician and political leader of these Socialists was Louis Blanc, whose theoretical views and political stands, especially during the years of exile, were not distinguished by their precision or consistency.

The role of Louis Blanc deserves special consideration. So far as I know, none of the numerous biographies of this man makes any special mention of his activities as a mason or as a member of secret societies in general.[11] Nor are there any traces of such activities in the Louis Blanc papers in the Bibliothèque Nationale in Paris.[12] But in histories of masonry, Blanc long has figured as one of the leading representatives of the Order of Memphis; although Blanc's name began to appear in such publications during his lifetime, he never protested its mention.[13] The absence of evidence of masonic activities in the Blanc papers means simply that the censorship to which they were subjected before being deposited in the Bibliothèque Nationale was thorough. Recent publications attest to Blanc's connections with revolutionary masonry. Bossu does not list him as a member of the Lodge of the Philadelphians, but he refers to Blanc's speeches at meetings organized by the Lodge (for example, at an 1870 banquet in honor of Paolo Tibaldi on his return from Cayenne). We learn from Bossu that in 1855 Louis Blanc was actually a member of the Supreme Council of the Order of Memphis.[14] This apparent discrepancy is explained easily. Blanc apparently had been connected with this order for a long time, and was indeed one of the organizers of its Supreme Council in London (after the Order had been banned by the Paris police in 1852–53); but he did not join the Lodge of the Philadelphians, which was organized to work among the French émigrés, because he considered the position of ordinary lodge member (even of a "Grand" Lodge) beneath him. When the Supreme Council was transferred to London, however, Blanc, as the Council's chief speechmaker, was able to direct its policy, and, at the same time, to influence the policy of the Lodge of the Philadelphians without officially becoming a member.

Two other points must be made about the Philadelphians in order to understand their role in the formation of the First International.

The first is the enormous interest of the Philadelphians in revolutionary movements in other countries, and their creation of a separate organization intended to maintain constant contact among revolutionaries in different countries. This organization was called the International Association, and it existed from 1855 to 1859. The statutes of this organization, the adoption of which was the only condition for membership, set forth as its principal tasks spreading "the doctrine of solidarity" and preparing to implement "the ideal of our hearts, the Universal Democratic and Social Republic." Arthur Mueller-Lehning, who devoted an entire work to the Association and assembled a number of valuable documents relating to its activities, called it "the first form of a proletarian International of a revolutionary and Socialist character."[15] It is difficult to accept this judgment.

Not only was the Association in fact composed exclusively of émigrés in England and America, it never tried to establish contact with workers' organizations; the words "workers" and "proletarian" never appeared in its statutes. In this respect the Association represented a definite step backward from the international organizations that the English Chartists had tried to create in the 1840's. Trying at first to use the disintegrating remnants of the

Chartist organizations as a base, the Association soon lost all contact with them, and its émigré character became increasingly pronounced. The leaders of the Association considered themselves Socialists and advocates of revolution, but in its basic structure the Association was clearly an organization of the conspiratorial type. It should be seen not as "the first form of a proletarian International," but rather as the last attempt to create an international organization of the Young Europe type.

That the International Association, the Commune Révolutionnaire, and the Philadelphians were all organizations of the old conspiratorial type is evident from their pronounced sympathy for individual acts of political terror. This is the second point I wish to stress here. Present-day historians, when studying revolutionary movements prior to the Franco-Prussian War, as a rule give very little attention to the question of terrorist activities, yet they are exceptionally important indicators both of the social and political attitudes of the day in general, and of the level of revolutionary tension in activist circles in particular. Tyrannicide was much more in the air during the Restoration and the July Monarchy than is now usually remembered; let us not forget that there were even attempts on the life of the young Queen Victoria. There is no need to stress the extent of terrorist activities in France. Very little was said about them openly, still less was written in the press, but many people thought about them. The literature of the day, police records, personal correspondence, and private archives force one to the conclusion that *all* the secret societies of the era were filled with people who were more or less sympathetic to terrorism. These sympathies outlived the Revolution of 1848. Indeed, sympathy toward terrorist attacks may be considered a reliable measure of the spread of revolutionary attitudes in Second Empire France. It is important to stress that the Philadelphians, too, and apparently all societies connected with them organizationally, must be regarded as sympathizing with individual acts of political terror. The attitudes of these groups toward the terrorist activities organized by Mazzini and his supporters leads us to this conclusion.

The Italian revolutionaries in Mazzini's organization were stubbornly preoccupied at the time with organizing attempts on the life of Napoleon III. Mazzini not only considered Napoleon III the most dangerous political opponent of Italian unification but personally regarded him as a traitor, and consequently sent to France group after group of terrorists whose mission was to assassinate Napoleon III.[16] Most of the terrorists came from English territory, with the assistance of Englishmen. The French press, reflecting government opinion, accused the English government of aiding the terrorists.

The most important terrorist outbreak was the attempt of Felice Orsini to assassinate Napoleon III with a grenade on January 14, 1858. The explosion missed its target, but 156 people, including guards and innocent passers-by, were killed. The indignation of the press—and not only of the French press—prompted the English government to take an unprecedented step: Simon Bernard, a French émigré and a friend of Orsini's, who helped him prepare the grenades, was put on trial in London. The hearing turned into a trial of Napoleon III. The jury deliberated only 15 minutes before unanimously acquitting Bernard.[17]

This trial, of course, was preceded and accompanied by polemics in the press. The International Association's *Bulletin de l'Association Internationale* defended both Bernard's actions and tyrannicide in general.[18] *La Commune Révolutionnaire, The Reasoner* (the organ of the Free Thinkers, who had connections with the Philadelphians), and similar publications carried articles in the same spirit. When Simon Bernard died several years later, only his friends and allies from the Philadelphians spoke at his funeral: Adolphe Talandier, Gustave Jourdain, Joseph Holyoake, and Félix Pyat.[19] We might add that, as mentioned earlier, in 1870 the Philadelphians arranged a banquet in honor of Paolo Tibaldi, who was then returning from Cayenne, where he had served part of a term of life imprisonment at hard labor in connection with another attempt on the life of Napoleon III. The speakers at the banquet were Louis Blanc and Gustave Flourens, and the chairman was Talandier; all of them were Philadelphians.[20]

### *The Philadelphians, Mazzini, and Garibaldi*

Between 1850 and 1855, the Philadelphians were active as a group that welcomed all proponents of revolutionary Socialism among both French and foreign émigrés. Their sharpest blows were then directed against Mazzini, who had become the militant spokesman for all the anti-Socialist émigrés. This isolated the Philadelphians and their organizations from the Italian émigrés, who were under Mazzini's influence. Personal friendships between Philadelphians and Italian émigrés, and the active assistance the Philadelphians gave Mazzini's terrorist enterprises did not lessen the gulf. This is why we do not find Italian names among the members of the International Association, and why the Association had no publications in Italian.

The situation began to change in 1858–59, when political preparation for Piedmont's war against Austria began. The war brought substantial changes both in the international situation and in the émigrés' state of mind. The question of Italy's unification became one of general interest. Mazzini's speeches, which called for the relegating of social problems to a second place behind the unification of Italy, brought forth the opposition of Socialist émigré circles. The International Association responded immediately (December 1858) with a special manifesto criticizing Mazzini's position. Characteristically, among the manifesto's signatories one finds neither the leaders of the Commune Révolutionnaire, nor of the Philadelphians, nor even the old leaders of the International Association itself.[21] The explanation for this, confirmed by police reports in the Vienna Staatsarchiv, is that a struggle was raging in the Association around the anti-Mazzini manifesto.* It looks very much as if the rank and file tried to save the Association, while the leaders, who were Philadelphians, were burying it. The reason is clear: the leaders were moving toward a new policy, the core of which was rapprochement with Mazzini.

Napoleon III's assistance to Piedmont and Austria's military defeat called forth lively pro-Napoleonic sentiments, even in genu-

* The *Wochenberichte* (weekly reports) of the Berlin police explain the struggle and the subsequent crisis in the Association by the discovery that John Mackay, the Association's new Secretary-General, was an agent of the French police. (Report of February 15, 1859, in the Vienna Staatsarchiv, Informationsbureau.) Since Mackay remained at his post, there can be no doubt that the majority of the active members of the Association put little stock in the accusation. Furthermore, it is unlikely that the discovery of a police informer (and there were a number of them among the French émigrés) would have been sufficient in itself to shake the Association. The crisis reflected in the police documents was undoubtedly precipitated by deep political divisions within the Association.

inely leftist émigré circles. Hopes that Napoleon III had decided to "ally himself with the revolution" and become the "executor of the will of the late republic"[22] were to be cruelly disappointed, yet it was the defeat of Austria that made possible Garibaldi's victories, which were hailed by democrats throughout the world. Garibaldi's extraordinary popularity enabled him, on October 5, 1860, to come forth with a plan to organize a special International Legion to be made up of volunteer divisions of French, Polish, Swiss, German, and other nationalities. The Legion's primary task, of course, was to aid in Italy's struggle for liberation. Later, Garibaldi promised, the divisions would aid in the liberation of their homelands. Ludwig Mieroslawski was placed at the head of the Legion. This plan set in motion widespread agitation and activity, which persisted even after the plan itself was abandoned.[23]

The movement to support Garibaldi became the center of the Philadelphians' activities during the second phase of their history, 1859 to 1864. Bossu cites a quotation from *Le Monde Maçonnique* for 1874, which states that in 1859 Garibaldi, Mazzini, Charles Bradlaugh, and Louis Blanc were members of the London Lodge of the "United Philadelphians."[24] Bradlaugh, as is evident from his biography, actually did join this lodge in March 1859,[25] but it is unlikely that Mazzini or Garibaldi, who occupied prominent posts in the Italian masonic movement, would join a lodge of French émigrés. What seems to be true, however, is that around that time they reached some sort of agreement with the Philadelphians on joint activities. The existence of such an agreement is beyond dispute; only the form of the agreement is open to speculation. In the 1860's, then, Mazzini, Garibaldi, and the Philadelphians formed a bloc that replaced the International Association of 1855–59.[26]

A number of other countries joined in the bloc's undertakings, notably Belgium and Switzerland. The major project of these men became the convocation of an international democratic congress and the creation of an international association. After considerable preparatory work, an official decision to hold the congress was made on the basis of a report given by Johann-Philipp Becker at a conference in La Chaux-de-Fonds, Switzerland, on July 20, 1863. All the preparatory work for the congress was carried out in the name of Garibaldi, who signed the official invitation, which was dated

Geneva, September 7, 1863. Together with proposed Statutes for the new association, the invitation was sent out to leaders of democratic and republican movements in all the countries of Western Europe. The congress was held in Brussels, September 26–28, 1863. Its president was Pierre Coullery, from La Chaux-de-Fonds.* The vice-chairman was Becker.[27] The other executive officers are not known. The congress adopted a resolution to create an Association Fédérative Universelle de la Démocratie, but it issued no documents, and the report of its activities went unpublished.[28]

The Brussels Congress passed almost unnoticed by the outside world. The reason for this was the concentration of the congress on Garibaldi and his movement at a time when that movement was obsolescent. The congress adopted a resolution on Garibaldi's trip to London, planned for the spring of 1864, which emphasized the importance of agitation among workers' groups and democratic organizations.[29] No doubt the leaders of the congress argued among themselves about the trip. Some of them shifted their attention to negotiation with the English government for its support in further struggles against Austria.

The trip took place as planned. The enthusiasm with which Garibaldi was met by thousands of people indicated the magnitude of his personal popularity and that of the cause for which he stood. But in government circles he did not receive the support on which the behind-the-scenes organizers of the trip had reckoned. The game of extending nationalist liberation movements no longer had a place in the policy of the English government or the government of Napoleon III.

The Philadelphians in London played an active role in organizing the reception there for Garibaldi. In the French colony they organized a special society called La France Libre and published a small pamphlet entitled "La France Libre et Garibaldi,"[30] but their behind-the-scenes role in various English democratic and workers' societies was far more important. They organized welcoming committees for Garibaldi and planned welcoming speeches. But the significance of their work was slight in view of the collapse of important political negotiations, to which I now turn.

* For a more detailed account of Coullery's political activities and the role of the section in La Chaux-de-Fonds, see pp. 15–16 above.—Editor.

*The Philadelphians' Second Phase, 1859–1864*

The second period of the Philadelphians' activity (1859–64) differed from the first (1851–59) on essential points. The slogan "République Démocratique et Sociale Universelle" was dropped, even from publications addressed to a French audience. It does not appear, for example, in the pamphlet "La France Libre et Garibaldi." The pamphlet's presumably subtle account of the disputes of 1848–49 completely overshadowed any thought of political influence on the masses in 1864. True, revolutionary aims were expressed openly by the revolutionary leaders whose documents are included in the brochure, that is, by Garibaldi, Mazzini, and Blanc, as well as by the official delegates of the Philadelphians whose names are not mentioned in the pamphlet. However, now the major concern was not that of the previous period, Socialist agitation, but the day-to-day relationship between Italian democrats on the one hand and French democrats on the other. The Philadelphians openly disassociated themselves from the aggressive aims of Napoleon III. They stressed the importance of peace and international solidarity, but cast overboard not only the Universal Republic, but also the entire non-Italian part of the program of national liberation. No mention was made of Garibaldi's 1860 promise that the divisions of his International Legion would carry the struggle to their own countries once Italy had been liberated. Though perhaps reluctantly, Garibaldi did agree to subordinate his own plans for the London trip to the diplomatic calculations of those who hoped to secure the support of the "great powers" of the West. These powers, however, regarded their recent wager on the national liberation movement as a card already played. They were now willing to pay a small part of the expenses for wrapping up Garibaldi's movement, but nothing at all for extending it to other countries.

Although the general trend was a retreat from revolution, it is important to note here that, largely under the leadership of the Philadelphians, quite different notes began to be sounded—notes of attempts to escape from great-power diplomacy, of attempts to appeal to the masses. These new notes were sounded with special clarity in the work of the Belgian and Swiss allies of the Philadelphians. It was these two countries that bore the main burden of preparations for the international democratic congress in Brussels, preparations that, in contrast to the Philadelphians' tradition, they linked with organizational efforts to broaden their own mass organizations. It was not at all accidental that these pioneer builders of the earliest organizations that formed the First International dated its birth not from the London meeting of September 24, 1864, at which neither the Belgians nor the Swiss were present, but from the Brussels Congress of September 26–28, 1863.[31]

Yet in its structure the Brussels Congress itself and the Alliance Fédérative Universelle de la Démocratie it organized were still too intimately tied to the old traditions of secret societies of a conspiratorial character. (These traditions were as persistent in Belgium as in France.) The congress was held in complete secrecy, without a single line about it in the newspapers. Not only was the Alliance built on the principle of individual membership; it had, in general, nothing to do with workers' organizations (the term did not even appear in its statutes, as it had not appeared in the statutes of the International Association), and its national sections were organized whenever as few as three members of the Alliance of the same nationality got together. All the members undertook to keep secret the names of the other members and of the congress participants. Neither the program nor any other document concerning the Alliance has ever been published.[32]

In this second period in the development of the London Philadelphians, then, what progressive element there was came not from London, not from the Philadelphians themselves, but from their Swiss and Belgian allies.[33] We do not know what the attitude of these allies was toward the Philadelphians' organization and political ideology. There is reason to suppose that some kind of tie linked London with both Brussels[34] and Geneva,[35] along the lines of the Order of Memphis, but there is no reliable evidence of this. During the period that the policy of the London Philadelphians was being made by the Mazzini-Blanc-Bradlaugh bloc, the Philadelphians took a step backward rather than forward.

In 1862–64 the Philadelphians' path crossed that of a group of Paris workers, who had come to England to acquaint themselves with the English labor movement. In outlook and composition, the two groups could hardly have been more different. The legal English labor movement was of little interest to the exiled conspirators who were the Philadelphians. Indeed, they were inclined to regard it with a measure of suspicion, if only because it was a legal movement, which attempted to create legal workers' organizations. Such a movement was beginning to revive in France, where it was more or less tolerated by the police. As members of old underground societies, the Philadelphians had learned to distrust anything the police tolerated.

The leaders of the Paris workers' groups were men of a different generation. They had not taken part in any secret organizations and had no inclination whatever in that direction. They had risen to the top with a new surge of a labor movement which, for all its peculiarities and defects, had strong, organic ties with the proletarian masses and was responsive to their changing needs and attitudes. They came to England for short stays which always had a specific purpose. Their basic purpose, however, was always the same: to acquaint themselves with the life of the English workers, with their working conditions, and with the organizations they had built. These workers came to England with the expectation of returning to France. In order not to become exiles themselves, they had to be very circumspect in their public pronouncements. They did not give speeches about the Universal Democratic and Socialist Republic, the favorite rallying cry of the Philadelphians, but constantly stressed their ties with the workers' organizations of France and their desire to establish permanent ties with similar organizations in other countries, particularly those in England.

The Philadelphians and the Paris workers represented two radically different approaches to the problem of international organization. In this early period, when Europe was beginning to emerge from the reaction that followed the defeat of the 1848 revolution, it was possible for these profound differences to go unnoticed. Yet they existed, and would assert themselves as soon as concrete social and political issues were raised.

The First International grew out of the second of these two approaches, out of the contacts established by leaders of the French labor movement with representatives of the English workers' organizations. But a great role in the creation of the First International was played also by representatives of the Philadelphians. All the attempts of the Philadelphians over a decade and a half to create an international organization based on conspiracy had ended in failure, yet the outward masonic form the Philadelphians had adopted helped preserve their old cadres. The organizational traditions which the Philadelphians preserved, and which were lacking among the legal workers' organizations, enabled the Philadelphians to be of technical service to the representatives of the French and English workers' organizations in 1862–64.

*The Philadelphians and the Founding of the First International*

The part played by individual Philadelphians in 1864 was enormous; Victor Le Lubez, to name only the most important, personally undertook the tremendous work of organizing the meeting of September 28, 1864, at which the General Council of the First International was elected. But even while giving Le Lubez and other Philadelphians their due, we must not forget that they never for a minute abandoned their conspiratorial traditions, and from the very beginning planned to use the new International, an alliance of workers' organizations, for the purpose of strengthening their own organization. Whenever possible, they tried to place their own people, who shared their views on tactics, in leading positions in the new International. The General Council of the International was selected by Le Lubez, and included a large and influential group of Philadelphians.[36]

We do not know enough about the members of the General Council to establish precisely how many of them were Philadelphians or their allies,[37] but we do know that of eight non-Englishmen elected to the first General Council, six were Philadelphians or Mazzinists, who, as we have seen, were then allied with the Philadelphians. And the influence of the non-English members of the General Council was much greater than their number would suggest. By November 29, the membership of the General Council had increased to 58, and the new members were primarily candidates proposed by Le Lubez. The French group in the General Council grew from three to nine, eight of whom were Philadelphians; and the number of non-English members who were definitely allies of Le Lubez—among whom I count all the Italians and Poles of Emile Holtorp's group—grew from six to 18 at the meeting of November 29, an increase, that is, from 19 per cent of the total membership of the General Council to 31 per cent.[38] Given the more regular attendance of the non-English members at the meetings of the General Council, it is clear how great the influence of the Philadelphians and their allies must have been, the more so since the Philadelphians had allies not only among the Poles and the Italians but also among the English and other national groups.[39]

This grouping, which counted no less than one-third the membership of the General Council, naturally had a decisive voice in all questions raised in the Council. There is no need to assume, of course, that this grouping acted as a disciplined bloc. Even the known members of the Philadelphians' lodge in the General Council disagreed on a number of issues, and no one even thought of invoking discipline. But the grouping's general agreement on basic questions was inevitably reflected in the course of its overall behavior. The struggles inside the General Council, at least in its initial period, cannot be correctly understood without reference to the existence within the General Council of the bloc of Philadelphians and Mazzinists.

The principal enemy of the Philadelphians, the man who prevented the First International from becoming a front for their activities, was Karl Marx. After Marx's bitter experience with the attempted revival of the Communist League in 1850–51, he refused to take part in any league or society created abroad. He made his first exception to this rule in the case of the First International, for reasons made clear in his correspondence: this International was being built by "real forces" that represented the open labor movements of France and England.[40] The impression he carried away from the meeting of September 28, 1864, was a good one. "Very nice fellow," he wrote about Henri Louis Tolain; he was favorably impressed, too, by George Odger and William Randal Cremer, who headed the International as representatives of the English trade unions. The good impression made on him by the leaders of the new organization, and above all his general evalution of the importance of a workers' international, decided Marx: he joined in the work of the International.

From the very first, Marx was confronted with the Philadelphians. Scattered remarks in his letters indicate that he had been aware of their existence before, and had been informed, for example, of the Brussels Congress of 1863. But he did not attach much significance to them; he had long since written off all secret, conspiratorial organizations. But in 1864, when the Philadelphians helped to launch the International, he did not regard them as harmful. He could not help but evaluate their work in the International favorably, and Le Lubez personally made a rather good impression on him. In the realm of theory and over-all policy he doubtless considered them great confusionists, but the harmful effects of their daily work in the International became clear to him only as time wore on.

Marx's attitude during the drafting of the programmatic documents for the International indicates that at first he wished to avoid a direct clash with the Philadelphians, which would have deprived the International of a large number of valuable members. The programmatic document drafted by Le Lubez was clearly out of the question, but it was easy to reject his draft on purely literary grounds. Marx was thus forced to write his own program, which was enthusiastically received by the Philadelphians ("worthy of enthusiasm," wrote Le Lubez).[41] But Marx had to compromise on the Statutes. The important concession was not the inclusion, in modified form, of a number of organizational proposals put forth by the Italians. It was especially important that Marx agreed to include, as he wrote to Engels on November 4, 1864, "two sentences about 'obligations' and 'rights,' ditto about 'truth, morality, and justice.' "

This passage in Marx's letter is often quoted by historians, but no one seems to have explained why Marx felt it necessary to add in writing to Engels that these words were "put in such a way that they cannot bring any harm." This remark makes strange reading, as do the notes of the Moscow editors of the works of Marx and Engels to the effect that the two sentences in question were introduced into the Statutes "upon the insistence of the other members of the commission," and that therefore Marx was not responsible for them.[42] Yet it is hard to imagine Marx's including in a document written by him important statements with which he seriously disagreed. As a matter of fact, the phrases in question did not violate any basic precepts of Marx's: they stated that there are "no rights without obligations" and "no obligations without rights," and that all members of the International "would recognize truth, justice, and morality as the basis of their relations with each other and with all people, irrespective of the color of their skin, their faith, or their nationality." Today these words sound a bit pompous, but in substance they are unexceptionable, and one wonders why Marx felt he had to justify including them in the Statutes. The reason is simple: these phrases were something in the nature of slogans for the Philadelphians, which defined their position on basic social and political questions and which seem to date from the early years of the July Monarchy. Our evidence is still fragmentary and indirect, but this is the only hypothesis that explains why Marx hastened to explain to Engels his reasons for including these words in the Statutes of the International, and why he added that in the context, these words "could not do any harm." Harm would have been done if these words had been taken to indicate general agreement with the Philadelphians' social and political ideas. It was this danger that Marx took measures to forestall in his general presentation of the Statutes. Obviously he agreed to include the two statements because the Philadelphians on the editorial commission insisted, and because Marx then considered their participation essential to the success of the International.

The desire to preserve the cooperation of all those who helped organize the September 28 meeting guided all Marx's actions in the struggle between the Parisian workers and the Philadelphians that broke out in the International in 1865. All the documents the International issued in 1864–65 were written by Marx, and they naturally reflected his views. But when he opposed the Philadelphians, he did so in such a way that they could continue to work for the International. The conflict inside the International was not provoked by him, but by the Philadelphians, whose actions jeopardized the entire work of the International in France. Although it is not possible here to go into the history of the Paris conflict of 1865 at length, it is clear, first, that the aggressors were the Philadelphians and their allies, and second, that the basis of the struggle was the opposition of the old conspiratorial societies to the new workers' organizations. Not all those who sided with the Philadelphians were aware of these two facts, but they were what basically characterized the Philadelphians' behavior. At first Marx tried to find a compromise, and only when it became clear that the Philadelphians would settle for nothing less than total victory, and that this victory would mean the end of the International as a workingmen's association, only then did Marx throw his weight behind the Parisians.

The struggle was essentially a struggle for power in the General Council of the International. The key to understanding power relations within the Council lies in the composition of its major, policy-making subcommittee, which was appointed at the very first session of the General Council, October 5, 1864. The subcommittee was then composed of five Englishmen, including the Chairman and the Secretary of the General Council, William Randal Cremer, and four non-Englishmen: Marx, Le Lubez, the Italian Luigi Wolff, and the Pole Emile Holtorp. Apart from Marx, all the non-Englishmen were in the Philadelphian-Mazzinist bloc, which apparently also had support of at least one, and perhaps two, of the Englishmen; the bloc was thus able to steer the work of the subcommittee. After reviewing the dispute provoked by the Parisian section on September 19, 1865, the General Council selected a new subcommittee, made up of six Englishmen and five non-Englishmen.[43] Three Englishmen from the old subcommittee stayed on, including the Chairman of the General Council and the Secretary, and only one non-Englishman, namely Marx. Three Englishmen and four non-Englishmen joined the subcommittee for the first time, and not one of them belonged to the Philadelphian-Mazzinist bloc. Thus the formation of the new subcommittee meant a complete defeat of the bloc and was in particular a cruel blow to the Philadelphians, who had considered themselves the masters of the General Council.

To make the political significance of the altered composition of the subcommittee even clearer, it should be pointed out that it was at precisely this time that the leaders of the old-style conspiratorial societies attempted to launch their own new international organization. I refer to the International Republican Committee, which was then conjured up by Mazzini. We seem to have no information about this committee, but from the letters of Marx to Engels we know that besides Mazzini, its membership included Alexandre Ledru-Rollin, Gottfried Kinkel, Karl Blind, Heinrich Bolleter, and the Poles Emile Holtorp and Marian Langewicz.[44] These names make the political complexion of the organization clear.

Mazzini, who had abandoned the terrorist campaign against Napoleon III during the Franco-Austrian war, returned to it in 1863–

64 and even tried to extend it.[45] Ledru-Rollin had been a loyal ally of Mazzini in such activities as far back as the 1850's. Blind wrote articles for Karl Heinzen's German-American newspaper, *Der Pionier,* that at once expressed anti-Socialist views and advocated terrorism. Blind's stepson, moreover, had been arrested shortly before for trying to kill Bismarck, and there is no doubt that he acted under his stepfather's influence. Langewicz and Holtorp, too, had strong sympathies for individual acts of terror.[46]

Thus it is obvious that Mazzini's International Republican Committee was an alliance of proponents of individual acts of terror. When it became clear that the plans to seize control of the First International through the Philadelphians had collapsed, Mazzini took steps to form his own International, the International of extreme terrorist groups. This was one of the last cards played by the epigoni of the old conspiratorial societies.

*The Legacy of the Philadelphians*

The role of the Philadelphians in the formation of the First International, as it has been described in the foregoing pages, was enormous. The International, as history knows it, was born out of the struggle against the old methods of political conspiracy and secret organizations. Only against the background of this struggle can we understand the creation of the First International and its subsequent history.

The struggle at this stage formally ended in the autumn of 1865, when the known supporters of the Philadelphians were removed from leading posts in the International. But not only did the traditions of the Philadelphians survive in individual sections of the International, their supporters continued their work on an international scale. Although I do not wish to go beyond the chronological framework of this paper, the years in which the International was founded, I cannot refrain from indicating that not only was Mikhail Bakunin connected with the Philadelphians, but there were strong bonds between the Philadelphians and the Blanquists. And it was, after all, the Blanquists who dealt the death blow to the First International, when they forced Marx to move the General Council to the United States.[47]

Max Nomad

# The Anarchist Tradition

Anarchism, as a movement directed against the status quo, has shrunk, except in a few Spanish-speaking countries, to the insignificance of a motley of tiny, inoffensive groups. They continue to discuss their ideas, but to most of them even the once dread-inspiring term "propaganda by the deed," with its echoes of the spectacular terrorist acts that were frequent around the turn of the century, has lost all meaning. Yet there was a time, particularly during the 1860's and the early 1870's, when the names of Pierre Joseph Proudhon and Mikhail Bakunin, the two outstanding apostles of anarchism, were better known to the general public than the name of their contemporary Karl Marx, even after the appearance of *Das Kapital*.

The decline and virtual disappearance of anarchism as a factor in politics is sometimes explained by the alleged superiority of Marxist realism over the utopianism and romanticism of its rivals for the allegiance of the masses. To be sure, there were utopianism and romanticism in the teachings and the activities of the anarchists, but this alone does not explain their defeat. For there were plenty of those ingredients in the teachings of Marx too: the theories of the increasing poverty of the masses, of the disappearance of the middle strata, of the collapse of capitalism, to mention only a few. Despite those theoretical shortcomings and despite Marx's blind spots, those who rightly or wrongly call themselves Marxists are now the masters of a substantial part of the globe, and Socialist parties holding Marx in high esteem, though otherwise ignoring him, are a powerful political factor in most European countries. Hence there must be other, more valid reasons for the eclipse of anarchism, aside from the additional fact that the disreputable label may have been an impediment to the growth of the movement.

However, before that question can be tackled, a distinction must be made between anarchism as a *philosophy* opposing the principle of authority, and hence the state as its concrete manifestation, and anarchism as one of the branches of the *anti-capitalist movement* of the nineteenth and twentieth centuries, a movement representing specific class or group interests and changing both its doctrines and tactics according to circumstances.

Anarchism as a philosophy opposing the principle of authority proceeds either from the protest of the *individual* against all kinds of compulsion imposed by society or from the opposition voiced in behalf of the masses against the state and its institutions. Both branches of anarchist philosophy—that label did not come into use until it was coined by Proudhon—have age-old histories. They can be traced back to Greek history, with Aristippus of Cyrene voicing the individualist protest and Zeno the Stoic championing the social protest against the state. Similar ideas can be found in the writings of various mystics, such as the Gnostic Carpocrates, and in *The Net of the Faith* by Peter Chelcicky, who lived during the Hussite period and who may have inspired the Christian anarchism of Leo Tolstoy; in Etienne de la Boétie's *Discours de la servitude volontaire,* which, as many suspect, was probably written by his friend Michel de Montaigne; in *The Law of Freedom,* written by the "True Leveller" Gerrard Winstanley during the Cromwellian Revolution; in Sylvain Maréchal's *Manifeste des égaux,* written at the time of Babeuf's conspiracy; in William Godwin's *Political Justice*; in Edmund Burke's (yes, Burke's) *Vindication of Natural Society,* which, as others have said, is not a satire directed against Bolingbroke, but the actual expression of the youthful Burke's sentiments. In modern times, such ideas occur in the works of Thoreau, Stirner, Spencer, Nietzsche, and Ibsen. One might also add to the list American individualists such as Josiah Warren, Lysander Spooner, and, finally, Benjamin R. Tucker (who did call himself an anarchist)—champions of a sort of individualist anarchism, which never won a following among the workers.

None of these ideas had any relevance to the anarchist movement that flourished at the time of the First International and during the subsequent decades, even though some Marxists, such as Georgi Plekhanov, who were eager to discredit their critics from the extreme left, disingenuously harped on the "bourgeois individualism" of Max Stirner as the source of modern anarchism.[1] For the real fountainheads were the writings of Proudhon and Marx, the teachers of Bakunin, who was the actual father of modern revolutionary anarchism.

To be sure, Stirner's super-individualism did play a certain role in the thinking of some French anarcho-bandits of the first two decades of this century, particularly the famous "tragic band" headed by Auguste Bonnot. But their exploits had nothing to do with any aspect of the anarchist movement—whether Proudhonist, Bakuninist, Kropotkinian, or syndicalist. Nor did they contribute a single penny to the war chests of these movements. They believed neither in the class struggle nor in the realizability of any social ideal. Theirs was the philosophy of an illegal parasitism of underdogs tired of their drudgery, a proletarian counterpart, as it were, of the Nietzschean "anarchism" of some ultra-plutocratic opponents of the income tax and the welfare state.

*The Proudhonists and the "Collectivists"*

The "anarchist tradition" may be said to have started with Pierre Joseph Proudhon (1809–65), not only because Proudhon coined the term—he was the first writer to call himself an anarchist in the original etymological sense of "an-archy," that is, "without government"—but also because during nearly two decades his ideas had numerous adherents among French-speaking workers, and because his following was represented at the congresses of the First International.

Proudhon's books—there are over 50 of them, including 14 volumes of correspondence—are no longer read, not only because there are no longer any Proudhonists, but also because his main ideas are altogether out of tune with the present age, even in the opinion of anarchists who hold his name in great esteem. And there is the additional circumstance that, despite the brilliance of his style, he was often hard to understand. His vocabulary is the despair even of specialists in anarchism, such as Max Nettlau, anarchist biographer of Bakunin and historian of anarchist ideas and movements, who devoted more than 50 years of his long life to the study of his subject.

Proudhon wrote on a great variety of subjects, but he is remembered chiefly for his "Property is theft"—a phrase which, by the way, was not original with him, for the Girondist Jacques Pierre Brissot had said essentially the same thing more than 50 years before the appearance of Proudhon's *What Is Property?*, which contained that answer. His ideas—they are summed up in his last, posthumous work, *On the Political Capacity of the Working Classes*—are anything but bloodcurdling appeals to revolt and expropriation, two concepts usually associated with what is commonly called anarchism. To be sure, their point of departure is the rejection of the state and of property (except property acquired by one's own toil), a rejection based on Proudhon's fundamental principle, *justice*. For the authority of the state he wanted to substitute a single norm, namely, that agreements must be kept. For the privilege of capital, Proudhon wanted to substitute the principle of *mutuality*. The instrument Proudhon suggested for the realization of this principle he called a "People's Bank," which would grant free credit to producers and would facilitate the exchange and distribution of their products. Persuasion, not violence, was to be the tactic for attaining this aim.

Proudhon's ideas had a certain appeal to skilled workers and to some intellectuals. The basis of that appeal was the realization that all past revolutions had resulted mainly in changing the ruling personnel, but not in overcoming the basic evil of economic inequality. The skilled workers to whom Proudhon appealed—they were engaged mostly in small handicraft industries—saw in the People's Bank a shortcut to their longed-for freedom as independent, small producers operating either individually or through producers' cooperatives. These workers, as a rule, did not take to the conspirator Auguste Blanqui and his following of malcontent, déclassé intellectuals, for they saw in these revolutionists merely power-hungry job-seekers. The few intellectuals who joined Proudhon did so apparently because in their opinion only an appeal to the workers' economic interests, e.g., the remedy of "free credit," could serve as a basis for a mass struggle against the status quo.

In this connection it may not be amiss to point out that Proudhon's "negation" of the state was not to be taken literally. He saw the realization of the idea of "an-archy," that is, "non-government," as something that was centuries away. For the time being his "negation" went no further than hostility to administrative centralism. The elimination of that evil, he hoped, could be realized by dividing France into 12 autonomous provinces and shearing Paris of its central authority.[2] There was no place in the world of his ideas for either labor unions[3] or strikes for higher wages.[4]

A few months before his death Proudhon hailed the idea of the International Workingmen's Association (the First International), which at the time of its founding was not controlled by Marx, and which Proudhon hoped might be an instrument for the propagation of his ideas. Therefore a number of his followers, all self-educated skilled workers, joined the new organization.

In the First International the Proudhonist anarchists—they called themselves *mutuellistes*—constituted what might be called the very moderate right wing of that organization. They harped on the panacea of the "People's Bank" (that is, mutual credit), and consistently rejected such measures as abolition of the right of inheritance, expropriation, nationalization of land, and socialization of industries. Their only "radicalism" consisted in their insisting—unsuccessfully, to be sure—that only manual workers be admitted as delegates to the International.* That proposal was directed primarily against the Blanquists, who had not yet joined the International, and who were, almost without exception, malcontent, déclassé intellectuals, mostly students and journalists, who professed Socialist principles and were known to aspire to a revolutionary dictatorship.

While the more or less orthodox Proudhonists were opposing all anti-capitalist motions advanced by other members of the Interna-

* At the turn of the century that ex-horny-handed professional jealousy was to find its counterpart in Gompers' and later in the syndicalists' hostility to the socialist politicians, and also in the antagonism of the German social-democratic ex-horny-handed trade-union leaders to their college-bred comrades in charge of the Socialist Party apparatus. Both leaders of the Proudhonists within the International, Henri Tolain and E. E. Fribourg (originally skilled workers), ended their careers as respectable middle-class politicians. Tolain, the one who had insisted on barring intellectuals, became a senator after 1871.

tional, some of Proudhon's followers began to move in the direction of what was then called "collectivism." They included such figures as César De Paepe and Eugène Varlin, who combined Proudhon's rejection of the state with the idea of expropriation of the capitalists and collective ownership of the means of production.* They had arrived at these non-Proudhonist heresies when they began to realize that the growth of large-scale industry left the workers little hope of economic independence, and that to defend their interests, the workers would have to organize in labor unions and strike for higher wages, two altogether non-Proudhonist concepts. The ideas of expropriation and collective ownership, which were then shared by many members of the First International, combined with Proudhon's opposition to government ownership, gave rise to the concept of ownership and management of industries by labor unions,[5] an idea which, less than three decades later, was to reappear in modified form as one of the basic tenets of syndicalism.

*Enter Bakunin*

From 1868 on, the idea of a revolutionary, "stateless" collectivism, as professed by Varlin, found in the International an inspired spokesman, Mikhail Bakunin (1814–76), a Russian revolutionary exile, who since the 1840's had been under the ideological influence of both Proudhon's anti-statism and Marx's concepts of the class struggle and the materialist interpretation of history. There was also undoubtedly in Bakunin's thought an echo of Carbonarism and of the Blanquist traditions of conspiracy and insurrection.

Apart from these basic elements of his philosophy, Bakunin's views were in constant flux. After his escape from Siberia in 1861, he was, until 1863, interested only in Slavic nationalism, which was unrelated to either anarchism or anti-capitalism. It was only in 1864 that Bakunin decided to devote himself exclusively to the radical movement in the West. Yet it was four years before he joined the International. He was apparently repelled by the moderation of the Proudhonists, on the one hand, and, on the other, unwilling to

* César De Paepe, the former Proudhonist, who for a while was moving in the same direction, eventually became a Marxist and one of the founders of the Belgian Socialist Party. Eugène Varlin perished during the Paris Commune of 1871. He is venerated by the syndicalists as one of their precursors.

play second fiddle to Marx, whose mind he admired—in a famous letter to Marx in 1868 he declared himself his disciple[6]—but with whom he disagreed chiefly on the question of tempo and on which of the two was to be the supreme leader of the European revolution in the making. Moreover, he needed time to elaborate both his own theory of a decentralized form of Socialism and the strategy that would secure him a position of power within the International.

The result of Bakunin's meditations was the *Revolutionary Catechism* (1866),[7] which became the credo of the International Brothers, a secret organization Bakunin founded in Italy, apparently as early as 1864. This may, of course, have been an additional reason for Bakunin's delay in joining the First International. He had a sort of International of his own, composed mostly of devoted Italian followers, though in a letter to Alexander Herzen written in 1866 he claimed that he had followers in practically every country. (This *Revolutionary Catechism* is not to be confused with the notorious document called *Catechism of the Revolutionist,* written several years later, which the anarchists generally attribute to Bakunin's discredited disciple Sergei Nechayev.) The ideas set forth in the 1866 *Catechism* show that there was no essential difference between what the Bakuninists planned to do "on the morrow of the revolution" and what the Marxists might do under similar circumstances. There was no hint there of the immediate abolition of all government, which Bakunin advocated in many of his later utterances.[8] On the contrary, under Bakunin's post-revolutionary system there were laws, penalties, and prisons, just as there were elected "public, judicial, and civic officials." There is, however, in contrast to the centralism of the Marxists, a far-reaching political decentralization, with the greatest possible autonomy of the provinces within the nation and of the municipalities within the provinces. To be sure, this was to be the transitional phase before real stateless "anarchy" could be established. But this was the case, too, in Marx's "dictatorship of the proletariat" which was to precede what in Marxian parlance was called the "withering away of the state"—in other words anarchism, but without the disreputable and confusing label.

Bakunin's economic program, as propounded in the *Catechism,* was similar to, only less "radical" than, what 60 years later was to be called the New Economic Policy (NEP) in the Soviet Union. The land was to be given to the peasants, the forests and subsoil were to be socialized, but industry would remain in the hands of its capitalist owners. The transition from this semi-capitalist post-revolutionary system to full "collectivism" would be effected gradually by the abolition of the right of inheritance and the development of producers' cooperatives. The great difference between Marx's economic program and that of Bakunin consisted in the fact that under Marx's "communism," as it was called at that time, all means of production would be taken over by the government, whereas according to Bakunin they would be controlled by producers' cooperatives, or, as he called them, "workers' associations."

Simultaneously with the *Revolutionary Catechism,* Bakunin offered his International Brothers another document, called *Organization.*[9] In that document he made a distinction between the "International Family," which was to play the part of the Central Executive Committee, and the "National Families," which might be compared with the various Communist parties at the time when the Communist International enforced strict discipline over all affiliated parties. The degree to which the "International Family" was to dominate the subordinate bodies is clearly indicated in such sentences as "The National Family of each country is formed in such a way as to be subject to absolute and exclusive control of the International Society" and "All members of the national Junta are appointed by the central directorate, to which the national Junta owes absolute obedience in all cases." *Organization* was an anticipation of Lenin's and Stalin's methods under an anarchist guise.

Having laid the groundwork for his future international activities, Bakunin left Italy in 1867 for Switzerland, to be in closer contact with the malcontents of various nationalities who might be receptive to his revolutionary plans. However, the first step in his campaign was an act of great "stupidity," as he admitted two years later. He joined the League for Peace and Liberty, a society for middle-class pacifists composed of liberal lawyers, politicians, and journalists. This was not a group that an irreconcilable champion of the underdog and preacher of the destruction of the state had any chance of winning over to his ideas. Bakunin left the League when all his radical proposals were rejected by its conventions.

Before retiring from the League in 1868, Bakunin became a member of the Geneva section of the First International. He was joined by a number of International Brothers from various countries, mostly political exiles. To them the aging, romantic rebel was a charismatic figure, the personification not so much of the longing for a faraway "stateless" ideal as of the hope for an immediate revolution in their respective countries—a revolution that would enable them to take over. One of his followers at that time was the Serbian student Nikola Pashich, who four decades later was to become the creator and strong man of pre-Tito Yugoslavia. It goes without saying that, as in all revolutionary movements, the ranks of Bakunin's followers included, in addition to the common run of job- and power-hungry educated déclassés, a number of disinterested idealists, such as the famous French geographer Elisée Reclus and the Italian dreamer Carlo Cafiero, a wealthy aristocrat who had been slated for the diplomatic service.

When Bakunin's followers joined the First International, they were already members of a secret organization variously referred to as the "Alliance of Social Revolutionists," the "Secret Alliance of Socialist Democracy," or, briefly, the "Secret Alliance." This organization was virtually identical with the International Brotherhood founded by Bakunin during his stay in Italy, though the International Brothers may have been the inner circle of the Secret Alliance.

So much mystery surrounds Bakunin's conspiratorial activities that even the most authoritative historians of anarchism—themselves followers and admirers of Bakunin—disagree on a very essential point. Thus the Swiss James Guillaume, who was the Western follower closest to Bakunin, in his voluminous history of the International actually denies the existence of that Secret Alliance. He may have done so because he wanted to clear Bakunin and himself of Marx's accusation that they were secretly intriguing against the First International in order to gain control of it. On the other hand, Max Nettlau—who was not a contemporary of the First International, to be sure, but was the generally recognized "Herodotus of Anarchy"—in his *Der Anarchismus von Proudhon zu Kropotkin,* the second volume of his unfinished history of anarchism, leaves no doubt that the Secret Alliance actually existed.

It goes without saying that with regard to the control of the International, Bakunin harbored the same ambitions as did Marx. Both hoped to use it for the consolidation of their power in the event of the revolution they were anticipating. They differed in only one important respect: Marx was willing to wait for an international conflict that would precipitate a revolution, whereas Bakunin and his followers put their hopes in spontaneous or organized uprisings to be extended and controlled by the International Brothers. Bakunin thought that one hundred Brothers would be sufficient for that task.[10]

As mentioned earlier, these International Brothers—there were never as many as a hundred of them—were the core of the Secret Alliance. Apart from this secret body, which was unknown to the public, Bakunin's followers formed an open international organization called the "International Alliance of Socialist Democracy." Bakunin opposed its formation because, it seems, he felt that the existence of an international organization openly competing with the First International might weaken his "legitimate" opposition to its leaders.[11] He was overruled, however, by his own followers, who shortly after the founding of the open Alliance applied for the admission of their organization to the First International. That application was rejected, but the individual sections of the Alliance were admitted as local organizations.

The existence of the two alliances, the one open and the other secret, placed Bakunin in a peculiar theoretical position. By 1868 his views had evolved beyond the position he had taken in his *Catechism* of 1866. He had become acquainted with former Proudhonists, and had adopted their principle of expropriation and collective ownership, together with the Proudhonist hostility to government ownership. This basic revolutionary idea Bakunin now put before his followers in the *Program and Aim of the Revolutionary Organization of the International Brothers.*[12] This work was his true and definitive gospel, to be realized after the successful overthrow of the old regimes. Before this happened, however, he wanted to avoid antagonizing the peasants, who as owners of property were opposed to the idea of expropriation. Hence, in a public statement at the Basel Congress (1869) of the First International, he still advocated the abolition of the right of inheritance—an idea he had propounded in his *Revolutionary Catechism* of 1866—as a painless, delayed-action, installment-plan expropriation, even though he had abandoned this idea when he was converted to the "collectivism" of the former Proudhonists. At the Basel Congress, these ex-Proudhonists pointed out that after a victorious revolution resulting in the expropriation of the capitalists and the establishment of a collectivist form of production, the abolition of the right of inheritance would be meaningless.[13] Bakunin was, of course, aware of this himself, but he clung to the old formula for the practical reasons I have just mentioned.

Bakunin's intimate followers must have been aware of this game of two truths, but as practical revolutionists they saw nothing objectionable in anything that would serve the cause of immediate revolution. Similarly, in order to outdo Marx in radicalism, they were ready to call "abolition of the state," or anarchism, what in fact was merely the replacement of centralized governments by autonomous provincial or local governments.

As against Bakunin's following of déclassé intellectuals from economically backward countries such as Italy and Spain,* Marx could lean for support chiefly on the less desperate malcontents of the economically more advanced countries, particularly the German-speaking countries. Marx could also depend on the British trade unions, to whom he was a lesser evil than the Bakuninist firebrands. Similarly, Marx's rank-and-file following consisted largely of the better-paid skilled workers, while the Bakuninists appealed chiefly to the generally underpaid or starving workers and peasants of their native countries. Some of the French Proudhonists switched their allegiance to Marx instead of to Bakunin. Marx could also count on the support of the Blanquists, even though temperamentally and sociologically this group of impatient, educated déclassés was closer to the Bakuninists. The Blanquists took the Russian's thunderings against the seizure of power at their face value, not realizing, as Marx did, that behind them was concealed Bakunin's desire for personal dictatorial power. (Bakunin's revealing state-

* Bakunin had few followers in Paris, not because the French capital lacked the potentially revolutionary educated déclassés, but because the latter had a glamorous leader of their own, Auguste Blanqui, who was just as quick on the revolutionary trigger as Bakunin and whose reputation as a rebel was even older.

ment about the "invisible dictatorship" his organization would exert after the successful revolution was at that time still unknown to outsiders.)[14]

With the support of these diverse elements and aided by the disarray in Bakunin's camp—Bakunin's Italian followers had refused to attend the crucial Congress of the International at The Hague in 1872—Marx succeeded in having Bakunin and his closest associate, James Guillaume, expelled (September 2, 1872) from the International for participation in a secret organization whose activities were harmful to the International. An additional reason for Bakunin's expulsion was his alleged commission of a dishonorable act of "swindling."* This attempt to rob a famous rebel of his good name, an act of character assassination now condemned, apologetically, by most Marxist historians, was to poison well-nigh forever the anarchists' personal feelings toward Marx.

In a pamphlet written shortly before Bakunin's expulsion, Marx placed all blame for the conflicts within the International on Bakunin's intrigues and lust for power.[15] He was apparently unwilling to face the fact that for the educated déclassés who formed Bakunin's following, immediate revolution, as preached by their leader, was the only alternative to hopeless destitution. To Marx, they were simply the "dregs of the bourgeoisie,"[16] whose plight did not interest him, particularly since the economic situation of his own educated following in the economically more advanced countries, though not quite satisfactory, was at any rate not so desperate as that of their Spanish and Italian counterparts.

The real cause of Bakunin's expulsion and of the subsequent fatal transfer of the International to New York was revealed in 1893, in a statement made by Friedrich Engels at the Zurich Congress of the Second International. Engels said that in 1872 Marx felt that the situation on the Continent was becoming "too dangerous for the old organization to be maintained."[17] The "danger," as the Marxist historian Franz Mehring put it, consisted of the possibility of futile uprisings (*Handstreiche*) which, in Engels' opinion, could result in "persecutions" and "unnecessary suffering."[18] These

* Bakunin had failed to return 300 rubles which he had received from a Russian publisher as an advance on the translation of Marx's *Kapital*.

uprisings might have been the work of either the Bakuninists or the Blanquists. Ironically, it was against the Blanquists, who had helped Marx get rid of Bakunin, that the transfer was directed.

*The "Anti-Authoritarian International"*

After the expulsion of Bakunin and Guillaume, their followers assembled during the same year (1872) at St.-Imier, Switzerland. The delegates represented Spain, Italy, and the Jura, as well as France, Holland, and Belgium. They did not consider themselves "expelled." On the contrary, they refused to recognize the official General Council of the First International, and looked upon themselves as the continuation of the body virtually liquidated by Marx.

The reunion at St.-Imier led to the formation of what is sometimes called the "Anti-Authoritarian International," which held conventions until 1877. It was not an outright anarchist International; some of the delegates professed views midway between anarchism and democratic socialism, while others were moderate British trade unionists. Not all of them were actually anti-authoritarians; the only "plank" they shared was opposition to the authority exerted by Marx in the General Council of the International. During their struggle against their Marxist rivals, even the ultra-authoritarian followers of Ferdinand Lassalle sent delegates to one of the congresses.

In the course of the debates held at the Geneva Congress (1873), the arsenal of anarchist ideas was enriched by the concept of the general strike as a tactic of social revolution.[19] The concept was originally proposed by the Belgian delegates, who stood halfway between anarchism and democratic socialism. It was supported by a number of other delegates; the representatives of the Jura Federation also stressed the necessity of strikes for higher wages, thus emphasizing the importance of labor unions. No definite decision was adopted on this point, but it is now generally believed that this was the first step in the direction of what was later to be called either "anarcho-syndicalism" or "revolutionary syndicalism."

The last convention of that "Anti-Authoritarian," or, more precisely, anti-Marxian, International took place in 1877, in the Belgian industrial town of Verviers. It was attended exclusively by anarchists, for most of the other participants at the former congresses of that International had decided to hold in Ghent, Belgium, what they called a "Universal Socialist Congress," whose aim was to unite *all* elements of the European radical and labor movements. Possibly it was an attempt to revive the old International, which had officially expired in 1876, with some former middle-of-the-roaders, like the Belgian ex-Proudhonist and near-Bakuninist César de Paepe, definitely intent on joining the Social Democratic camp. Some anarchists took part in that congress, too, and voted against the two main planks of democratic Socialism adopted by the majority: government ownership of the means of production, and participation in parliamentary struggles for power. Of the anarchists' own Congress in Verviers, it can be said that it had a special place in the history of anarchist ideas, for it marked the beginning of the transition from Bakuninism to a new phase of anarchism dominated by the ideas and the personality of Peter Kropotkin.

The disintegration of Bakuninism had begun even before Bakunin's death, in 1876. It had started two years earlier, in 1874, when the revered leader covered himself with shame and his movement with ridicule by wasting the entire war chest of the hoped-for revolution on the childish project of improving the villa in which he lived.[20] Shortly after that disaster, Bakunin's followers attempted to start an uprising in Italy; the attempt misfired. Another attempt, in 1877, was equally unsuccessful. The masses, supposed to be potentially revolutionary and always ready to rise, proved as disappointing as the judgment of Bakunin.

Bakunin's closest and most active followers reacted in two different ways. Some of them moved over to the Marxist camp. They had apparently never been taken in by the mystique of the anarchist "abolition of the state," behind which they were able to discern the will to power of their erstwhile teacher—a sentiment in which they heartily concurred in the innermost recesses of their all-too-human souls and hungry stomachs. However, the economic situation in their countries was improving. Industries were springing up, offering prospects for the organization of labor unions and labor parties, with jobs for organizers, lecturers, and journalists. The once-starving and hence fiery Don Quixotes of immediate revolution were turning into sensible Sancho Panzas of law-abiding gradualist socialism, using the vocabulary of Marxism to predict an inevitable revolution in an unpredictable future. Outstanding among them were Jules Guesde and Andrea Costa, the founders of the French and the Italian Marxist parties. The "dregs of the bourgeoisie" became the cream of the proletariat.

However, there were others, idealists and romantics, such as Elisée Reclus, Errico Malatesta, and Carlo Cafiero, who stuck to their anarchist guns and were joined by Prince Peter Kropotkin, who had escaped from a Tsarist dungeon in 1876. These pure-in-heart dreamers, joined by some implacable haters, rejected any idea of receding from their irreconcilable position. But they also rejected the idea of blindly accepting their departed teacher's views. Sobered by the scandal mentioned above, they may have taken a second look at some of his theories. Apparently in deference to his great prestige among the rank and file, they never publicly criticized his theories; but the ideas they gradually evolved implicitly rejected most of the tactical and theoretical tenets of "collectivist anarchism," as Bakunin's version of anarchism is usually called.

For Bakuninism, they gradually began to realize, was a contradictory combination of libertarian, anti-authoritarian philosophy *in abstracto* and dictatorial, authoritarian practice *in concreto*. They certainly recalled the letter Bakunin had written on February 7, 1870, in which he demanded of his followers absolute submission to his authority.[21] Nor could they forget what he had written about the "invisible dictatorship" that their secret organization would have to exert to keep the revolution on the right path.[22] Even the economic aspect of his "collectivist anarchism" was found wanting. The means of production were to belong to producers' cooperatives, whose members were to receive the full value of their labor. This, however, implied the necessity of statistical or accounting commissions to estimate the worth of a worker's output—bodies that one way or another would smack of government authority.

To eliminate all these "impurities," they decided in favor of a very loose, well-nigh atomized form of organization, with no trace of the hierarchical principle of the International Brothers. They also devised a simon-pure ideal, which they called interchangeably either "communist anarchism" or "anarchist communism." Under that system, they believed, everybody would work voluntarily according to his abilities and consume according to his needs, satisfying his requirements out of the well-stocked storehouses. Authorship of that ideal system is usually credited to Kropotkin, who is generally recognized as the theoretician of communist anarchism. The fact is, however, that the idea was "in the air" during the late 1870's, and that Reclus, Cafiero, and Malatesta were as much its fathers as Kropotkin.

Only pure-in-heart idealists like these men could actually believe in the workability of such a system. Being quite naïve about economic facts, they were convinced that the capitalist system produced such an abundance of goods that for a long time after the revolution there would be enough for everybody, even in the event of widespread loafing. Eventually, they were sure, everyone would voluntarily adhere to the idea of solidarity. They based their hopes on the inherent goodness of man, and on the principle of mutual aid allegedly governing animals and humans alike. One of their later converts, Ferdinand Domela Nieuwenhuis, the founder of the Socialist movement in Holland, put it this way: "Why speculate on man's evil passions rather than on his generous sentiments?"

Only the anarchists of Spain and the United States remained for a number of years under the sway of Bakunin's ideas: the Spaniards because, having a mass following among both the workers and the peasants, they still hoped for a revolution in their lifetime, something conceivable only under the slogans of the not-quite-pure anarchism of the old apostle; the Americans, or more exactly the German-American anarchists of New York and Chicago, because, as former Social Democrats, they quite naturally took to Bakunin's ultra-radical crypto-Marxism rather than to the ultra-utopian dreams of Kropotkin.

Some of Bakunin's views were taken up, about two decades after his death, by the Polish-Russian ex-Marxist Waclaw Machajski, author of *The Intellectual Worker* (1898). Apparently taking his cue from a passage of Bakunin's *Statism and Anarchy* (1873) about the spurious "proletarian" character of a Marxist dictatorship, he argued that what the Marxist Socialists were aiming at was in reality not the emancipation of the working class, but the rule of a neo-bourgeois class of officeholders and managers—in short, of a non-capitalist middle class. And, just as inconsistent as Bakunin, he postulated a revolutionary dictatorship of his own secret organization. Because of his violent criticism of Socialist gradualism, he was in his time generally classed as an anarchist, though he himself rejected that label. His views are of some interest because they either directly or indirectly inspired those writers who emphasize the "managerial," i.e., "non-proletarian," aspect of the various anti-capitalist theories.

*The Social Revolutionary Congress of London, 1881*

During the late 1870's and early 1880's the ideas of Kropotkin and his close associates were making gradual headway among opponents of the de-facto gradualism of the growing or budding Marxist parties. On the initiative of some of these groups and of some extreme left-wing Socialists, arrangements were made to hold an international revolutionary—but not strictly anarchist—congress in London in 1881.

The debates at that congress reveal the confusion prevailing in the minds of the participants.[23] In the first place, the congress was honeycombed with agents provocateurs. Their number has never been definitely established, but outstanding among them was a certain Serreaux, editor of *La Révolution Sociale,* a periodical published in Paris with funds supplied by the chief of the Paris police.* Besides those professing anarchist views, the delegates included German, French, and Belgian left-wing Socialists, whose only bond with the anarchists was the advocacy of immediate revolutionary action. They were essentially Blanquists, even though some of them used a Marxian vocabulary. They believed in the seizure of power rather than in the immediate "abolition of the state." Their views were shared by Johann Most, who was then in prison. A reluctant anarchist, his political philosophy, apart from his super-emphasis on terrorist acts, was a hybrid of Bakuninist, Blanquist, Marxist, and Lassallean ("iron law of wages") ideas. It seems that he ac-

* When at last he was unmasked, he was merely confronted with the evidence of his role, and that was all—even though revolutionary tradition would have expected them to deal with him in the good old fashion of underground revolutionary vendetta. It seems, however, that with the passing of Bakuninism the old-time conspirators were largely succeeded by dreamers or phrasemongers, with a few romantics like Errico Malatesta or Charles Malato trying in vain to maintain the old spirit.

cepted Kropotkin's altogether utopian communist anarchism only when, thoroughly disenchanted, he no longer cared one way or another.

Of the same Blanquist bent was young Malatesta, in whom the man of action prevailed over the theorist, and who believed in collaborating with extreme left-wing Italian Socialists in order to bring about a political revolution, the establishment of a democratic republic. He expected a social revolution to follow immediately. His opinion was not shared by Kropotkin, who epitomized his views on that subject as follows:

> We will become [merely] an army of conspirators if we believe that it suffices to overthrow the government. The next revolution must, from its very start, set about the seizure of the entire social wealth by the workers in order to convert it into common property. Such a revolution can be accomplished only if the industrial and agricultural workers will themselves carry out the seizure. To that end they will also have to carry on their own action during the period *before the revolution*; this is possible only if there is a strong workers' organization. The revolutionary middle class [Kropotkin obviously had in mind the educated déclassés] can overthrow the government; it cannot make the revolution. Only the people can do that.... Hence we have to make every effort to organize the masses of the workers. We, the small revolutionary groups, have to submerge ourselves in the organization of the people; we have to take our inspiration from their hatred and from their hopes, and help them transform these into action. When the masses of the workers are organized, and when we join them in order to arouse in them the spirit of revolt against capital—and there will be many occasions for that—only then will we be justified in expecting that the people will not be cheated out of the next revolution as they have been cheated out of the previous ones, and that this revolution will be the social revolution.[24]

One of the means that, according to Kropotkin and his friends, would "arouse the spirit of revolt" was what the communist anarchists called "propaganda by the deed"—terrorist acts of retaliation or protest against representatives of the existing system. That tactic had not been in the armory of the Bakuninists; they believed that the masses were essentially revolutionary, and hence needed no terrorist fireworks to stimulate their spirit of revolt. All that was necessary, according to Bakunin, was an organization of conspirators, who at the proper moment would capitalize on the revolutionary potential of the masses. That view was no longer shared by Kropotkin and his friends. It was replaced by a sort of revolutionary "education" of the masses through acts of revolt, or "propaganda by the deed." Originally that sort of "propaganda," as first discussed at the Berne Congress of the "Anti-Authoritarian" International (1876), referred to small attempts at local insurrection.[25] Somewhat later—after such actions had proven to be quite ineffectual—the term was applied to individual acts of protest.

Propaganda by the deed occupied a prominent place in the discussions at the London Congress of 1881. The assassination of Tsar Alexander II, which had occurred earlier the same year, had made a great impression on the delegates. There was, of course, a difference between the terrorist acts of the Russian revolutionaries of the Narodnaya Volya, who expected to intimidate the Tsarist regime into granting constitutional reforms, and the acts of violence contemplated and later carried out by the anarchists, which were to serve merely as "awakeners" of the masses. Moreover, while Russian terrorist acts were, as a rule, organized affairs, the anarchist "propagandists by the deed" were mostly loners who were intent upon indirect suicide. The chronicle of anarchist terrorism is filled with acts of desperate protest, tragic retaliation (the assassination in 1897 of the Spanish Prime Minister Antonio Cánovas del Castillo, who had ordered the torturing of hundreds of innocents), and bestial stupidity (the assassination of the Austrian Empress Elizabeth in 1898). With only two exceptions, when they resulted in the liberation of political prisoners in Spain and Italy, they hurt the movement they were supposed to serve, and blackened its image in the mind of the masses they were supposed to "awaken." Except in Spain, such acts did not occur after the turn of the century, when the anarchist movement took another direction.

No anarchist terrorist acts of any significance had been carried out at the time of the London Congress, yet much time was devoted to discussing the necessity of studying chemistry; the implication was obvious.[26] The main ideas animating the participants of the congress were expressed in the following resolution:

Whereas the International Workingmen's Association [those assembled in London assumed the original name of the First International] deems it necessary to add propaganda by the deed to oral and written propaganda; and, furthermore, whereas the moment of a general conflagration is not far distant, and the revolutionary elements of all countries will be called upon to do their utmost—the Congress urges all organizations affiliated with the I.W.A. to head the following proposals:

It is absolutely necessary to exert every effort toward propagating, by deeds, the revolutionary idea and to arouse the spirit of revolt in those sections of the popular masses who still harbor illusions about the effectiveness of legal methods.

Those who no longer believe that legality will bring about the revolution will have to use methods that are in conformity with that aim.

The persecutions directed against the revolutionary press of all countries prove the necessity of organizing an underground press.

Whereas the agricultural workers are still outside the revolutionary movement, it is absolutely necessary to bend every effort toward winning them to our cause, and to keep in mind that a deed performed against the existing institutions appeals to the masses much more than thousands of leaflets and torrents of words, and that propaganda by the deed is of greater importance in the countryside than in the cities.

Whereas the technical and chemical sciences have rendered services to the revolutionary cause and are bound to render still greater services in the future, the Congress suggests that organizations and individuals affiliated with the International Workingmen's Association devote themselves to the study of these sciences.[27]

The congress decided to form a new, open International, to establish a correspondence bureau in London, and to hold another congress the following year. However, nothing came of these decisions. It was 26 years before the anarchists held another congress—this one altogether their own.

At the time of the London Congress, Kropotkin believed in the need for two kinds of organizations—an open one and a secret one. The former was to be concerned with the bread-and-butter struggles of the masses, while the latter would consist of very small groups, apparently engaged in direct action.[28] In a letter written in 1902 to Jean Grave, his outstanding French follower, Kropotkin made a similar proposal "for an International of the workers engaged in the class struggle (Alliance Ouvrière Internationale), combined with a more intimate alliance of persons who knew each other within that organization."[29] However, neither in 1881, nor in 1902, nor during the interval between these years did an international organization of this kind materialize. With the collapse of Bakunin's camouflaged struggle for power, those malcontents who would not join the camp of gradualist Marxism became preachers of or believers in a faraway ideal, which they could not possibly expect to be realized in their lifetime. With nothing except hatred of the status quo and the vague ideal of "anarchy" to hold them together, they constituted a practically unorganized quasi-religious sect, protesters in word or deed against the world's injustices.

The violent defiance of authority implied in individual terrorist acts incidentally resulted in something that had not been envisaged by the romantic champions of post-Bakunin anarchism. The supernal beauty of their anarchist-communist ideal made it clear to all but the most unsophisticated of the rank and file that a revolution in behalf of that ideal was out of the question during their lifetime. This meant that, aside from immolating themselves, all they could do in defiance of the status quo was attend meetings, distribute leaflets, read anarchist periodicals and pamphlets, and occasionally exchange blows with the police. They would also, as Victor Adler, leader of the Austrian Socialists, put it, hope that "somewhere, sometime, someone would kill some person in power, and feel happy when such a thing happened."

However, not all rank-and-file followers were satisfied with such harmless forms of protest against fate. Some of the malcontents were adventurous types, who, if untouched by propaganda, would simply have joined the criminal underworld as an escape from a life of permanent drudgery. Having heard of a new evangel that extolled revolt against the law, they gladly embraced it as an ideological cloak that enabled them to draw a line between themselves and the common run of crooks with no philosophy.

In many cases it was even simpler than that. Jean Grave, Kropotkin's leading follower in France, once put it this way: "Since the bourgeois press has persistently presented the anarchists as criminals and maniacs, many criminals and maniacs have come to believe that we are their party." The result was a wave of burglaries, robberies, and similar crimes, whose perpetrators posed as, or considered themselves to be, anarchists—in some rare cases making small contributions to the cause. This gave the movement a very black eye, and hence activities of this kind were persistently encouraged by agents provocateurs. The ideologists of anarchism were quite distressed about it, but not all of them felt that they could publicly repudiate these converts. Some of them took the position that criminals were victims of society, and therefore it did not behoove anarchists to join the chorus of those who attacked them. In one particular case the exploits of two fanatical anarcho-bandits—most of the others were cynics rather than fanatics—who specialized in cop-killing and who ended on the gallows, unwittingly contributed to the destruction of a flourishing pro-anarchist mass movement in Austria during the early 1880's. A robbery during which they murdered an entire family—the children, one of their admirers explained to this writer in 1904, were "too noisy" —generated revulsion among the workers in Vienna, who at that time were receptive to anarchist ideas.

Sporadic acts of violence, which during the last two decades of the nineteenth century were, in the public mind, the main characteristics of anarchism, were not the only anarchist activity. When conscripts reported for military duty, anarchists distributed appeals to the recruits urging them to disobey their officers when ordered to fire on striking workers. And at election time, appeals were published urging the voters to abstain from going to the polls, thus refusing to recognize the state. In actual practice, however, this kind of propaganda could hurt only the Socialists, for the workers whom the abstentionist leaflets or speeches reached were potential Socialist voters. At the turn of the century, a candidate of the anti-Semitic Christian Social Party of Austria running for parliament in Florisdorf, an industrial suburb of Vienna, actually used anarchist-anti-parliamentary leaflets—apparently copied from some anarchist publications—with the intention of discouraging the workers from voting for his Socialist opponent.

Reduced to the insignificance of a noisy, quasi-religious sect, the anarchists showed vitality only in the Spanish-speaking countries, particularly in Spain itself. This was due to a peculiar circumstance: in 1868 an Italian emissary of Bakunin's in Madrid and Barcelona struck almost virgin soil when he began his work on behalf of the First International. As a result the first Spanish sections of that body, formed the following year, had a distinct anarchist cast. By relating their propaganda to the wage struggles of the workers, the first Spanish leaders of the International established in their country so firm a tradition of championing working-class interests that no amount of later Marxist competition was able to weaken it. The cruel persecutions by the government and the hopeless economic plight of large sections of the intelligentsia, and of both the industrial workers in the north and the landless peasants in the south, have contributed to perpetuating that mood to the present day.

*The Anarchists and the Second International*

Despite their antagonism to the democratic—particularly the Marxian—Socialists, whom they usually referred to as "Authoritarians," the anarchists repeatedly made strenuous efforts to be heard at the International Socialist Congresses called by the democratic Socialists after the formation of the Second, or Socialist, International in 1889. There were two reasons why the anarchists tenaciously insisted on being admitted to those assemblies despite the unwillingness of the democratic Socialist majority to have anything to do with them. In the first place, the anarchists did and do consider their philosophy as one of the shades of Socialism. For Socialism, in its widest sense, embraces all currents opposing private ownership of the means of production. The anarchists often called themselves "libertarian" or "anti-authoritarian" Socialists, and hence they were unwilling to concede to the democratic Socialists the monopoly of the concept of Socialism.

In the second place, they had tacitly abandoned Bakunin's idea of an immediate anarchist revolution, which logically would entail the establishment of a dictatorship by the anarchist minority. Hence the more realistic elements among the anarchists had come to the conclusion that communist anarchism could be ushered in only after the establishment of a democratic Socialist system, a system that would enable them, through experimentation and example, gradually to persuade the majority that a form of voluntary collective ownership was preferable to a government-owned economy. They were therefore ready to serve as a sort of independent, militant, ultra-left-wing ally of the Socialists and to help them to bring about a democratic Socialist revolution. Malatesta was the best-known representative of this trend. It did not occur to him or to his friends that the enormous majority of the Socialists, despite their lip service to the "inevitable" social revolution, at that time definitely favored a gradual transition from capitalism to Socialism, and that as a result they could do without the assistance of the anarchists.

It may not be amiss to mention here that in his *L'Anarchie: Sa Philosophie, son idéal* (1896), as well as in other works, Kropotkin wrote that every phase in the development of a society is the "resultant" of the various social forces at work. Applied to the concept of the social revolution, this idea could only mean: those whom the anarchists called authoritarian would exert pressure to entrust the state with the organization of production; they would be opposed by the anarchists, who would favor entrusting voluntary organizations with this task. The resultant of these two opposing forces would be midway between these two tendencies, toward a decentralized form of democratic Socialism with much local autonomy and ample scope for producers' cooperatives. It was a tacit, scientifically camouflaged retreat from utopia.

It was not the anarchist ideal, then, but the cult of violence that motivated the Socialists' refusal to admit the anarchists to their congresses. Eager to attract voters, they were unwilling to be associated in the public mind with men whose terrorist acts branded them as assassins or maniacs. They also resented the abstentionist, anti-parliamentarian propaganda, which if successful would threaten their election to the various representative bodies.

The anarchists were not prevented from participating in the first congress (or rather two congresses) held in Paris in 1889. A split in the ranks of the French Socialists had resulted in the simultaneous holding of two international gatherings: one called by the French Marxists (called "Guesdists," after their leader Jules Guesde, a former anarchist), which was attended by delegates from practically all countries; the other called by the followers of Paul Brousse, also a former anarchist, who had become the leader of the extremely moderate "Possibilists." The latter gathering was attended by representatives of the British trade unions, among others. The anarchists had delegates at both assemblies. They were not bothered by the Socialists, who were preoccupied with the problem of two rival international Socialist congresses.

However, violent battles were fought at the three subsequent congresses of the Second International. At the Brussels Congress of 1891, only Ferdinand Domela Nieuwenhuis, founder of the Socialist Party of Holland, who had become an anarchist, was given an opportunity to speak on two questions of tactics that separated the anarchists from the Socialists: participation in parliamentary elections, which the anarchists rejected, and the general strike to prevent war, which the anarchists advocated but which the Socialists refused to endorse. Two years later, at the 1893 International Socialist Congress in Zurich, the anarchists were forcibly ejected, and a resolution was passed to the effect that in order to be admitted to future congresses, a delegate had to recognize the necessity of using the ballot as a tactical weapon. This, however, did not prevent the anarchists from appearing again at the next congress, which was held in London in 1896. This time they came not as delegates of anarchist groups, but as representatives of the labor unions of France and Holland, which at that time were under anarchist influence.

Their admittance to the Congress through a back door, as it were, was possible because the Socialists had sent an invitation to all Socialist parties and, with no strings attached, to all labor unions. At the time, the British trade unions were wholly uncommitted politically, and the Socialists were eager to impress the world with the fact that labor organizations of *all* countries participated in their congresses. Hitherto they had avoided stating outright that anarchists would not be admitted to their congresses, apparently believing that such a statement would give undeserved publicity to people they despised as cranks and nuisances.

However, the vitality of the anarchists, who had been instrumental in the formation of the French Confédération Générale du Travail (CGT), gave them pause. Anarchism, in its syndicalist version, which used the Marxist class-struggle vocabulary familiar to the Socialist rank and file, threatened to become a really dangerous competitor. Hence the Socialists assembled at the London Congress adopted a decision expressly stating that anarchists would be refused admission, which meant that the doors would be closed to them even if they had credentials from bona-fide labor unions. After that the anarchists no longer attempted to participate in international Socialist congresses.

Though there were no anarchists at the International Socialist Congress in Paris in 1900, a distant echo of the anarchist tradition, as it were, was sounded by—of all persons—Aristide Briand, who defended the general strike as a weapon that would be instrumental in overthrowing the capitalist system.[30] In the early 1890's, Briand had been closely associated with Fernand Pelloutier, who was then elaborating the theory of syndicalism. Though Briand was never an anarchist or a syndicalist, he saw the endorsement of the general strike as a very practical way to bolster his popularity at the expense of his Marxist rivals (the so-called Guesdists) who opposed that idea. (In 1909, when he became Premier, Briand broke the general strike of the railwaymen by mobilizing them and threatening them with court-martial.)

Another echo of anarchist propaganda was heard at the Amsterdam Congress of the Socialist International in 1904. On that occasion a right-wing Socialist (Jaurèsist) member of the French Chamber of Deputies said that a defense of the general strike was necessary to dispel the misconceptions of many French workers who thought that by voting the Socialist ticket they were merely "assisting the careers of wire-pullers and climbers." For this reason he thought that the Socialist members of parliament should also "endorse the general strike."

The naïve Machiavellianism of that back-bencher must have amused the German Socialists, who were dead set against the general strike because, under the Kaiser, supporting it was not very safe. But they were not amused three years later, when, at the Stuttgart Congress of the Second International in 1907, Gustave Hervé, a French extreme-left Socialist, asked the Congress to endorse the general strike and the military strike as means to prevent war. More than a decade earlier, these same ideas had been preached just as futilely by the anarchists at the International Socialist Congresses. Hervé was therefore often called a syndicalist, but he was nothing of the kind. He was an irresponsible half-fanatic and half-mountebank, who enjoyed the plaudits of the ultra-radicals and was ready to suffer imprisonment for the pleasure of posing as a sincere, ultra-revolutionary "insurrectionist." He eventually became a fascist.

Three years later the idea of the general strike, "above all in the war industries," was advanced at the International Socialist Congress in Copenhagen in 1910. This time the former Blanquist Edouard Vaillant, a prominent leader of the left wing of the French Socialist Party, and Keir Hardie, leader of the Independent Labour Party of England, were the sponsors. It was, no doubt, a concession to the revolutionary mood of many French workers and to the incipient syndicalist movement in Great Britain. The general strike was voted down as it had been on all previous occasions.

Another vestige of the anarchist tradition was the adoption of the general strike by many Socialist leaders—both extreme-left-wingers, like Karl Liebknecht and Rosa Luxemburg, and "revisionists," like Eduard Bernstein—not as an instrument of social revolution, to be sure, but as a weapon for obtaining political concessions, such as the extension of the franchise for the Prussian Landtag.

### *The Anarchist Congress of Amsterdam*

Frustrated in their attempts to present their views at the conventions of the Second International, the anarchists attempted to hold an international congress of their own during the World's Fair in Paris in 1900. The organizing committee had received reports about the movement in the various countries, but at the last moment the gathering was prohibited by a government that, ironically, included both Alexandre Millerand, once a leading Socialist, and General Gaston de Galliffet, the Minister of War, who three decades earlier had headed the military operations that crushed the Paris Commune.

It was seven years before another attempt to hold an international convention succeeded. That congress met in Amsterdam in 1907. Its main feature was the debate between Errico Malatesta, the most romantic representative of post-Bakunin anarchism, and Pierre Monatte, the outstanding spokesman of a new school of anarchism, usually designated as anarcho-syndicalism, which had emerged in the mid-1890's, partly as a revulsion against the wave of terrorist acts, which were often senseless even from the anarchist point of view and which were discrediting the cause of anarchism.

The first champion and originator of the new current had been Fernand Pelloutier, a former Guesdist who, in his "Letter to the Anarchists," had appealed to his comrades to devote themselves to the labor movement. It was due to his efforts that in 1895 the French trade unions, hitherto mere vote-gathering appendages to competing Socialist parties, combined to form the Confédération Générale du Travail, a new organization that would be under the political control of no party or sect. Its leaders, some of whom were anarchists, called themselves "revolutionary syndicalists" (the term "anarcho-syndicalists" was adopted chiefly by their non-French emulators.

The basic theory of syndicalism, as evolved by Pelloutier (whom the syndicalist philosopher Georges Sorel credits with originating the idea), is a compound of Proudhon's hostility to politics and politicians, of Marx's insistence on the class struggle, and of Bakunin's revolutionary activism. The labor union was the workers' basic *groupement d'intérêts,* that is, the organization for the protection of the material interests of the workers, regardless of their political affiliations. It could, therefore, embrace all workers in a given occupation. Its tactical method was direct action (including sabotage), and its chief weapon the strike—the ordinary strike for the improvement of the workers' material conditions within the capitalist system, the general strike for the overthrow of that system. The labor union was also the basis for reconstruction after the victorious social revolution, which would follow in the wake of what the syndicalists called "the expropriatory general strike." Not the individual unions but the national federation of all unions would then take over the management of the socialized industries and of all public affairs, thus eliminating the state. The idea of the general strike and of the role of the labor unions after the social revolution had been aired twenty years earlier by the Jura Federation of Bakunin's organization. It did not occur to the syndicalists that the capitalist state, "eliminated" by the "expropriatory general strike," would be replaced by a new state with a new ruling class—the self-taught officials of the labor unions. It was only after the Bolshevik Revolution that most French syndicalists, dropping the last vestiges of anarchist anti-statism, adopted the slogan "*au syndicat le pouvoir,*" i.e., all power to the labor union, which of course meant all power to the union leaders. Syndicalism, without the anarchist prefix, thus eventually became one of the heretical variants of Leninism.

The initial success of the French syndicalists, who at the turn of the century got control of the bulk of their country's labor unions, stimulated the rise of similar movements in other countries. Soon enough, however, the non-French converts to syndicalism saw themselves faced with a situation that doomed them to failure. Unlike the labor unions in France, those in other countries were under the firm control of unified, centralized Socialist parties, and their officials in the unions lost no time in eliminating anarchists who tried to win the unions over to their views. As a result the anarcho-syndicalists resorted to the formation of their own revolutionary unions.* This was contrary to the basic principle of authentic—i.e., French—syndicalism, which required that there be no dual unions, that the unions, as such, include all workers regardless of their views, and that no special ideological label be attached to the unions. Otherwise they would become sectarian organizations rather than organizations embracing all workers on the basis of their common class interests. Needless to say, the various "syndicalist" unions created outside of France remained sectarian bodies never succeeding in offering any serious competition to the long-established labor unions.

The acceptance by a large number of anarchists of the basic tenets of syndicalism, which were more persuasive than Kropotkin's idea of independent, free groups taking charge of reconstruction after the revolution, gave the anarchist movement a temporary shot in the arm. This encouraged the anarchists to attempt once more to establish an international organization. The outcome was the convocation of an international congress in Amsterdam in 1907.

The main subjects discussed at the Congress were "Anarchism and Organization" and "Syndicalism and Anarchism." Propaganda by the deed, once the core of anarchist "dreadfulness," was disposed of in a resolution containing the rather noncommittal statement "Such acts, with their causes and motives, should be understood rather than praised or condemned."[31] The arguments of anarchist

* The defunct IWW (Industrial Workers of the World) of the United States, though professing many ideas similar to those of the French syndicalists, was largely an autochthonous growth, owing its origin less to anarcho-syndicalist influence than to the cleavage between the unskilled and migratory workers on the one hand, and the skilled craftsmen of the AFL on the other.

opponents of all kinds of organization—they constituted the lunatic fringe of the movement—were torn to shreds by most of the speakers. There was, however, no smooth sailing on the question of syndicalism. The arguments of Pierre Monatte—who after the Bolshevik Revolution was to concoct a sort of combination of syndicalism and Leninism ("all power to the unions")—were countered by Errico Malatesta. Malatesta was in favor of the anarchists' participating in the labor movement, for this would give them an opportunity to make contact with the masses. But he objected to the anarchists' becoming union officials, because then they "would be lost to propaganda, they would be lost to anarchism."[32] He also attacked what he called "an over-simple concept of the class struggle." As he put it, "Because of the universal competition under a system of private ownership, the workers, like the bourgeoisie, are subject to the law of universal competition. Hence there are no classes in the proper sense, because there are no class interests."

Malatesta also criticized the idea of the general strike as the magic weapon of working-class emancipation, for it was no substitute for the violent conflict with the armed forces that would occur as soon as the starving strikers attempted to seize food supplies. (The syndicalists, by the way, were fully aware of that, but they preferred not to expand on it.) Malatesta concluded with the argument: "Syndicalism, an excellent means of action because it places the working masses at our disposal, cannot be our only weapon; nor should it make us lose sight of the only aim worthy of an effort: Anarchy!"[33]

Such questions as anti-militarism, alcoholism, and Esperanto were also discussed at the congress. One of the resolutions adopted declared that an Anarchist International had been formed, with an International Bureau composed of five members. Its task was to keep in touch with the anarchists of the various countries and to maintain international anarchist archives. For two years a monthly bulletin was published by the Bureau, whose seat was in London. Shortage of funds and lack of interest on the part of the various groups affiliated with the International resulted in the discontinuation of the bulletin and finally in the demise of the organization in 1911. It seems that the anarcho-syndicalists were engrossed in the affairs of their respective unions, and not much interested in maintaining contact with the "pure" anarchists, whom they despised as either crackpots or naïve romantics. The "pure" anarchists, for their part, saw in their more practical comrades chiefly union bureaucrats on the make.

This view, by the way, was eventually borne out by events. The French unions, the inspiration of anarcho-syndicalists in other countries, eventually reverted to type. As the French unions grew in membership and were able properly to remunerate their officials, their leaders gradually became respectable and lost their enthusiasm for sabotage, direct action, violent demonstrations—in short, for everything that smacked of prison bars. And when World War I broke out in 1914, the great majority of them forgot their antipatriotism and became stanch supporters of their country's war effort.

That war proved a blow to the "pure" anarchists as well. Peter Kropotkin, Jean Grave, Charles Malato, Max Nettlau, and other bearers of famous names came out in defense of their respective countries, thus throwing overboard one of the oldest anarchist tenets, namely, that all forms of government are unworthy of defense. The fact that some of the famous old-timers, including Malatesta, Emma Goldman, and Alexander Berkman, stuck uncompromisingly to their guns, could not offset the disarray created by the fall from grace of the almost deified Kropotkin, whose anarchism, in the opinion of some ultra-radical critics, turned out to be a sort of crypto-democratic gradualism, which viewed the coming Russian Revolution, as he wrote in 1892 in his *Conquest of Bread,* as destined not to go beyond the ideas of the Revolutions of 1789 and 1848.[34]

### *The Impact of Bolshevism and the Anarcho-Syndicalist International*

The gradual extinction of the anarchist movement, outside the Spanish-speaking orbit, was hastened by the Bolshevik Revolution of 1917. Most of the anarchist rank and file and many of the leaders, including such figures as Emma Goldman and Alexander Berkman, enthusiastically hailed Bolshevism's defiance of the capitalist world. This indicated that anarchism had attracted the most discontented elements prior to 1917 chiefly because they assumed anarchism to be the most rabid enemy of capitalism, and not because it is the "negation of the state," which theoretically is its main feature. Once capitalism was under serious attack, many anarchists were cured of their great aversion to the idea of "proletarian dictatorship," and were ready to forget the main tenet of their faith, the "negation of the state." Consequently the anarcho-syndicalists and syndicalists who did not use the anarchist prefix were invited by the Bolsheviks to participate in the founding Congress of the Third, or Communist, International, to be held in March 1919. To make it easier for those invited to overcome their doctrinaire reservations, the Communists decided to set up what they called the Red Labor Union International ("Profintern"), which was to include all revolutionary labor unions regardless of their political philosophy. That body was to be altogether independent of the Third International. The syndicalists agreed to participate in 1921 in the first congress of that purportedly independent International. However, most of them balked when they realized that the organization was dominated by the Communist labor unions. The harsh measures the Soviet regime had taken against the Russian anarchists who refused to collaborate, and the extermination of the entire staff of the Ukrainian anarchist guerrilla leader Nestor Makhno after they had helped the Red Army defeat the Whites, likewise contributed to ending the flirtation between anarcho-syndicalists and Communists.

As a result, the anarcho-syndicalists decided to create an International of their own. It was founded at a congress held in Berlin in December 1922, and was called officially the International Workingmen's Association, a name identical with that of the First International of 1864–76. In its early years it was usually referred to as the "Berlin International" because its headquarters were in the German capital prior to the Nazis' seizure of power. It goes without saying that the non-syndicalist anarchists stayed out of the organization. Among them were a small number of pure idealists, who dreamed of revolution but knew or felt that they were powerless in the face of the spiritual subjection of the masses to either their traditional masters or to Socialist or Communist leaders. But most of them were sectarians or cultists of one kind or another, intent on verbally defying the accepted views or scandalizing their fellow men without incurring risks for their bravado. Among them were people interested chiefly in sexual freedom, Tolstoyism, Esperanto, anti-alcoholism, sterilization by the Steinach method, and whatnot. There was nothing revolutionary about them, except the once dread-inspiring label.

The Berlin International was at its outset dominated by the personality of Rudolf Rocker, an ex-bookbinder, who was the author of many books on anarchism and other subjects. A refugee from German police persecution during the early 1890's, he lived in London until the collapse of the Kaiser's government, when he was able to return to Germany. While in London he was prominently active among the Yiddish-speaking immigrants, whose language he had learned (he himself was not Jewish). Those he helped educate were later to become prominent as leaders and organizers of the needleworkers in New York. After his return to Germany, the policy Rocker and his followers adopted during the three-cornered struggle between Socialists, Communists, and Nazis was the rejection of all violence and refusal to manufacture instruments for killing. This was a rather pathetic comedown after a long revolutionary tradition. During the 1920's, Rocker's German following consisted of the members of the Freie Arbeiter-Union; there were approximately 30,000 of them, mostly secessionists from the Socialist-controlled giant trade unions. The most important section of the Berlin International was beyond question the Spanish Confederación Nacional del Trabajo (CNT), which, before its destruction at the end of the Civil War, claimed a membership of about one million. In 1924 it did not exceed 200,000.

The French syndicalists, who had once controlled the unions of their country, had in the meantime been reduced to insignificance. When, as a result of the conflict between the Socialists and the Communists, the Confédération Générale du Travail was split, the anarcho-syndicalists and the syndicalists proper joined the Communist-controlled Confédération Générale du Travail Unitaire (CGTU). A few years later the anarcho-syndicalists broke away from that organization to form their own CGT Syndicaliste Révolutionnaire, which, according to figures published by the Berlin International, had only 7,500 members in 1928. It exerted no influence whatsoever, and disappeared at the outbreak of World War II.

Next to the Spanish CNT, the strongest unit that joined the syndicalist International was the Italian Unione Sindacale. Led by anarchists and syndicalists, it included various unions dissatisfied with the moderate Socialist leadership of the Confederazione Generale del Lavoro. At its height, shortly before being suppressed by the fascists, it had approximately 100,000 members.[35] There were also small anarcho-syndicalist or syndicalist organizations in the Netherlands, where the originally strong pro-anarchist unions had shrunk to insignificance; in the Scandinavian countries, where they were strongest in Sweden, yet still of no importance when compared with the regular, Socialist-led unions; and in Latin America, particularly Mexico and Argentina, where anarcho-syndicalist influence was later greatly reduced by Communist competition.

In 1932 the seat of the anarcho-syndicalist International was transferred to Amsterdam, whence it migrated to Madrid during the Civil War, to find its ultimate asylum in Stockholm. There it has been functioning since 1939—the central organization of an insignificant movement with branches or twigs in various countries. Hopelessly outbid in radicalism by the sundry varieties of Leninism, it is completely unknown to the general public.

*Conclusion*

The eclipse of the anarchist movement as a political force was the result of economic and political circumstances that altered the mode of thinking of those opponents of the status quo who called themselves anarchists. Those opponents were far from constituting a socially homogeneous group. At the outset of the movement, a few years before the founding of the First International, anarchism appealed chiefly to skilled workers, who hoped to attain economic independence without resorting to any illegal, revolutionary methods. These were the Proudhonists. They disappeared because the bootstrap methods they proposed had lost all meaning in the wake of the development of large-scale industry.

Proudhonist anarchism, or mutualism, was followed by Bakuninism, whose moving force was the déclassé intelligentsia of the underdeveloped countries—precisely that social group which the Proudhonists had opposed because they considered its members aspirants to power and not champions of the working class. It is beside the point that Proudhon's bêtes noires were the Blanquists, who differed from the Bakuninists only in their verbiage, not in their intentions. Unlike the Proudhonists, the Bakuninists were insurrectionists, hoping for an immediate revolution. They disappeared as an organized group when they realized that the masses were not ready to rise at their call and when the further economic and political developments of their respective countries afforded job opportunities for the educated in general and enabled the militant déclassés to become gradualist Socialist or trade-union leaders of a growing industrial working class.

These defectors from the camp of anarchism were succeeded by an unorganized motley of ultras—intellectuals, semi-intellectuals, and self-taught workers—who formed a psychological rather than a political or social category. They were a mixture of elements who would accept neither the status quo nor its gradualist opponents, such as the Socialists and the trade unionists. Their irreconcilability found expression in the adoption of a millenarian ideal, in whose immediate realization they did not believe, and in propaganda for violent acts of protest against the existing system. However, neither their faraway ideal nor their violent protests appealed to the nonromantic masses. As a result, the more realistic among them sought contact with the masses by engaging in radical labor-union activities, as anarcho-syndicalists. But in this phase, too, anarchism met with defeat. For labor unions, even if originally controlled by ultraradicals, eventually become moderate as they grow larger, and so do their once fiery officials after they attain a middle-class standard of living. Those few anarcho-syndicalist leaders who preferred to remain true to their principles, or who would not submit to Socialist or Communist control of the unions, as a rule became leaders of small separatist unions and were doomed to be ignored by the masses.

And, finally, it was the Bolshevik Revolution whose proletarian mystique and anti-capitalist reality deprived the anarchists of most of their rank and file and of many of their leaders.

Nevertheless, it cannot be said that the anarchist movement will die without leaving a trace in history. In the opinion of many historians, including the Bolshevik biographer of Bakunin, Yuri Steklov, the methods advocated by Bakunin were "in many points practically an anticipation of Soviet power and a prediction, in general outline, of the course of the great October Revolution of 1917,"[36] and Bakunin's Secret Alliance was the Third International within the First. It may also be said that basically Leninism is a hybrid of Bakuninist activism and Marxist terminology.

It is beside the point whether the anarchists are particularly proud of this strange sequel to the most romantic chapter of their history.

# The Second International

Gerhart Niemeyer

# The Second International: 1889-1914

What was the Second International besides a name and rudimentary organization (instituted eleven years after the founding congress), consisting of an International Socialist Bureau and a Permanent Executive Committee? The name and the organization are concrete enough, but did they represent anything of reality? If so, what kind of reality was it? There were eight periodical congresses, plus an extraordinary one. There were member parties, some of which even called themselves "sections" of the International. The word "section," invoking the idea of a mere part of an integral whole, begs the question it is intended to answer. Was the Second International essentially nothing but a group of intellectual dreamers, who convened every few years to compare their notes? Or was it a mass movement with real unity, transcending national boundaries and joining millions of workers of various countries? Was the International a source of influence on the members, channeling their energies and aspirations? Was it a federal structure, or rather a kind of league of nations? Was it an organization for action, or one mainly for pronouncements? Was it the framework for a new "people," or a new "church?" Did it make any difference in the course of events, in the minds of its members, or in the minds of its opponents?

These questions, or some of them, have usually been asked by historians who have themselves taken part in the Western Socialist movement, and who look back on the International as something they still cherish for all the devotion once bestowed on it. The International, however, is a phenomenon of significance to all of us, not merely to the faithful remnant. As we learn to understand it, we begin to understand our own mind, and the paths and byways on which it has traveled.

*The Victory of the Salle Petrelle*

One wonders whether to call by the name of "Socialism" or even "labor movement" all the political groupings to the left of the bourgeois parties that existed by the end of the 1880's. Is there a common denominator for the Proudhonists, Blanquists, Marxists, Fabians, trade unionists, Possibilists, anarchists, radical pacifists, who felt drawn together as if they all pressed toward a single hope and formed part of a single enterprise? One might attempt to relate them to each other as various types of reactions to what they considered capitalism, although as soon as this is said exceptions spring to mind. The fact that they did feel drawn together, however, is significant. Trade unions in the 1870's and 1880's demanded an international congress. The French Possibilists, no friends of the Marxists, sent out the call for one in 1889. The French and German Marxists, not to be outdone, called for a congress of their own. Two congresses, meeting in Paris at the same time, surely impressed on the minds of participants and onlookers the question which is the real, the true one? It was this unspoken question that lent significance to the contest between the two meetings. Thus when the Marxist Salle Petrelle eventually won out over the Possibilist Rue de Lancry, something decisive was felt to have taken place. What was it? First, the meeting with the supposedly Marxist stamp refused to unite with the other one. This was a move of exclusion, even though nothing as yet existed from which to exclude. The refusal to unify sharpened the contrast between the two meetings, which made the congress at the Salle Petrelle appear as the Marxist one. Its ascendancy set the stage for further moves to establish and define an international identity. Thus out of the multitude of vaguely socialist, revolutionary, oppositional, millenarian, reformist, nihilist, and other groups was carved something that a great number of parties and organizations in various countries could call "we."

Second, Engels' desire to impress the Marxist stamp on the new entity could not be realized either through the badly split French, among whom Marxism was weak, or through the English, among whom it was practically nonexistent. These two parties, however, had taken the initiative in calling the Congress of 1889. Thus in fact Engels' insistence shifted international leadership to the German Social Democrats, who counted themselves among the Marxists.[1] The Second International thereby acquired a national center of gravity, German Social Democracy. Other parties, to be sure, raised questions and advanced their ideas, but in a good many cases it was the German reaction to these questions and ideas that became the accepted principle. An understanding of German Social Democracy is thus indispensable for an understanding of the Second International.

Third, the victory of the Salle Petrelle over the Rue de Lancry meant the establishment of a set of symbols as the accepted understanding of historical reality. No organization emerged from the Congress of 1889, nor were leaders nominated and elected. The group that went home from the Salle Petrelle had, however, implicitly subscribed to three symbols of the *Communist Manifesto,* represented by these slogans:

(a) "Workingmen of all countries, unite!"
(b) "Society is splitting into two great hostile camps: bourgeoisie and proletariat."
(c) "Every class struggle is a political struggle."

The inescapability of the class struggle, the commitment to struggle in the arena of politics, i.e., government—these constituted the dividing line marking Petrelle off from Lancry. The remaining symbol is one to which separate attention will be given later. It is most important to emphasize, though, that the Second International draw its identity first of all from a set of symbols rather than an organization. In that respect it differed from both the First International and the Third. The significance of the Second International must therefore be sought in the relation of the accepted symbols to the given reality.

### *The Total Critique of Society*

The struggle for the definition of a collective identity continued during the Congresses of Brussels, Zurich, and London as a move to exclude the anarchists. Although the anarchists had not been invited to Brussels, they came, claiming that they belonged by virtue of their hostility to capitalism. "We are Socialists too." They were ousted, mainly because of their obnoxious conduct. Their exclusion, however, was justified in terms of a criterion for membership: the International would include only groups and organizations that had accepted the need for political struggle. The anarchists, by contrast, had insisted on direct action. Underneath these two modes of action lay two different attitudes toward society. The anarchists were antinomians. They regarded the entire existing society and all who enjoyed any kind of power in it as totally and hopelessly depraved. They rejected any kind of obligation to that society. They disdained any action through that society's structure or institutions. To them all existing governments were tyrannies, and all those who maintained them or profited by them were existentially wicked persons. "I am not striking an innocent person when I strike down the next best bourgeois," said an anarchist in an attempt to justify his attack on a customer in a Paris restaurant in 1894.[2] This total critique of society was based on the assumption that the Revolution represented a real or true order of human existence in accordance with human nature, while at present men are subject to a regime that does violence to human nature. Thus Bakunin could believe that the "unleashing of brutal passion" contained the promise of a new world, which must arise from the "destruction of the public order." Meanwhile the anarchists, fancying themselves citizens of that new world, disdained to dirty their hands by touching the decaying body of the old.

It seems simple enough to exclude antinomian utopists from the Socialist family. In fact, however, the matter was far from simple. The International had contrasted its own commitment to "political action" with the anarchists' "direct action." Since the anarchists, too, wanted to realize the overthrow of the existing regime, one cannot understand this dichotomy to mean "political action" versus "unpolitical action." It meant, rather, "one type of political power" versus "another type of political power." In the resolutions of the International we find spelled out what "one kind of power" meant: the power of registered parties, the power of armies, the power of magistrates, the power of mayors, the power of ministers.* In other

* The Zurich Congress of 1893, for example, recommended "to the workers of all countries the struggle for, and exercise of, political rights, which are necessary to

words, the members of the International had committed themselves to a contest with bourgeois parties for control of the potestas as instituted in the structure of the existing society.[3] This seems simple enough. It turned out, however, that the exclusion of the anarchists by no means rid the International of the total critique of society—the tendency to concentrate all hope, value, and obligation exclusively on the future society and radically to deny them to the present. In the recurrent debates on the general strike, on the road to power, and, above all, on war, the anarchists were silent but influential partners of the parties who thought that with the expulsion of the anarchists in 1896, they had laid the ghost of revolutionary radicalism forever.

*The Debate on the General Strike*

The protracted debate on the general strike is particularly instructive in that it brought to light ambivalent and contradictory attitudes prevailing in the International. The general strike appeared in five different ends-means configurations. First the debate dealt with the political strike intended to bring about certain constitutional changes, as, for instance, the political mass strikes in Belgium in 1886, 1887, 1891, and 1893, which aimed at the extension of suffrage to the workers. Second, the rising anarcho-syndicalist movement looked upon the general strike as a revolutionary act that would dissolve the existing order and transform society into a stateless economic community. These two mutually exclusive ideas converge on the same instrument. Both envisage the general strike as a blow against the powers that be; but the first seeks a partial change that ultimately would strengthen the existing society, whereas the second intends a total revolution leading to a new world.

In a third view, the general strike was conceived of as a "revolutionary exercise," a link in the chain of strategic maneuvers eventually leading to a victorious final battle. Fourth, the one-day general strike planned in connection with May Day, the first action attempted by the new International, was intended to bring about the self-identification of a worldwide proletariat, as opposed to separate

---

impress the demands of the workers on all legitimate and administrative bodies and to conquer the means of political power, so as to convert them from means of capital's domination into means of the proletariat's liberation."

national entities. In that context, the use of the term "world strike" in the preparation of the agenda of the Zurich Congress is significant. Finally, from 1891 on the International again and again discussed the general strike as a means of stopping an international war.

One can distinguish three patterns of assumptions and expectations in these ends-means configurations. Broadly speaking, they are (1) the action of a newly rising social group in making its way to political power and a position of influence; (2) the total rejection of the existing society and the breakthrough to a new life; and (3) the gestation and mobilization of a new supranational force capable of arresting the evils of the contemporary society without total revolution. In spite of these utterly different purposes, the means is identical: stoppage of work in all or at least all key industries, in hopes of paralyzing the life processes of society. In regard to the anticipated effects, however, predictions varied considerably. Some felt that unless a general strike was organized by power machinery that could compare with the state, the ensuing repression would destroy the workers' movement and wipe out whatever gains had been made. Others predicted that a general strike would force the government to disperse its troops to such an extent, particularly along the railroads, that the factories would be left defenseless.[4] The various precedents did not lend themselves to any definite conclusion, especially since they were regarded as specimens of the same genus, "general strike," without distinction of underlying motives. In Belgium a general strike movement, broken off in one instance without damage to the organizing forces, eventually led to universal suffrage; in Holland a general strike collapsed with disastrous consequences; in Sweden, a general strike was conducted and terminated with disciplined order but did not attain the desired results. In Italy, general strikes had been both socially effective and politically unproductive. On the other hand, the events of January 1905 in Russia once more seemed to underscore the suitability of the general strike as a decisive revolutionary action.

The debate in the International, far from clarifying and sifting these experiences, mostly focused on the general strike as such, in semi-detachment from its potential ends. Some of the ends implied in the debate did not even belong to Socialism. Universal suffrage is a liberal-democratic objective. So is the prevention of international war. Insofar as these are utopian ideals, they clash with the Marxist ideology that had come to dominate the International. Whenever the general strike as such was discussed, as if it had a meaning of its own apart from any concrete political objective, the ideological outlook of anarchism reasserted itself in the same International from which it had supposedly been purged. While the debate avoided a thorough examination of the ends-means correlation and dwelt on the instrument, the general strike, as such, it did not even give much attention to problems of practice. The International made no effort to determine how best to organize a general strike, how to make it last, how to execute its maneuvers. It was as if a group of military planners were to talk about "chemical warfare" without coming to grips either with its potential strategic uses or with its technical and tactical requirements.

One cannot escape the impression that in these discussions the general strike had more of the meaning of a myth than of a weapon or an instrument. Not until 1907 did Georges Sorel give articulate expression to the general strike as myth. "Apocalypse," he said then, "which represented a scandalous ancestry to Socialists who wished to make Marxism compatible with the practice of politicians in a democracy, in reality corresponds perfectly to the general strike, which, for revolutionary syndicalists, represents the advent of the new world to come."[5] Leading members of the International had opted for the "conquest of the means of power," by which they meant "all legitimate and administrative bodies." As Marxists, however, they too were looking for a new world to be attained by the proletariat in emancipating itself. Marx's revolution is in itself a myth of freedom resulting from heroic action of the oppressed. Ferdinand Nieuwenhuis, Keir Hardie, Gustave Hervé, and others who were attracted to the general strike may not have heard of Sorel. The myth of self-redemption through revolution is older than he. Even before Marx, even before the French Revolution, the eighteenth century had engendered the notion of the "people in insurrection," the refusal to obey that would free mankind from all alien and oppressive powers.[6] In this tradition, the general strike must appear not so much as an instrument to be used with cold calculation but rather as a negative power, as organized negation, the constitution of an anti-society as an alternative to the present-day society. While the leaders of the Second International tried to find their way from a mythical action to a more sober tactical concept, while they sought to differentiate between "general strike," "political mass strike," "military strike," and "strike in strategic industries," they could never rid themselves of an unspoken question that can be read between the many lines of discussion of the general strike. Could the anti-society that would be constituted with the exodus of the workers from their factories break out of the existing order by which it was deemed enfettered?

In the discussions of the International, two replies were offered to this unspoken question. First, the practical politician asked a sober counterquestion of a purely practical kind. "Can we really move the required multitude of people to participate in a strike in which they have no economic interests?" Behind this question lay a problem that had occupied the International apart from the general strike issue: the relation between the Socialist parties and their political purposes on the one hand, and the trade unions on the other. Labor as such was organized in trade unions. The unions were for labor the prime instruments of existence, both economic and cultural. Political action was alien to the unions. Even though they paid their respects to the need for political action, they often felt bothered by it, much as businessmen felt bothered by the policies and conflicts their governments put athwart the path of trade. There was a time when it looked as if the International had to choose between a trade union and a political party base. That choice had been avoided, however; the unions had acknowledged the leadership of the parties, and the parties the needs of the unions, and a working relationship had been happily established. All the same, labor as such saw its organization in the unions, and the purpose of the unions in economic gains. Where the unions had not become syndicalist, as they had in Italy and Spain, their power to move masses apart from economic objectives appeared very doubtful.

The second reply can be represented by two statements: one by Henrietta Roland-Holst, in the resolution of hers that was adopted by the 1904 Amsterdam Congress,[7] the other by Rudolf Hilferding.[8] Henrietta Roland-Holst rejected the general strike because "it made every existence, including that of the proletariat, impossible." Hilferding observed, with respect to Germany, that "the ruling classes will always look upon the general strike as a question of to be or not to be." Roland-Holst was saying to the workers that there is only one society, not two. If the workers were to deny themselves the existence in which they were caught up along with all other men, they would find themselves not in a glorious, revolutionary, alternative world, but rather without any existence. Hilferding's observation is related to Roland-Holst's. A serious threat to the one existence in which all men are involved together must bring into play all the energies of self-preservation and all the means to this end of which a society disposes. Life, in the form of its social structure, will defend itself.

The argument of self-preservation was given a further turn by August Bebel, Wilhelm Liebknecht, Willem Hubert Vliegen, and others who strenuously opposed any endorsement of the general strike. They saw the general strike not as an instrument, but rather as a radical adventure.* Its positive results were wholly unpredictable. On the negative side, however, one could say with certainty that it would endanger the organization, rights, advantages, and political opportunities that had so far been attained by Socialist parties and trade unions. Not merely would the workers threaten "every existence," they would also draw destruction upon that particular niche in society they had carved out for themselves by hard work and long struggles.

While these counterarguments prevailed in the International, the remarkable fact is that many Socialists of different persuasions could not escape the fascination of the general strike mirage. They include Jean Allemane, Aristide Briand, Rosa Luxemburg, Rudolf Hilferding, Eduard Bernstein, Friedrich Stampfer, Kurt Eisner, and others who could not be suspected of anarchist leanings. One is forced to conclude that even the most sober advocates of step-by-step political advance could not eradicate from their minds the

* Vliegen said in 1904: "The general strike is neither a means, nor even *the* means of the proletariat." Quoted in J. Braunthal, *Geschichte der Internationale,* I (Hanover, 1961), 302.

myth of a counter-society, a "people in insurrection," a revolutionary, alternative existence, which could be summoned into being with one magic word as the masses left their places of work.

*Reformism Versus Revolution*

The issue of reformism versus revolution was related to that of the mass strike. In the International this issue came to a head at the Congresses of 1900 and 1904, as a result of two events: the entry of the French Socialist Alexandre Millerand into the bourgeois cabinet of Waldeck-Rousseau in 1898, and the publication in the same year of Bernstein's first proposals for revising certain basic assumptions of Marxism. One should distinguish between reformism, "Millerandism," and revisionism. Millerand's example could be—as indeed it was, at the Paris Congress of 1900—treated as an exception. Reformism in itself was a mere practical policy, a counsel of expediency. Bernstein's revisionism, however, struck at the core of the ideology. If that was a sensitive point, then the reaction to reformism and Millerand had to be sharpened by the fearful awareness that Bernstein was providing a theoretical justification for reformist practice.

The Paris Congress of 1900 and the Amsterdam Congress of 1904 were preceded by the German Social Democrats' Hanover Congress of 1899 and the Dresden Congress of 1903. Resolutions adopted by these two party congresses provided the ideas and the language for the subsequent resolutions of the International. One can therefore say that the question of reformism was settled for the International within the framework of German Social Democratic politics.

German Social Democracy—the very term indicates its character as a little world unto itself—formed a "state within a state." There were the unions, whose houses were to most workers their true home, with a string of organizations and associations clustering around them. There was the party, with an elaborate bureaucracy, a considerable press, and branch organizations in cities, regions, and states, with an electorate running into the millions even under oppressive laws. There were consumers' cooperatives, Social Democratic cultural enterprises, a Social Democratic literature, and Social Democratic taverns. Social Democracy has been described as a subculture that necessarily had to participate in the main culture of the existing society.[9] Bebel professed in a debate against Bülow that the Social Democrats wanted to attain "the highest possible development of the physical, intellectual, and political *Bildung* [i.e., culture] of the people ... to enable the last of the citizens to be a *Kulturmensch* [cultured person] ... to create a state that stands on the pinnacle of *Kultur*."[10] There was, of course, only one *Kultur* to which the society as a whole aspired. Bebel conceived of Social Democracy as "the leaven which forces bourgeois society ahead."[11] The participation of Social Democracy in the dominant culture, which Bebel acclaimed as a value, committed it to a reformist attitude.

Another force strengthening this commitment was the party bureaucracy, an extremely efficient machinery, disciplined like the *Beamtentum* of the Prussian state, proud of its business competence. It "was built primarily to compete with other political parties, to get members and voters, not to shatter the existing order."[12] The more successful it became, the greater its interest in perpetuating itself, the prerequisite of which was the preservation of the society that enabled it to function. The third conservative force in German Social Democracy was the trade union, which represented the workers existentially while the party represented a political revolutionary idea. The unions, essentially conservative in outlook, established an ever-closer link with the party's leadership, and every time they threw their full weight into the scale, they enabled the reformist attitude to prevail.[13]

The Social Democratic subculture, however, was not held together, as subcultures often are, by ethnic, linguistic, or other existential factors that may divide a subgroup from the dominant society. Rather, an artificial separation and alienation was supported by occasional seconding experiences. This alienation was provided by Marxism and its millenarian expectations. "The flags and symbols, the badges and pictures, the songs and legends of the 'fight for freedom of the working class' had served many as substitutes for a lost religion and for ... national patriotism."[14] In her autobiography Adelheid Popp describes how the reading of pulp magazines had kept her for several years in an imaginary world. When she encountered Socialism, she found it concrete: a theory that explained her material living conditions and promised a millennium, and a political movement that demanded her action. "I was now endlessly happy. I had a sphere of work which satisfied all my longings, but which I had considered quite unattainable for myself. It was to me the Promised Land."[15]

The poet Karl Bröger, writing of himself in the third person, describes his own conversion upon listening to a Social Democratic functionary on the subject of a strike: "He suddenly grasped the value and power of community and was anxious to support this newly found recognition. He began to talk about trade union problems, read what was worthwhile in this field, although he found it strange at first, and passionately accepted the doctrine of salvation. ... He believed the new order of life would come for all the poor, not just for one alone."[16] And Liebknecht, at the Hanover Party Congress, was quoted to this effect: "Islam was unconquerable as long as it believed itself to be unique.... As soon as it entered on compromise, it lost its conquering power ... it could not help this because it was not the true, world-redeeming faith.... Socialism, though, is this faith ... and Socialism cannot conquer and redeem the world if it stops believing in itself."[17] Bebel had written in 1879 a utopian work, *Die Frau und der Sozialismus,* which went further in millenarian optimism than any other book in the Marxist arsenal, and which was more widely read than the *Communist Manifesto*. Bebel himself was convinced that the revolution, the passage into that promised land, would occur within the lifetime of the people attending the Erfurt Congress of the German Social Democratic Party in 1891.[18]

The Social Democratic subculture was thus isolated from the main culture not by differences in custom, language, tradition, and existence, but rather by a millenarian ersatz religion.[19] The isolation of Social Democracy from German society was partly the fault of Bismarck and the Kaiser. The Social Democratic Party and its political fortunes, however, flourished through this isolation, which was deliberately maintained and cultivated when the leaders officially embraced Marxism in 1891. The allegiance of the entire movement was founded on ideological alienation from the main society. "This situation motivated the leaders to keep the party for decades in a kind of political ghetto, in order to avoid any kind of contaminating contact with the workings of bourgeois state mechanisms."[20]

Social Democracy thus lived in two worlds, thought in terms of two realities. Closely linked existentially with the surrounding society, sharing its cultural aspirations, wanting to enjoy its goods, it denied to that society ideological approval, postulated its destruction, and gave allegiance to a new order that would arise in the future. Apart from this ideological negation of the existing society, the subculture could have no intelligible identity. An attack on the ideological dogma of separation therefore hit Social Democracy at a most sensitive point. Hence the extremely strong condemnation of revisionism by the Dresden resolution:

> The Congress rejects [condemns] . . . a shift from our tactic based on the class struggle aiming at the conquest of political power through defeat of our opponents . . . to a policy of adjustment to the existing order. . . . The result of such a shift would be to transform a party . . . that is revolutionary in the best sense of the word . . . into a party that confines itself to reforming bourgeois society. . . . Therefore the Congress, in opposition to the existing revisionist tendencies, is minded not to mitigate but rather to sharpen the existing class conflict. . . . The Congress disapproves every tendency to mitigate class conflicts in order to facilitate a rapprochement with bourgeois parties.[21]

The Amsterdam Congress not only approved this revolutionary clarion call, but also the terms "rejects," "disapproves," "condemns," in opposition to Jaurès, the Belgians, the Austrians, and the English, but with the support of parties that found themselves basically alienated from their countries' political order. Ideological alienation, the affirmation of a millennium as an alternative to the present-day society, commitment to revolutionary destruction, citizenship in a mythical new order—these turned out to be appeals that could obtain a majority in the International.

Significantly, the operational part of the resolution committed the parties to work for the "interests of the working class, the securing of political liberties and equal rights, and for the extension of social legislation and the fulfillment of the cultural tasks of the working class." There is nothing revolutionary in this. It is a reformist program requiring the functioning of the existing society and its political order, and aiming to secure for the Socialists increased influence in the ongoing political process. The Amsterdam resolution and the Dresden resolution it embodies testify to the fact that the International, like German Social Democracy, had one leg planted firmly in political reality and the other, equally firmly, in a dreamland belonging to a millenarian myth. As G. D. H. Cole observed, somewhat naïvely, "The revolutionary phrases of the Dresden-Amsterdam resolution were on record; but they were singularly ineffective in preventing a continued drift in a reformist direction, either in Germany or elsewhere."[22]

*The Question of War*

The question of war occupied the International from the very beginning, and the first resolution against war was passed in 1889. No other problem in the history of the International was beset with such profound confusion. The war issue is generally considered the crux of the "failure" of 1914. A "failure" presupposes a confident expectation of achievement that was disappointed. What did the International set out to achieve in this respect? The record of its resolutions is by no means unambiguous. The record of its discussions reveals utter confusion, not only as regards the possibility of action on the part of the International, but even as regards the nature and significance of war or wars.

The first resolution, passed in 1889, laid down a strictly Marxist formula. "War, the disastrous product of the present economic conditions, will disappear only when the present mode of production has given way to the emancipation of labor and the international triumph of socialism."[23] There are three basic assumptions behind this resolution. First, *war* is treated as if it were an institution, or at any rate a kind of disease, a phenomenon that remains absolutely evil regardless of the political circumstances attending any of its concrete occurrences and that is unaffected by any considerations of justice. Second, war is attributed to the "present mode of production," from which it issues, presumably together with other evils that beset human existence. Third, war will disappear with the "international triumph" of Socialism, meaning the coming to power of Socialists in at least a number of important countries. The last was Kautsky's chief hope. He, together with other historians of the International, was quite aware of the confusion that attributed war "now to standing armies, then to the war plans of certain governments, and finally to the present economic conditions." As for Kautsky himself, "once the 'international triumph of Socialism' is attained, any danger of war will disappear."[24]

War is an absolute evil, a product of an absolutely evil world. That is the verdict of the International, expressing itself at its founding congress. The very fact of this congress, a response to Marx's "Workingmen of all countries, unite!" invoked another world to come, a world free from the evils of the present-day society. True, the "present economic conditions" supposedly could come to an end only through a proletarian revolution that was not yet in sight, though believed to be not too far away. But the International was already here. Its name attested to something that allegedly had an existence apart from nations and their conflicts. It seemed to offer a possibility, at least to the workers, of stepping out of their present existence, with its national boundaries, armies, and wars, of stepping through the looking glass and into a society that knew of no conflicts leading to war. The present-day world with its evils then did not have to be accepted. The International was already no longer part of it. It was something existentially new, a community of people untainted with the sins of the present society. Their "solidarity" constitutes a new society in embryo, a union of those who are free from the wrongs perpetrated by the rich and the mighty. The French original of the famous Socialist hymn contains a line that is lost in most translations: *"L'Internationale sera le genre humain!"*—the International will be mankind, i.e., the International is potentially a universal realm of harmony, free from the conflicts of existence.

The unreality of this assumption is such that two entirely conflicting courses of action can be derived from it. One of them was represented by the demand of Jules Guesde that the International do nothing about war as such, since it was but a product of capitalism and would automatically vanish together with other evils once capitalism fell. The other appeared in the repeated attempts of men like Hervé, Hardie, and Nieuwenhuis to put the International on record in favor of a general strike in case of war, i.e., an attempt to get the "new people" to step out of the old society, to stop it from functioning just at the critical moment when it had to fight for its existence. These resolutions, though never adopted, were reintroduced again and again, and the argument against them never penetrated to the full depth of the problem.

Those who opposed the Hardies and Hervés were in their way no less committed to the vision of a new world to come. They assumed that it was not yet here, not even in the shape of the International, but that the organizational strength built up by the Socialist parties in various countries contained the best promise of its eventual realization. Any diminution of this power meant a blow to the millennium. This was applied to the politics of nineteenth-century Europe, in view of the difference between the more democratic regimes and the more repressive ones, of which the worst was Russia. Engels had said in 1891, "If Russia, the hotbed of cruelty and barbarism, the enemy of all human culture, should attack Germany in order to partition and destroy her, . . . then we are as much concerned as those who rule Germany and we shall resist."[25] Similarly, Bebel had declared in 1880 that the Socialists had an interest in defending Germany against the Russians. The same Bebel, though, in his great debate with Jaurès in 1904, had denied that there was any significant difference between monarchies and republics as long as capitalism prevailed, rejecting Jaurès' policy of defending France's democratic liberties, if need be in cooperation with bourgeois parties. The 1904 debate, of course, dealt not with war but with reformism. Still, if Bebel could say in this context that there was no significant difference between democracy and autocracy as long as both were capitalist, then it was difficult to refute Nieuwenhuis, who in 1893 had argued, "If in Germany pamphlets are distributed saying that the Cossacks will come, one must ask oneself if this invasion would ultimately be such a disaster. Greece and Rome were invaded by barbarians, but their culture survived."[26] Soon after the 1904 debate Nieuwenhuis left the International, but this thesis was advocated as late as 1907 by Lensch, Hervé, and Schippel.

Still, if Bebel was inconsistent with himself, so was the International. Bebel's reasoning of 1880 had powerful spokesmen. Plekhanov said in 1893, "A military strike would disarm above all the cultured nations and deliver Western Europe into the hands of the Cossacks. Russian despotism would sweep away our entire civilization, and in lieu of the freedom of the proletariat we would get the rule of the Russian knout."[27] Engels arrived at the same result by a somewhat different line of thought. "People must realize that if France, in alliance with Russia, declared war on Germany, she would be fighting against the strongest Social Democratic party in Europe; and that we should have no choice but to oppose with all our strength any aggressor who was on the side of Russia. For if we are defeated, the Social Democratic movement in Europe is smashed for twenty years; if not, we shall come to power ourselves."[28] In other words, the "strongest Social Democratic party in Europe" is defended by the army of present-day German society, and Socialists had to support that army and Germany's independent existence because of the opportunities to come to power that they represented.

Engels' statement contains the word "aggressor." The longer the debate on war lasted, the oftener the International had to face the question of legitimate self-defense against an unprovoked attack. This, of course, was the old problem of the just war. A war can be justified by circumstances of attack and defense, or by the objects governments pursue through war. The Socialists had looked upon the Franco-Prussian War of 1870 as justified self-defense until Napoleon III had been captured at Sedan. When Prussia continued the war for annexationist goals, the Socialist attitude changed. As late as the Zimmerwald conference of 1915,* both the revolutionary and pacifist factions "recognized that a case might be made for the historical function of conquering states as the unifiers of continents."[29] When one looks upon war in terms of attack and defense, or of "historical function," one does not conceive of it as an abstract and absolute evil. Here Socialists dealt with the public use of violence against external enemies according to the cause it served, and that in turn in relation to concrete governments and their policies.

Once this approach was taken, the Socialists were deeply involved in the politics of the present-day world, interested not in peace as an abstraction, but in peace with justice, or in peace and national

* A group of Socialists who were disillusioned with the Second International met in Zimmerwald, Switzerland, in September 1915. At this conference the "Zimmerwald Left," including Lenin, called for the conversion of the international war into a revolutionary civil war. A second conference took place in 1916 at Kienthal.

survival, within the existing society. That, indeed, was the nature of their effort to meet the Balkan crisis of 1912. Victor Adler then spoke of a "proletarian foreign policy," worked out by the Congress of Basel in 1912. The "foreign policy" in this case consisted of sound enough advice to the European cabinets on how to get out of the diplomatic tangle. The word "proletarian" in this context was practically meaningless, but showed how the International could not take any practical step without invoking the socialist world to come, the society free from sin, composed of the new men. In fact there was nothing "proletarian" at all about the view Socialists took of the various war crises preceding World War I. They talked good, common sense, and their judgment was shared by many who had no part in Socialist ideology, and who had even less in a proletarian existence.

The same applies to a fourth approach to the problem of war: proposals for disarmament and arbitration. The Congress of Copenhagen in 1910 adopted a resolution calling on all Socialist parties to vote against all military and naval appropriations, to demand compulsory arbitration, and to work for general disarmament, the abolition of secret diplomacy, and the autonomy of all peoples and their defense against attack and oppression.[30] The last demand seemed not quite to accord with some of the others. At any rate, this package came to be the stock-in-trade of Socialist peace efforts. It was adopted again and again. We find it among the resolutions of 1893 and 1896, and also at the wartime Congresses of Copenhagen (January 1915), London (February 1915), and Vienna (April 1915). It is significant that this "anti-war" program had nothing Socialist about it. Ideologically, it was rooted in the bourgeois expectation of a steady and automatic increase of "reason" over tradition and prejudice, the assumption that a reasonable state would faithfully represent the people rather than the "vested interests," whose policies therefore reflected no conflict that could not be settled like any lawsuit.[31] In the liberal view war stemmed from the underdevelopment of reason and democracy. In the modern civilized world war was an anachronism. The full development of democracy, the shedding of all remnants of the irrational and tradition-bound past, would lift states above war. Neither capitalism nor the new proletarian men played any role in this vision of peace.

Why did this view find such strong support in the International? The millennium of universal and enduring peace is not the same as the Socialist millennium, even though the latter also counted on the end of war, together with the end of private property and exploitation. The pacifist millennium, however, fixed its attention on war to the exclusion of other evils. In the International, Hervé, for instance, seemed to be inflamed more with a passion for peace than for the establishment of Socialism, and he was not alone. One has the impression that the International attracted elements of various beliefs mainly because it stood for a radically transformed world, a "third age," a new society composed of new men, and it did not matter too much what concrete millennium one had in mind so long as it was a negation of the present. Later, however, incompatibilities came to light, when the revolutionary wing of Social Democracy increasingly emphasized the use of force in the irreconcilable class struggle, and postponed all hope for order and harmony to the day after the struggle's victorious termination. Then the reformist majority of the Socialist movement absorbed much of the liberal pacifist program that accorded so well with its own policies.[32]

The resolution adopted at the Stuttgart Congress of 1907 can be considered the climax of the International's anti-war discussions. Many conflicting arguments and elements are thrown together in the resolution's paragraphs. First, we have an assertion that war springs from capitalism's quest for world markets and the resulting "never-ending" armaments race, a view similar to the one presented later in Lenin's *Imperialism* and advocated by Rosa Luxemburg as early as 1900. In the very next paragraph, we find the attribution of war to the "prejudices of one nation against another," the typical liberal view. Summing up these two, the following paragraph asserts: "Wars are *therefore* [emphasis supplied] inherent in the nature of capitalism; they will only cease when the capitalist economy is abolished, or when the magnitude of the sacrifice of human beings and money . . . and popular disgust with armaments lead to the abolition of this system." This is straight Marxism as represented by Guesde: capitalism, not war, is the evil to be fought. Somewhat inconsistently, the second half of the paragraph seems to allow that war itself is an evil of such magnitude that "popular disgust" with it may lead to the "abolition of this system"—without indicating whether "this system" means war or capitalism.

Next follows a definition of the working class as the people of peace, the "natural enemies of war." This does not quite accord with Engels' and Bebel's readiness to go to war rather than knuckle under to the Russian knout. Nor does it subordinate enmity against war to hostility against capitalism, as did the previous paragraph. Essentially, however, this is the same kind of identification between the proletariat and peace that later enabled the Communists to call all nations they ruled "peace-loving" nations, even when they were engaged in aggressive military action.

The operative paragraphs of the resolution are mixed with enumerations of past activities and hopes for future success. Primarily the resolution demands: refusal on the part of the Socialists to vote for military appropriations; popular militias in lieu of standing armies (an "essential guarantee" against aggression); parliamentary pressure in favor of disarmament and arbitration; education in the spirit of the brotherhood of nations, socialism, and class consciousness; and "decisive intervention" to ensure peace—whatever was meant by that. The resolution ends with the two famous paragraphs introduced by Lenin, Luxemburg, and Martov, which exhort the "working classes and their parliamentary representatives" to do "whatever seems to them most effective" to prevent the outbreak of war, but, if they should fail in this, to "intercede for its speedy end," *and* to make use of the ensuing political crisis to "arouse the people" for a total revolution.* It is remarkable that in this, as in any one of the other resolutions, the International as such is not called upon to play a decisive part. The key to action is clearly not in its hands. In spite of the vague reference to a "decisive intervention," the resolution does not attribute power to act even to the Socialist parties. They are "to intercede," "to refuse to support," to use "pressure," to "educate." The International can

* The exact wording of the passage runs as follows: "In case war should break out anyway, it is their [i.e., the working classes' and their parliamentary representatives'] duty to intervene in favor of its speedy termination, and with all their powers, to utilize the economic and political crisis created by the war to rouse the masses and thereby to hasten the downfall of capitalist class rule." The text is taken from Carl Landauer, *European Socialism* (Berkeley, Calif., 1959), I, 344.

"strengthen and coordinate the endeavors of the working classes," it can "encourage" and "unite" Socialists.

That is all. In the real world, then, the International has no standing. In the real world, men are organized under governments and in nations. It is through their governments that societies are capable of action, not through parties or international bodies. The Socialists are real as parts of nations, as *parties,* which can endeavor to influence events but cannot take action on behalf of society as a whole. Each nation and its political order is paramount, so much so that the International refused to formulate general principles of socialist endeavor. Each of the member parties had to find its own line, in accordance with the life and structure of its own nation. Having recognized the pre-eminence of the various orders of existence that we call "nations," the International then pretended that a conflict of existence between nations is either "only in the mind," i.e., the mind of "prejudices" and nationalisms, or else rooted in an economic system which, after all, was supposed to embrace the entire world in one network of markets and production.

Between 1907 (Stuttgart) and 1914, the Socialists made much sense when commenting on the political errors of Europe's diplomats. It is significant that men with such excellent judgment in political matters should have been incapable of recognizing the irrationality of their own pronouncements against war. If many of them accused the International of "failure" in 1914, if their sense of failure led to a revolt against the Second International, and, from Zimmerwald and Kienthal to Moscow, to the founding of a new, the "true" International, it must be because in spite of all their emphasis on national order, national parliaments, national armies, national parties, they still somehow believed that the International had some kind of reality, which in the hour of crisis could be substituted for that of nations. Not that the voices of sound common sense were absent from the congresses and resolutions. They did indeed counsel against sweeping dictates of the International to its members; they insisted that all practical decisions had to be made within the framework of life as organized in concrete societies under concrete governments. But they did not lay the ghost of the ideology that again and again attributed to the proletariat, the International, the people, some kind of supranational existence and effectiveness. Thus the practical and sober minds themselves set up the great expectations by which they were later charged with "failure," "cowardice," and "treason."

*The Achievements of the Second International*

What was the International? How do we measure its success or failure? How can we judge it in retrospect?

There was by no means unanimity, among the Socialists, that the First International had failed or that it had to be revived. When Becker, in 1876, proposed reviving the International as a federation of national parties, Engels strongly opposed this. Engels, for one, felt (in 1877) that "the International has completed its work; it has attained its great aim, the unity of the proletariat throughout the world against its oppressors." The proletarian movement could be strengthened by grouping its national units around an international center only when great events of European importance were imminent. In that case, the international organization of the national units should be established not for propaganda but for action.[33] Did the Second International comply with Engels' directive?

Engels' concept was clearly a strategic one. His military mind thought of national parties as "units," and of the International as something comparable to an allied unified command. On a few occasions, the Second International tried to assume this role, with no more than meager success. Its pretenses, however, were far more complicated than Engels' clear-cut formula suggests. If one dates the Second International from 1889 rather than from the establishment of a Secretariat and an Executive Council, the tangible aspect of the International was at first no more than a series of congresses. Far more important, though, is the intangible aspect, the emotion stirred by the slogan "Workingmen of the world, unite!" an affirmation of something called proletarian solidarity. This, as Carl Landauer has rightly emphasized, was not a tactical necessity but "a matter of sentiment."[34] "International solidarity" was a profound experience. Of what? Liebknecht spoke in 1889 of "the world parliament of the workers, the first the world has ever seen."[35] A parliament represents a people, a commonalty. Liebknecht obviously had in mind a new society, the society of the workers, which would transcend national barriers. In the words of Pottier's song, this society was identified with "le genre humain," humanity as a whole. "Nous qui n'étions rien, soyons tout." We who were nothing will be everything. Lafargue declared in 1889, "You are all brothers and you have only one enemy: private capital, be it Prussian, English, or Chinese."[36] George Lansbury, at the 1896 Congress, described political actions of the International as "means directed toward the establishment of the 'International Socialist Republic.' "[37] Rosa Luxemburg demanded, in a draft resolution of 1907, that the International reply "to the worldwide alliance of the bourgeoisie and the government for the purpose of perpetuating war, through an alliance of the proletarians of all countries for the purpose of perpetuating peace."[38] Kautsky saw "international solidarity" as the necessary foundation of a socialist labor movement which alone could be a "reliable guarantee of world peace."[39] Edouard Anseele proclaimed at Stuttgart, "The community of political interests is stronger than racial instincts and patriotic notions, and socialist conviction is a much firmer bond than blood ties."[40]

All these formulations testify to the concept of a new community of new men, a new people constituting itself apart from the peoples as they were traditionally established under existing governments and within existing boundaries, a society identical with mankind as a whole, a life wholly transformed and utterly different from that of present experience. The International, representing this as-yet-unseen but coming realm, was to its members a quasi-religious experience. Its first symbolic celebration, and a powerful one, was May Day. May Day was meant to have a tactical use; actually, it did not produce tangible results, but it stirred profound emotions as an early manifestation of a worldwide proletarian community in the making. When the unions later sought to make a general cessation of work on May 1 more attractive to the workers, by offering them compensation for the work missed and protection against lockouts, they were rebuked by the Socialist parties, who wanted May Day to be an occasion for sacrifice.[41] At the Stuttgart Congress, a German choir sang the Lutheran chorale *Eine feste Burg ist unser Gott,* substituting for the word *Gott* the word *Bund*: A mighty fortress is our Union.[42] In Basel, the 1912 Congress met in the cathedral, marching in to the sound of pealing bells. By that time, the

International seemed to some of its members not merely a realm to be but actually a society in being. Anseele addressed the gathering, and through it Europe, with this claim: "The International is strong enough to speak to the powers that be in a tone of command, and, if need be, to follow up its words with action."[43]

All this had little or nothing to do with organization. The International was looked upon as representing a new truth of human existence, a "peculiar people," the proletarians, and an autonomous community that could articulate itself and even move world events without the help of governments or authorities.[44] In this sense it obviously created expectations that could not be fulfilled. It is subject to the same criticism which Adler hurled at the anarchists: "[They] resemble Archimedes, who looked for the point from which the world could be lifted out of its hinges and concluded that this point had to lie *outside* of this world."[45] The autonomous community of proletarians, a people transcending the boundaries of present political existence, humanity as a single society—all this lies outside the world of experience. The given world was rather represented by those "legislative and administrative bodies" and "means of power," which "must be conquered in order to convert them from means of capital's domination into means of the proletariat's liberation." In this sense, the International represented not the real but a dream world.

This representative aspect of the International, however, is only a part of the picture. Its structure is another. The structure of the Second International was not that of a "parliament," a representative and potentially authoritative assembly. It differed from the First International, which had constituted itself around a firm and powerful center, the General Council, functioning like a single party, with branches in various countries. The Third International, in turn, was an extension of the Communist Party of the Soviet Union, and was for most of its lifetime administered as a department of the Soviet government. Unlike both of these, the Second International acquired organizational structure only halfway through the period with which we are dealing. Five of its eight congresses before 1914 took place without the help of any permanent organization. From the beginning, the various national parties were considered paramount. Voting was by nations, each nation having two votes. Each national party insisted on the right to decide what had to be done under its particular circumstances.

The structure which emerged under these conditions was not that of a potential political community, but rather one resembling the League of Nations. Almost all the ambiguities and problems of the League of Nations are foreshadowed in the Second International. In 1889, the Congress meeting in the Rue de Lancry demanded "a maximum day of eight hours, fixed by international law."[46] The Report of the Economic and Industrial Commission at the 1896 Congress called for "socialization by national or international enactment."[47] Underlying these and similar statements is the idea of a positive law higher than national law, which without replacing national law superimposes itself on it. The same idea is found in the proposals for arbitration, which the International considered the most promising substitute for war. The organizational structure of the International also resembles that of the League of Nations. The Secretariat did not have the functions appropriate to a planning and directing body, like the General Council of the First International, but operated mainly as a clearing house. The Permanent Executive Council, a committee without any powers, had its parallel in the Council of the League of Nations.

A League of Nations pattern amounts to an attempt to institutionalize supranational laws and principles of rational behavior while leaving the national framework of human existence untouched. It presupposes, or rather postulates, a consensus among nations resembling that which supports governments within nations, but it refrains from creating representative leadership with powers equivalent to those of governments. It stands and falls with the underlying assumption: that the national components conceive of themselves ultimately as parts of a higher community, acknowledge this higher and wider community as a source of obligation overshadowing the obligation to the national community, and are in general disposed to conduct themselves in accordance with a pattern of universal reason articulated through periodic conferences.

The assumption is, of course, utopian. Some would call it idealistic, but then ideals, as Eric Voegelin has reminded us, are but fragments of utopias. An international organization is continuously charged with expectations that only a true government could fulfill. All the same, if it disappoints these expectations, its adherents resort to the ever-ready excuse that the organization is still developing, and that only unwavering optimism can help it grow. This same ambiguity attended the Second International. Victor Adler charged Guesde and his friends with "overtaxing the international congress." He himself, though, acclaimed the Secretariat as a "step from international solidarity to international organization. Thus the seeming unattainable dream has moved into immediate reality. ... The international congresses move now from mere sentiments and demonstrations to substantive discussions ... (to produce) generally binding principles for the Socialist parties."[48] This would not be an ambiguity if the ultimate pre-eminence of the national units were not simultaneously stressed. Engels rejected "any attempt to influence people against their will, [which] would only destroy the old confidence which dates back to the International."[49] Kautsky pleaded the necessity to act according to the conditions of time and place. "The mere invocation of socialist principles avails here for nothing."[50] Adler insisted "the International cannot direct us."[51] Jaurès even theorized that "the destruction of nations would diminish vital energy, impoverish the souls, decline the spirit" of the proletariat, which would lose more than other classes because it would lose the means of its liberation. The hope of the proletariat rested here in each nation rather than in an international organization.[52]

The International thus was constituted according to two different and mutually incompatible patterns. On the one hand, it invoked representatively a worldwide community of autonomous men united apart from, and even against, their nations and governments, who acknowledged their common bond with one accord and were ready to replace all of man's old order with this new humanity. On the other hand, the International organizationally constituted an international organization of national units, a supranational order that presupposed national orders as the framework of existence and action but at the same time overlay and guided national interests, a scheme for harmonizing national policies that would make a world government or society superfluous.

Each of these qualities of the International involved it in an insoluble inherent contradiction. The men who spoke of themselves as if they were no longer Englishmen, Frenchmen, Germans, Austrians, but citizens of a World Socialist Republic, represented by a World Parliament of the Workers, were at the same time leaders of parties that functioned in a political framework within national boundaries. Their laws were the laws of their nations; their liberties were the liberties won through their national traditions; their opportunities were the advantages they enjoyed within a constituted order that they shared with their countrymen rather than with workers of the world. They could not be effective party leaders and at the same time effective citizens of a new world community.

The Second International clung to two pretenses: that of a solidarity that could substitute for the mutual bond of countrymen, and that of a class struggle so irreconcilable that nothing but a completely different social system could eventually command the workers' political loyalty. It created two corresponding conflicts: supranational solidarity versus national interest, and revolutionary intransigence versus adjustment to national political systems. The two contradictions are clearly reflected in the two resolutions that can be considered the highlights of the Second International's twenty-five years: the Dresden-Amsterdam resolution of 1904, and the Stuttgart resolution of 1907. The question "what was the International?" must be answered in terms of pretenses in conflict with the relevant realities. The International brought together a number of men from many countries, who shared with each other an ideological fiction, a Second Reality, as well as a conflict between their fictitious world and the real world.* For twenty-five years, they combined their efforts to have the best of both worlds, and to that effect passed resolution after resolution in which they paid their respects to the Second Reality as well as the real reality, without ever being seriously tested by life. When that test finally came their ranks split, some clinging to the fiction and others to the reality, and the Second International for all intents and purposes ended then and there.

* The concept "Second Reality" (meaning a fixed idea about life, people and the world that someone is determined to embrace as if it were real) was created by the Austrian novelist Robert Musil, in his psychological novel *Der Mann ohne Eigenschaften*.

Institutions based on fictitious ideological assumptions still exist in the real world, where they act and have real effects, although neither their actions nor their results need have anything in common with their pretenses. What were the actions of the International, and what were its effects? The Second International, like the League of Nations, had real power to act only in regard to its own constitution and membership. Its major action in that field was the expulsion of the anarchists, which action in turn constituted the international Socialist movement around the core of Marxist dogma. Its other major action was the planning and proclaiming of an international demonstration, May Day, which became a first-rate vehicle for the propagation of the ideological fiction underlying the International. A third action, still in the realm of self-organization, established the leadership of the Socialist parties over the unions. It was a real action insofar as it prevented the constitution of an International of Trade Unions, or, what amounts to the same thing, prevented the International Congress of Trade Unions from playing the role of the Second International. A fourth action established the principle (mainly at the Amsterdam Congress) that each country could be represented by only one Socialist Party. This action, after the expulsion of the anarchists, secured acceptance for all the varieties of Socialists that remained within the International. This is all. No other decision of the International can be honored by the name of action. Particularly the celebrated resolutions were nothing but attempts to establish verbal compromises between ideology and reality on the one hand, or various versions of the ideology on the other. The search for formulas to which all thought they could subscribe without having to give up their most cherished positions became almost an end in itself. At any rate, it is difficult to see what end other than rhetorical reconciliation could be served by the so-called great resolutions that studded the successive congresses.[53]

With regard to the effects of the International, one can mention them only with great caution, for it is impossible to demonstrate that certain results would not have occurred if it had not been for the International. Still, it seems probable that the International was the major vehicle for the spread of Marxism throughout the European labor movement. Rivalry between Marxists and anarchists had been established in the First International. When the anarchists were rejected and expelled, in the Congresses of 1891, 1893, and 1896, this was almost automatically interpreted as a victory of Marxism. Marxism thereby became the international "bandwagon." Even in the German Social Democratic Party, Marxism was not fully adopted until 1891. The International helped to pull other parties along the same road. "Marxist phraseology was the lingua franca of the parties of the Second International."[54]

The unity principle, imposed on each country's labor party, meant that the revisionists and reformists remained in the same party, together with the adherents of the "permanent revolution" and the futurists. This produced a continuous mixture of revolutionary gestures and language with normal party activities aimed at electoral majorities and influence on legislature and administration. It prevented the Socialist parties from becoming totalitarian, unlike the Russian Party, which refused to accept the unity principle and insisted on excluding factions on ideological grounds. The same was true of the Bulgarians. As Cole put it, "What Amsterdam did bring about was more unity, not more discipline."[55] The same principle, however, counteracted the effort to subordinate unions to the political parties. In the interest of unity, unions could push the parties to adopt their point of view. Carl Schorske has shown that in Germany, on issue after issue, the unions prevailed whenever they decided to throw their weight into the scales.[56] In Germany, their influence was reformist; in Latin countries, it was usually radical. If the International could not assure to the Socialist parties ultimate leadership within the labor movement, it did stimulate the foundation or at least consolidation of groups into single Socialist parties.

These were results within the labor movement. Other effects of the International transcended the movement as such and had significance for the whole of our civilization, a significance which again can only be speculatively affirmed but which is of very great importance all the same. First, the twenty-five years of the International proved conclusively that there is no "revolution of the proletariat." Although the repeated resolutions of the International cannot be classified as actions, the member parties and their leaders took these resolutions most seriously. Again and again, they rejected language that committed them to a practice of total revolution. Again and again they affirmed their determination to bid for votes, to try to win positions in local government and administrative bodies, to influence legislation, and in general to advance in accordance with the rules of the democratic game. This was the language of people who wanted to obtain for the workers a place at the table, rather than the language of revolutionaries. Anyone who had taken the trouble to study the positions taken by Bebel, Jaurès, Adler, Vandervelde, and others could have proved long before World War I that Marx's assumption of a revolutionary proletariat was false. The existing society was in no danger of being violently overthrown.

Nobody, however, did learn this lesson from the International. For the International had another general effect. Its ideological pretensions, and the unity it imposed on revolutionary and reformist elements, caused the various Socialist parties, and the International itself, to use revolutionary language of a most radical kind. The case of German Social Democracy is very instructive in this regard. If we ask to what extent the workers developed a culture which, though separate, participated in the main culture, it is not the integration of Social Democracy but rather its continued isolation that strikes us as most remarkable. That isolation, as we have seen, was artificially maintained by words and symbols. One might even say that contrary to the proverb, in the case of the Socialist parties their words spoke louder than their actions. It was the effect of their gestures and language that drove a deep wedge of alienation between the workers and the rest of the people, an alienation that had no counterpart in the workers' actual existence. When the existence of the whole society was at stake, as in 1914, the alienation turned out to be artificial, only to reappear all the same when the danger was past. Thus, though largely ideological, this alienation became a political reality. After 1918 it prevented the growth of the new republics into well-integrated democracies. It contributed to a civil-war atmosphere that may have accounted, at least indirectly, for most of the violent events in Western Europe between 1920 and 1939.

Finally, the International raised vastly exaggerated expectations, which led to a "failure" trauma among European Socialists. True, a good many leaders in the International claimed that they were "not surprised" by the actions of Socialist parties during the first days of World War I.[57] If they actually had foreseen what would happen, however, they had failed to prevent the overambitious formulations of Stuttgart and Basel. The pretenses of the International were accepted at face value until the last minute by the Socialist labor movement of all countries. Thus the leaders experienced a fall from great heights. There were examinations of "guilt," recriminations for "betrayal." Everybody felt that something had gone wrong. Nothing had gone wrong, of course; everybody had behaved just as one could have predicted and should have expected he would behave. But reality was measured by the false yardstick of ideology, and by that yardstick reality was found wanting. The trauma of guilt and betrayal, in turn, had become a political reality. It was this reality which made it possible for Leninism to spread from Russia over the whole of Europe. Lenin stood against the Second International. In the light of the assumed failure, he seemed to have been right all along. When Lenin used the beginnings of Zimmerwald and Kienthal to found a Third International, he could appeal to large parts of the European Socialist parties and pry them away to form separate Communist parties.

The historians have dealt gently with the International and its leaders. They have seen it as a feeble though noble enterprise. They have acclaimed its founders and leaders as men and women of great idealism and selfless concern. They have hailed the vision of a world community of peace and justice. They have pitied and deplored its failure as the work of blind and atavistic patriotic passions. Underlying all this is an attitude which identifies itself with the French Revolution and its dreams of emancipation. Ultimately, this judgment of the historians is a bit of ideology, too. We must learn to see phenomena like the International for what they are.

It is true that the founding fathers of the International were devoted, selfless persons. That in itself does not mean very much. Who will doubt that the Tsarina in her devotion to Rasputin was driven by motives of the highest purity? Yet most historians do not hesitate to condemn these motives as superstitious. We have seen that the congresses of the International brought together persons whose outlook on life and the world was dominated by a Second Reality, a substitution of fixed ideas for perceptions and experiences of real life. Is a person less to blame for clinging to his cherished Second Reality than for clinging to superstition? The leaders of the International have been acclaimed for the nobility of their vision. Whence did they derive their notions of nobility? Who or what was the measure of value for them? How realistic, or even how careful were they in identifying the roots of evil, the obstacles to human nobility? Their own discussions were full of contradictory statements in that regard. Did they stop to even notice these contradictions? Did they feel any responsibility for clearing them up? If not, were they not willing to treat their own fancies as vastly more important than reality, to cling to their positions or even only their terminology at the expense of reality? And can one consider this attitude altogether harmless?

Not even the most ardent defenders of the International have called it beneficent. It could have had the beneficent effect of dispelling the false fear of the proletarian revolution had not its own reckless ideology reinforced the false impression. The alienation between workers and other people that this ideology perpetuated beyond any basis in fact was by no means harmless. It is only now, three-quarters of a century after the International, that the effects of this alienation are being overcome as workers acknowledge that they are in every way a full-fledged part of their communities. In the Europe of the Second International, workers were actually on their way to this integration. The Germany of Bismarck, for whatever reasons, had taken some exemplary steps, and the England of the Reform Act had made gradual advances in labor legislation inevitable. Other European countries had to follow suit. Without the International, European labor might have become as integrated a part of the existing society as labor did in America in the twentieth century, and it would have done so earlier. The revolutionary and utopian ideology, however, stood in the way of this development. It created fears and counterfears, and these helped to nourish the fascist and Nazi movements as much as they nourished the Communist movement. One wonders whether one can wholly absolve the idealistic dreamers of Amsterdam, Stuttgart, and Basel from responsibility for this. Dreams, after all, are the opposite of reality. As men, we are born into a world that was before we were and will still be there after us. Our responsibility is to know it, to know our own condition in it, and to know as much about the meaning of our transient existence as is accessible to us. The heroes of a new world a-fashioning in Paris in 1889 believed themselves noble because they were creating a human existence that discarded all previous existence. Their assumed role was that of masters of human nature, authors of a new morality, planners of a new earth to replace the old heaven. If Prometheus is to blame, so were they.

Carl Landauer

# Social Democracy

## *The Origins of Social Democracy and the Elements of its Creed*

The change in name of the German Socialist Party in 1891, from Sozialistische Arbeiterpartei (Socialist Labor Party) to Sozialdemokratische Partei (Social Democratic Party), though motivated partly by tactical considerations, marked an important stage in a process that was not confined to Germany. The great hiatus in the history of Socialism in the nineteenth century was the severe repression that followed the failure of the Paris Commune in 1871. In almost every country in which Socialism was an active movement, it went into that test for survival as a number of sects whose organizational bonds were loose or even nonexistent, and who were groping for a common ideology but were handicapped by antagonistic beliefs in different panaceas. Although the Socialist movement that came out of the period of severe repression had by no means achieved full doctrinal unity, and in some countries, notably France, not even organizational unity, the ideological differences were diminished, and those which remained were for the most part buried under generally accepted formulas. Rifts would come to the surface again later, but for more than two decades the degree of unity was sufficiently high for well-coordinated and, on the whole, effective action. Coordination was facilitated by the re-creation of an international forum: the Second International was formed at the end of the 1880's, and, based as it was on more unified movements in the individual countries, it represented a firmer structure than its predecessor of the 1860's and early 1870's, the International Workingmen's Association or First International.

The components of the Social Democratic creed were not new, and even in the period of the First International, if not earlier, they had begun to coalesce. It was the essential completion of that process of coalescence, together with a growth in membership and vote, and an increase in organizational strength, that had created a new phenomenon: a workers' party with a philosophy of its own, a party strong enough to play an important role in parliamentary constellations and increasingly forced or tempted to accommodate itself to the requirements of that role.*

What were the ideological bases of Social Democracy? The movement, obviously, was the heir of democratic liberalism and of utopian socialism. From the first, Social Democracy took the demands for universal suffrage, for control of the government by the governed, and for the protection of civil liberties; from the second, it took the idea of socialization of the instruments of production. The Social Democrats' version of this concept was closer to the ideas of the Saint-Simonians than to those of Owen or Fourier, because their programs tended toward a substantial measure of centralization in the management of resources and not toward "associationism." Another basic ingredient was identification with the working class, which was regarded as the force that would establish the socialistic and completely democratic society of the future; this was an inheritance from Karl Marx and Ferdinand Lassalle. Democracy and Socialism were seen as two aspects of the same con-

* The name Social Democracy was no more new than the elements of the Social Democratic faith. In the spring of 1849 in France, the party called La Montagne—in emulation of classical Jacobinism—effected a reconciliation with the Socialists, whom it had fought a year earlier, and the party resulting from this rapprochement—still more middle-class than labor in its social composition—was called Parti Démocrate-Socialiste. See Georges Renard, *La République de 1848* (Paris, 1906), pp. 136f; Pierre Joseph Proudhon, *Les Confessions d'un révolutionnaire,* in *Oeuvres complètes,* IX (Paris, 1868), 269ff; and Karl Marx, *Eighteenth Brumaire of Louis Bonaparte* (New York, 1935).

In Germany the Eisenachers, one of the two Socialist sects from which the Socialist Labor Party was formed in 1875, called itself Sozialdemokratische Arbeiterpartei; the newspaper of the other sect, the Lassalleans, was called *Der Sozialdemokrat,* and the same name was adopted for the paper—printed abroad and smuggled into Germany—of the Sozialistische Arbeiterpartei during the period of repression. Yet with all these antecedents, it was still of symptomatic significance that the German Socialist Party, as soon as it had regained legal status, added the word "democratic" to its name.

cept: democracy could not be fully realized without at least a close approximation of economic equality, and this would become possible only when the instruments of production were controlled by organized society. On the other hand, since equality was seen as a fundamental value, it would have seemed grossly inconsistent to confine it to the economic sphere and concede to any person or group exclusive or preferential political power. Since Social Democrats upheld the validity of the class struggle, it was inevitable that they occasionally acted with intolerance toward workers who did not share their creed, and who expressed their dissent by actions that to the Social Democrats seemed to violate the obligation of working-class solidarity—by joining, for example, a company union. But the Social Democrats always explained these actions as concessions to the imperfect character of the present class-ridden society, and they tried to keep them within narrow bounds. They were far from the idea that because present-day society contained fundamentally immoral features, immorality was legitimate whenever it served the cause of Socialism. On the contrary, the Social Democrats had a tendency toward ethical purism even in present-day politics, and, considering themselves the protagonists of humanitarianism, worked for the abolition of the death penalty, educational reforms, and the emancipation of women, and—most important—against war. Social Democracy thus played an important role as an ethical force in a period in which scientific skepticism had undermined the religious basis of ethics.

Social Democratic humanitarianism, however, was in irreconcilable contradiction with the Social Democratic belief in revolution, which had been inherited from radical democrcay. This contradiction did not remain entirely unnoticed, and the revolutionary creed not only declined under the influence of factors strengthening evolutionary tendencies—as will be explained later—but was occasionally subjected to softening interpretations even by believers in revolution, who held, for example, that revolution is not necessarily to be understood in the "hayfork sense of violence" (*im Heugabelsinne der Gewalt*). Yet at least in the earlier phase of the Social Democratic movement, it was understood by the masses in precisely this sense.

The identification with the labor movement influenced Social Democracy not only by making it a class party, but also by transmitting to it a strong faith in organization as an end in itself. Labor unions are necessarily based on solidarity, on the thought that "an injury to one is an injury to all," and on organization as the one means of putting this principle into practice. It is in the union tradition to treat splitting, "dual unionism," for whatever reasons, as a grave sin, because it impairs the unity of action that for an organized class is the first requirement of success. Since Social Democracy committed itself to the task of strengthening the labor unions by serving them politically and undershoring them ideologically, it was only logical to establish within the party the same high regard for organizational unity as existed within the unions. For a party, however, ideas and programs are more important than they are for unions, which are primarily instruments for accomplishing practical tasks. To what degree is it morally legitimate for a political party to demand of its members acquiescence in ideas that may help to unify the party but that some individuals cannot affirm in good conscience? The high value placed on organizational unity was something not found in the predecessor movements of Social Democracy. The sense of the importance of unity often clashed with the desire of right-wingers and left-wingers to follow their own convictions; it was a constant cause of friction between the working-class majority of the movement, which had been nurtured by the labor-union tradition, and the few intellectuals, whose primary allegiance was to truth as they saw it, rather than to organization as an end in itself.

## *The Influence of Marxism*

Prior to World War I, the great majority of Social Democrats, except in Great Britain, considered themselves Marxists. The merging of the sects into a fairly cohesive movement would not have been possible without the wide acceptance of Marxist formulas. Marx not only had supplied or transmitted many of the ideological elements of the Social Democratic creed, but also had already welded some of them together. Specifically, Marx had more forcefully than any other writer contended that it was the historical task of the working class to build the Socialist order, and the duty of Socialists to protect and promote the interests of the working class, to strengthen it for the accomplishment of this task. The most important contradictions in the Social Democratic ideology also go back to Marx: the means-ends conflict involved in simultaneous beliefs in democracy and humanitarianism and in the necessity of a revolutionary class struggle—which, according to the logic of Marxian dialectics, ought to have been a ruthless war, not amenable to limitation by the rules of democracy or by the commands of humanitarian ethics. Not only did Marx fail to make this consequence of the dialectical concept of the class struggle explicit, but several of his statements would seem to preclude the dialectic interpretation. In the famous passage of his speech of 1872, for instance, he declared that in countries without a bureaucratic tradition—such as Britain and the United States—the transition to Socialism might occur within the framework of a democratic constitution.[1]

Another contradiction which Social Democracy inherited from Marxian thought was that between determinism and activism. Marx had rejected the approach of the utopian socialists, who had searched for the ethically most desirable form of society. Marx, who professed not to believe in a "superclass" ethic—although there are reasons to doubt the firmness and the consistency of his disbelief—thought that the search ought to be for the historically inevitable form of society. Marx considered success in this search possible because he thought that technology would determine the development of social forms in a calculable way, and that such calculations would establish the inevitability of Socialism. But if Socialism was inevitable, was there any point in planning for its realization, and especially of making sacrifices to assure its coming? In spite of many efforts, neither Marx himself nor any Marxist has ever given a completely satisfactory answer to this question.

For the Social Democrats, however, Marxian determinism offered an easy way to avoid describing in detail the future society, a description which by necessity would have been vulnerable to attacks, sophisticated and unsophisticated. It was safer to rely on the argument that history would solve these problems. Thereby, however, a gap was opened in the Social Democratic program: there were postulates for immediate reforms, and there was a philosophy of history which implied that the society of the future would conform to some very general principles, but there was no bridge between the two, no explanation of how present action could so modify present institutions—by revolutionary or by evolutionary means—as to make them conform to those principles. Political action for reforms within present-day society was vigorous; the belief in the society of the future, still a source of hope, played a slowly declining role in the thoughts of the Social Democratic workers and even of the leaders. At the end of World War I, when the historical hour seemed to call for the establishment of Socialism, Social Democracy found itself without guidance. Nor could the Marxists of the left, who by that time had separated from Social Democracy, find any guidance in their creed: they had to enter a long period of experimentation with human lives and human destinies which has not yet ended.

In general, Social Democracy in all countries assimilated those elements of Marxian thought which fitted into its political strategy and pushed the rest into the background. Marxian economic analysis, for instance, was widely studied and was taught in the courses of instruction organized by Social Democratic parties, but with an emphasis somewhat different from that of Marx's own writings. Whereas Marx had made the basic proposition that human labor is the source of all value the first step in a causal analysis whose truth or untruth was supposed to be independent of ethical judgments, the ethics merely implied in his writings were made explicit and given a central position in Social Democratic ideology. From the contention that labor was the cause of all value was derived the postulate that workers should receive the full value of the product, regardless of the role of capital and land in its production.

Many of the ideas transmitted by Marx to Social Democracy were of course a heritage from earlier phases of history. Marx himself, for instance, was deeply influenced by the tradition of the Great French Revolution, and Marxism was one of the vehicles by which Jacobin ideas reached Social Democracy. Marx was also, in a sense, a disciple of the French and English humanitarian philosophers of the seventeenth and eighteenth centuries, and a conveyor of their ideas. Even the most determined secularists among these philosophers were deeply influenced by the Hebrew-Christian tradition of the value of the human person, and Marxism was one of the carriers of this tradition, all the professions of "materialism" by Marx and his disciples notwithstanding.

Marxist influence was most conspicuous in Germany and Austria, but it was very nearly ubiquitous within the Socialist movement, although sometimes indirect. Even in Britain, where the Labour Party eventually became an embodiment of the Social Democratic spirit, Marxist influence was not confined to the relatively narrow circle of the Social Democratic Federation, which considered itself a stronghold of Marxist orthodoxy. Just as their contacts with Marx and especially Engels had influenced the Chartists in an earlier period, the collaboration of leading British trade unionists with Marx in the First International undoubtedly left an imprint on their minds. Some of the Fabian leaders, though they were for the most part critical of Marx, had studied his writings before formulating their program. In France and Italy, a Marxist spirit was transmitted to the Socialist parties through a number of intermediaries, ranging from personal friends of Marx and Engels like Paul Lafargue and Antonio Labriola to deviationists still steeped in Marxism, like Benoît Malon, Filippo Turati, and Jean Jaurès.

*Non-Marxist Roots*

In addition to the ideological strands that originated in or ran through Marxism, a multitude of others reached Social Democracy. Lassalleanism, however, which is sometimes mentioned in this context, was much more a channel of Marxian thought than an independent influence. At least Lassalle himself was in most respects precisely what Marx and Engels considered him to be; despite their vituperations against him, they considered him their disciple and a popularizer of Marxism. A more independent source of influence came from Lassalle's disciple, Johann Baptist von Schweitzer. Probably the best Marxist economic theoretician living in Germany at the time, he also contributed more than anybody else to the development of a parliamentary strategy for the Social Democrats, a task for which neither Marx nor Engels had any taste and about which they had hardly anything to teach their followers. For the future character of Social Democracy, von Schweitzer's careful attention to the details of meliorative legislation and to the art of gaining the best results in this field through parliamentary combinations was an important determinant.

Important influences of a non-Marxist character originated in Great Britain. Social Democracy, as it has finally come to exist, is unthinkable without the influential role that labor unions played within the party. The classical land of modern unionism is England; although independent roots existed in most countries, and especially in France and Germany, it was not before the New Model unions in Britain had emerged from the debacle of Chartism, and their character and successes had become known on the Continent, that the labor unions there began their ascent to a position of social power.

Even more interesting is the development of the cooperative idea. It also originated in the main in Great Britain, where Robert Owen gave the idea its first strong impetus. French and German conservatives (B. J. B. Buchez, Victor Aimé Huber, Friedrich Wilhelm Raiffeisen) and liberals (Herman Schultze-Delitsch) took up this idea around the middle of the nineteenth century. Although Lassalle's efforts in this field failed to avoid the dead-end road of producers' cooperatives, his influence probably helped prepare the German workers for the idea of consumer cooperatives, which became an important part of the German labor movement. But in relation to the size of the country and the spending power of the working class, the cooperative movement was probably most important in Belgium, where British influence merged with the Proudhonian tradition of *mutuellisme,* mutual economic support, as a principle of working-class action. It was this confluence of the British tradition of consumers' self-help with Proudhonianism and Marxism that made the Belgian working class a model of the proletarian "subculture," which will be discussed a little later.

The influence of the French Revolution reached Social Democracy in part through Marxism as an intermediary, but in part without Marxist mediation; in particular the Jacobin combination of patriotism and radical democracy made its own way. Although Marx's thoughts on nationhood are certainly not summed up in his statement that "the workers have no fatherland," the fact that he, along with Engels, made this statement shows that he was much less a believer in the value of the nation than were the spiritual heirs of the Jacobins. The record of the French Revolution was studied by Social Democrats as it was by all the protagonists of popular sovereignty in the nineteenth century. Even without the influence of Lassalle, whose main difference from Marx lay in a greater appreciation of the nation-state, and without the influence of the Paris Commune, in which the Jacobin spirit (in a proletarian version) was predominant, it was probably inevitable that the belief in the nation would exist below the surface of Social Democracy with more strength than the Marxist formulas let it appear. In 1914, this belief broke through the surface.

One element of Marxism was almost entirely eliminated not by external influences but by the growth of the movement: Social Democracy lost the survivals of elitism which are still found in Marxian thought. This is not the place to determine the extent to which Marx was influenced by the Blanquist idea of a minority of professional revolutionaries who would destroy the existing system, seize power, and only after a period of transition have the new regime legitimized by the vote of a now-enlightened electorate.[2] In Marx's own mind, this idea was counteracted by the belief that "the emancipation of the proletariat must be the work of the proletariat itself," which implies a workers' mass movement. Yet the *Communist Manifesto* still leaves room for the role of a revolutionary elite, which, though it has "no interests separate and apart from those of the proletariat as a whole,"[3] also claims that it represents the future of the movement,[4] and that to safeguard that future according to its own understanding, may act independently of the will of the present majority of workers. Although Engels himself wrote in 1895 that "the time of revolutions made by small, conscious minorities leading unconscious masses has passed,"[5] elitism was still of great importance in the late nineteenth and early twentieth centuries, as the Leninist conception of party organization and the revolutionary-syndicalist cult of the "active minority" showed, but it existed only on the fringes of Social Democracy and was rejected by the core.

### *Pulls in Opposite Directions*

The ideology of a movement can be effective without being consistent. In spite of internal contradictions, the mixture of elements in the Social Democratic creed proved viable but unstable. The conflict between revolutionary dialectics and evolutionary-democratic philosophy was always present, and continually threatened the organizational unity of the movement. There was always a pull to the right and a pull to the left, both originating from inner tensions that were reinforced by external circumstances.

The pull to the right had its most important cause in the growth of the movement. Social Democracy did not consist merely of true believers; it had outgrown the limits of the old Socialist movement and had taken into its orbit masses of workers and some people from the lower-middle class. Many of these supporters were primarily interested in the reforms Social Democracy might achieve in the present. Social Democrats, the left wing no less than the right wing, were always interested in numbers; to the left-wingers the increase in the Social Democratic vote seemed to be a portent of revolution; to the right-wingers it was a promise of greater parliamentary strength and the increasing effectiveness of reformist activities. But large numbers could be kept within the party only by success in passing meliorative legislation. Work along this line connected the party with present society, and tended to push the idea of a social revolution, which would overthrow that society, into the background. Moreover, successful parliamentary work by a party that, for all its strength, did not have a majority in any major country, required collaboration with other parties, contrary to an extreme interpretation of the class-struggle concept. From parliamentary collaboration it was only a step to electoral alliances, which, to the dismay of the left wing, the Belgian, French, and German Social Democrats at various times concluded with the liberals (Délégation or Cartel des Gauches, Grossblock). And these alliances, by leading to the question of how a common victory could be exploited, sometimes ended in proposals to form a coalition cabinet. At this point, to be sure, resistance within the movement proved overwhelmingly strong in the pre-1914 period, as the Millerand case demonstrated; it took the war to weaken this taboo sufficiently to make the participation of Social Democrats in war cabinets and the coalition cabinets of the interwar period possible.

The inner tendency toward reformism was strengthened by influences from the outside. In all countries, the left-wing liberals looked upon the Social Democrats as potential or actual partners in an alliance to preserve or achieve political democracy, and sometimes also as defenders of culture against clericalism. But such allegiances had a number of presuppositions. Liberals had to accept the principle of state intervention for the protection of the weak, for only through successes in the field of social progress could the Social Democrats justify collaboration with bourgeois parties in the eyes of their own followers. On the other hand, no liberal party would have been able or willing to accept allies who acted according to the recipe of the *Communist Manifesto,* supporting the bourgeoisie until a common victory was achieved, and then using, "as so many weapons against the bourgeoisie, the social and political conditions" established by that victory.[6] Therefore the left-wing liberals, while increasingly receptive to the idea of social reform, tried to persuade the Social Democrats to temper the spirit of class struggle and revolution sufficiently to make collaboration possible.

The liberals, however, were not the only possible allies, and concentration upon democratic demands was not the only way for the Social Democrats to move to the right. In an earlier phase of the Socialist movement, a number of conservatives had tried to establish contact with Socialist workers and intellectuals against the liberal bourgeoisie. This had been among the motives of "Tory-Chartism," of Louis Napoleon's social pretensions, of Bismarck's contacts with Lassalle and von Schweitzer, of Rodbertus's approach to the German Socialists. But the motivation had not been entirely tactical; vague ideas about an "organic" society supplied some ideological foundation for the rapprochement.*

By the time Social Democracy had emerged from the Socialist movement of earlier periods, very little was left of these efforts. The only conservative group that here and there concluded an alliance with Social Democrats was political Catholicism, which through the Encyclical *Rerum Novarum* had been oriented toward meliorative social legislation. Such alliances were formed in Germany in the Bavarian elections of 1905 and the national election of 1907. They foreshadowed the post-1918 alliances between German Social Democracy and the Catholic "Center" Party to defend the Weimar

* In this context it is of some interest that the word Socialism, before it became identified with any school that we now regard as Socialist, was used by Catholic writers as a term for the organic society that they wanted to build, in contradistinction to atomistic individualism. See Karl Grünberg, "Der Ursprung der Worte 'Sozialismus' und 'Sozialist,'" *Archiv fuer die Geschichte des Sozialismus und der Arbeiterbewegung,* II (Leipzig, 1912), 372–79.

Republic; the Catholic-Socialist alliance in Belgium in 1925 for the promotion of social reform; and the efforts, unfortunately futile, to establish collaboration between the Italian Socialists and the Catholic Popolari for the purpose of keeping fascism out of power.

The pull to the left originated with a number of factors: the class character of the party, which made it susceptible to extremism whenever class relations were particularly strained, e.g. during a major strike; the survival of Marxian dialectics, with its implication of a final revolutionary struggle with no holds barred, in the phraseology of the movement (and every so often the purist would insist that formulas must be taken seriously); finally, the existence of non-democratic institutions in various countries, such as suffrage restrictions, that seemed to bar the legal way to power for Social Democracy and made armed revolution or the revolutionary mass strike appear an indispensable weapon.

The outside forces which pulled Social Democracy to the left were probably not quite as strong as those pulling it to the right. Not only had anarchism been driven from Social Democracy in the 1880's and 1890's, but Social Democracy had become fairly well-insulated against anarchist influence; in the eyes of the average Social Democrat, an anarchist was always suspect of serving as an agent provocateur. It was not quite the same with the offspring of anarchism, revolutionary syndicalism. As trade unionists, the syndicalists had important interests in common with the Social Democratic workers; especially in Latin countries, the anti-parliamentarian attitude of the syndicalists found some echo in the Social Democratic ranks. The indignation over the Millerand affair sprang not only from orthodox Marxism but also from skepticism directed against the whole parliamentarian game, and against ministerialism as its logical consequence; the revolutionary syndicalists had sown the seeds of this mistrust. Another force pulling the Social Democrats to the left came from the Russian Narodniki and the more modern representatives of the same movement, the Socialist Revolutionaries. Their influence, reduced but not eliminated by the hostility and contempt of the Russian Marxists, directly affected only the Social Democrats of Russia, but through them it reached the fringes of the rest of the Social Democratic movement.

With the Revolution of 1905, the influence of Russian events upon the Social Democratic parties of Western and Central Europe took on more importance. Most deeply affected was the German party, and this was due not only to geographic proximity. The Russian revolution secured a spectacular—though only in part durable—success through a general strike, which broke the resistance of the Tsarist government against the establishment of a constitution with a national legislature. Germany had constitutions on both the federal and the state levels, and the national legislature was elected on a fairly democratic basis. In the state of Prussia, however, suffrage was restricted through extremely high property qualifications, which minimized Social Democratic influence; because of the complicated federal structure, the Prussian diet exercised an indirect but powerful influence on the policies of the Reich. Could not the strategy that had proved so effective in Russia be successfully applied to blow up the Prussian barrier?

A substantial portion of the German party took up this idea with enthusiasm. Most of the advocates of a mass strike were leftists, but even some of the moderates were carried away. On the other hand, a number of orthodox Marxists had reservations about a general or mass strike, because it would have made the party dependent on the labor unions, whereas Marxists generally asserted the primacy of the political organization. As time went on, the misgivings about the mass strike plan grew: the unions opposed it, and the majority of the leadership considered it a weapon that might backfire, by giving the government a pretext to suppress the Social Democratic organization and by destroying its ability to find allies in the legislature. In the end, the support of the mass strike idea was very nearly confined to such extreme leftists as Rosa Luxemburg.[7]

The net effect of the mass-strike issue was unfavorable to the left wing. Prior to the debate over that issue, no division within the German party was visible on the surface except that between a right wing, which was regarded as at least semi-heretical, and the rest of the party. After the mass-strike debate, there was a threefold division: a right wing, a center group, which comprised the majority, and a small left wing. In other words, the left wing had become isolated from the majority because the majority had learned to fear being driven into adventures that would mean the end of Social Democratic power. In other countries, this indirect effect of the events in Russia was not quite so clear, but the result was essentially the same: on the eve of World War I, international Social Democracy consisted of three clearly distinguishable wings.

### *Social Democracy in the Interwar Period*

The threefold division of the last years before the war bears an obvious resemblance to the division into "Majority Socialists," "Independents," and Communists, which established itself as a consequence of the war and of the war-created revolutions. The merger of the "Independents" and the "Majority Socialists" in the early 1920's—on the national level in Germany, and on the international level through the formation of the Socialist and Labor International from the remnants of the Second International and from the components of the Vienna International—seemed to repeat the rapprochement between the reformist right wing and the center group in the last prewar period. Obviously this resemblance was no accident, but it does not prove that the prewar differentiation into three wings, which foreshadowed the postwar separation, would have led to a split even without the war. Not only the war itself, but perhaps even more the attainment of power by member parties of the prewar International under very different circumstances in different countries created a strain that broke the organizational unity of international Social Democracy.

Social Democracy, as it emerged from the ordeal, was both weaker and stronger than it had been in the prewar period. It had lost in numbers, and it was now in competition with an independent party on the left. But by losing the leftist Marxists, Social Democracy had gained much in inner coherence. By acquiring a share of governmental power in some countries, and the possibility of deciding the fates of governments in others, it had now entered a phase of necessary experimentation: how could the instrumentality of the state, if no longer restricted in its effectiveness by the many fetters on the popular will of the prewar period, be used to promote the development of society in the direction of Socialism?

Only for very few years could Social Democracy devote itself with some measure of freedom of action to the utilization of the new possibilities. The economic disturbances of the first postwar period destroyed political democracy in Italy and caused a temporary polarization of political sentiment in Britain and France—a polarization that was unfavorable to a party which no longer was the most radical of all political action groups. Social Democracy thus was engrossed in combating the most serious immediate dangers and could not attend to more fundamental problems. After 1929, economic distress and the end of democracy in Germany restricted the possibilities even more. Nevertheless, the character of Social Democracy, its fundamental philosophy, its strategy, and its dilemmas were clearer at the end of the interwar period than they had been before 1914.

The core of Social Democratic philosophy was humanitarianism, although this was often obscured by the verbal and faint ideological survivals of the revolutionary class-struggle concept. Living man was not to be regarded as an easily expendable tool of history, as the Communists essentially believed; Social Democrats believed in the value of the individual man. The kind of Socialism the Social Democrats wanted was humanitarianism applied to the economy. The economy was to be so shaped, and if necessary so modified, as not to require for its establishment a suspension of the rights of man as citizen. This was the fundamental difference between Social Democracy and Communism. Trotsky, the deepest thinker among the Soviet leaders with the possible exception of Bukharin, sensed this very well when, in his final summing-up, the pamphlet *Their Morals and Ours,* he recognized the conflict over the means-ends problem as the decisive difference between his own position, which with some justification he regarded as that of pre-Stalin Communism, and the attitude of Social Democrats and former Communists who had strayed in the direction of Social Democracy.*

Social Democratic humanitarianism, Social Democratic belief in democracy as the only form of government that can be humanitarian, was now freed, except for small remnants, from the ethical relativism of Marx, who—though inconsistently—had tended to-

* Trotsky's formulation of the issue, however, was in one respect misleading. The question was not whether any goals can sanctify some means that would otherwise be illicit; of course, a speed law can be broken to save a human life, and in the opinion of many of us, at least prior to the nuclear age, a war could be legitimately waged to save human freedom. The real question is what goals can sanctify what means, and whether there are not some means, especially terrorism, that cannot be sanctified by the goal of building a new social order, because—apart from other reasons—they spoil the human beings who will have to form the new order.

ward the belief that all ethics were class ethics; it was freed, too, from the incubus of the idea of a dictatorship of the proletariat, which Marx had never defined. But the responsibility for government action, which Social Democracy had now incurred, brought its own difficulties: government must use coercion against recalcitrant citizens and at least the threat of force against external opponents, and even if in both respects it exercises great restraint, its action will cause human suffering, or at least offend humanitarian feelings. Moreover, Social Democratic governments or governments supported by Social Democrats could not immediately liquidate all the historical commitments of which they basically disapproved. When a Social Democratic government in Germany ordered troops to shoot down Communist workers who tried to seize power, when British troops acting under the authority of the first or second Labour government had to defend colonialism in various parts of the Empire, a shadow fell on the Social Democrats' claim that they were trying to make society more humane. When Social Democrats refused to commit themselves to unilateral disarmament—from a feeling of responsibility in a still-strife-torn world, or out of an obligation to fulfill coalition agreements—the pacifists within and without the movement saw in this attitude a betrayal of old principles.

The truth that in political life even a humanitarian cannot do more than try to make government action as humane as possible under the circumstances is too complicated to be easily understood by masses. Social Democracy was helped, however, by the demonstrations of extreme brutality that the Communists and fascists supplied as early as the 1920's. In the eyes of the majority of workers the Social Democrats might be inconsistent humanitarians, but as long as they had power the atrocities of totalitarianism could not occur. It took the misery of the Great Depression to make many workers forget or overlook this object lesson.

Although the rise of international fascism made large numbers of workers rally around Social Democracy, it was from its beginning a danger rather than a boon to the Social Democratic movement. To a number of Marxist theoreticians, but also to a considerable number of workers, fascism seemed to be an expression of capitalism in its last phase; therefore, for a workers' party to ally itself with political representatives of capitalism to stave off the fascist danger was deemed a hopeless undertaking. Yet the Social Democratic parliamentary leaders knew no other way—because there was no other way—to keep the fascists down except coalition with non-fascist bourgeois parties or legislative support of bourgeois governments. These were the motives of the toleration policy which the German Social Democrats extended to the Brüning government, of the alliances which French Socialists concluded with the middle-class Radicals and which found their climax in the Blum cabinet,* and of similar arrangements in Belgium and Scandinavia. The degree of resistance which these policies found among the workers differed widely from one instance to another: it was great in the case of the toleration policy, small in the case of the Blum cabinet. Yet one aggravating factor was always present: since the height of fascism coincided in time with the depth of the Great Depression, most of the coalition governments or governments supported by Social Democrats were unable to create satisfactory conditions for the workers. In many instances, they saw no other way out of their financial predicaments than to cut welfare benefits or reduce wages. The Social Democratic workers hated to see their party assume responsibility for these measures, either directly or by dampening the workers' opposition in order to keep non-fascist governments in power, and therefore they wanted to believe that this policy of the "lesser evil" would be fruitless; consequently, many of them did believe it, and this benefited the Communists. It would have benefited them even more if the Communists had not on occasion entered into compromising semi-alliances with the fascists, foreshadowing the Hitler-Stalin pact of 1939, and if they had not, at least up to 1934, treated the Social Democrats everywhere as the main enemy in the very shadow of the fascist threat.

For another reason, too, the rise of fascism limited the freedom of action of the Social Democrats: it made it more difficult for them to find partners for parliamentary alliances. Whereas the Social Democratic ranks themselves proved almost impregnable to fascism as long as democracy existed, the middle-class parties lost many of their followers to the fascists; some were reduced to insignificance. Consequently, these parties often feared that by close

* That the latter received even Communist support was due to a peculiar international situation, which produced a temporary rapprochement between the Soviet Union and the West.

relations with the Social Democrats, who were a main target of fascist propaganda, they would lose even more. Moreover, some bourgeois parties believed that the rise of fascism, whether welcome or unwelcome on balance, would at least offer them an alternative to a coalition with Social Democrats, or to buying their support for or toleration of bourgeois governments. Only in Germany and Austria was this game played to the end, with disastrous results for the bourgeois players. But the feeling that the dictators were "riding the wave of the future" was a major handicap to Social Democratic action in the whole period, and contributed to shortening such periods of Social Democratic participation in power as that of the Blum cabinet in France.

The greatest factor benefiting Social Democracy in the long run was not a product but merely a concomitant of fascism—the destruction of the myth of the beneficent effects of unregulated capitalism. Like fascist power, this development was in the main an offspring of the depression. What happened in the United States between 1929 and 1932 had all but destroyed laissez-faire economics. Out of a merger of elements of Jeffersonian and Jacksonian thought with the ideas of Theodore Roosevelt and a sprinkling of Marxism —a mixture even more inconsistent than Social Democratic ideology and almost as unstable, but equally viable—there developed a body of practical measures and attitudes in many ways similar to those which Social Democracy had produced in Europe.* Except for this development, it would hardly have been possible for American governments to cooperate as closely as they did, in the period following World War II, with European governments led by Social Democrats. But for the moment, the domestic trend in the United States had little influence upon the European scene, where Social Democracy had to fight its battles.

* The interwar period also saw developments in the field of theory that helped to consolidate Social Democratic thought. Aside from the debate on Socialist economics, which is discussed below, there was much criticism of the Marxists' economic interpretation of history, at least in its more extreme version, which tends to regard the development of production technique as the sole determinant of all changes in ideas and institutions. This kind of "historical materialism" leaves no room for an autonomous development of ethics, and thus severely limits the significance of the ethical appeal that is an essential part of Socialist reformism. In the interwar period, the most influential critic of the Marxists' overemphasis on the technological factor in history was the Belgian Henri de Man, in his book *The Psychology of Socialism* (New York, 1928).

*The Social Democratic "Subculture"*

Before turning to the effects upon Social Democracy of the defeat of fascism in World War II and the prosperity of the 1950's and 1960's, it is necessary to discuss some of the inner developments that began prior to World War I but came to full fruition only after 1918. The first among these is the building up of what has been termed a proletarian or Socialist subculture.[8]

The connection of labor unions and cooperatives with the Social Democratic parties meant an extension of Social Democratic influence from the political sphere to the economic life of the individual worker. The practical reasons for that connection were reinforced by a community of spirit: not only the common creed, but also the suffering and dangers incurred for the common cause, had implanted in the minds of the Social Democrats a strong feeling of solidarity, and therefore it seemed natural to them that they should also stand together in economic life. Social Democracy and the unions and cooperatives under its influence thus formed more than a cluster of organizations for practical purposes: they represented a sort of widespread brotherhood, a life community, held together not only by considerations of expediency but also by strong ties of sentiment.

Gradually, this community of life was rounded out by the growth of a comprehensive body of workers' organizations devoted to leisure-time activities and cultural advancement, with the Social Democratic Party, the labor unions, and the cooperatives in the center. A whole sphere of institutionalized life developed, in which a Social Democratic worker could move almost from cradle to grave among people holding fundamentally the same views of society. Like labor unions and cooperatives, many of these organizations were born of practical needs either of the individual, of the movement, or of both; the consequences, however, reached beyond any purpose of immediate practical expediency.

The party had a great interest in developing a staff of organizers, editors, and parliamentary experts, who were trained not only in the performance of technical tasks but also in the fundamentals of the common creed, and who possessed a fair measure of general education beyond the elementary schooling provided for them by the state. Almost all Social Democratic parties therefore instituted a system of courses to educate such a staff. The party also had an interest in some technical services, growing out of workers' leisure-time activities. At mass meetings, there was need for first-aid stations; the "Worker Samaritans," proud of the knowledge they had acquired in special courses mostly given by Social Democratic physicians, usually manned such stations. In election campaigns, messengers had to be at the disposal of party headquarters; a workers' bicycle club took care of this task. On May Day and similar occasions, workers' athletic clubs and workers' singing clubs gave performances. The workers' touring club, the Nature Friends, acquired political significance after World War I, when the other Alpine clubs, at least in Germany and Austria, were permeated by a nationalistic spirit; the huts of the Nature Friends then became refuges for all Alpine hikers and climbers who were antagonized by the cult of ethnic and racial hatred in the mountains, and thus came to be a visible sign that the creed of human brotherhood was the creed of the Social Democratic movement.

The reasons for which party members joined these and other workers' societies (there were also, for instance, theater societies, reading clubs, chess clubs, burial societies) grew largely out of the economic and social stratification of society. Workers could not afford the membership fees charged by those clubs which were not specifically designed for workers, and because of differences in manners and educational level they did not feel comfortable in a club whose membership was mostly middle-class. In some of the clubs workers would probably have been blackballed if they had tried to join. There was also a positive motive for the workers to form their own societies: a desire to share hobbies and recreational activities only with those to whom one was tied by the bond of a common conviction.

Here and there, the idea cropped up that those societies whose activities had cultural significance should work toward a "proletarian culture," free from the corrupting influences of capitalism. This idea played a role in the large workers' theater organizations in Germany and Austria, the People's Theater (*Volksbuehne*). Although these theaters cultivated first naturalist and later expressionist drama at a time when other private and government-supported theaters shied away from these "modernistic" trends, the innovations did not lead to a separate proletarian culture but were eventually accepted by the public at large. Thus the hopes of some West European Social Democrats that the workers could do more than find access to the existing middle-class culture proved just as illusionary as the later concepts of "Proletkult" or Socialist Realism in the Communist countries. In fact, in most areas the workers did not even prove particularly receptive to cultural innovations, but remained bound by Victorian traditions still longer than some parts of the middle class. The innovating role of the People's Theater was due more to some especially gifted directors who were led to the workers' organization by political sympathy—Erwin Piscator of Berlin was an outstanding example—than to initiative from the audience. In the later interwar period, however, the intellectual elite of young workers was beginning to push beyond the inherited tradition.

The proletarian "subculture" had a two-pronged effect. On the one hand, class feelings were reinforced: the emergence of the subculture was sometimes regarded as a confirmation of the Marxist idea that within the womb of the old society the workers would form a society of their own, which in the end would break into the open. On the other hand, the subculture's organizations gave the workers an access to the culture of the age; they became less of a culturally deprived group. The subculture thus helped prepare for the reduction of educational class differentials that came after World War II. In this respect, the workers' cultural organizations —and here the word "cultural" should be taken in a broad sense, to include sports and other hobbies—may be compared to immigrant societies in the United States, which on the one hand tended to keep the immigrant apart from native American society while, on the other hand, teaching him American ways through the influence of earlier immigrants of the same origin, in terms to which the newcomer was accustomed and at a time when he would not be fully receptive to Americanization in any other form. As in the case of immigrant societies, there is little doubt that the function of the workers' societies as a cultural bridge proved to be more important in the long run than their reinforcement of class barriers.

*The New Economic Theory of Socialism*

Another significant development within Social Democracy, beginning prior to World War I but becoming particularly important in the interwar period, concerned the economic program. To pre-Marxian Socialists, and still on the whole to Marx and Engels, capitalist profit seeking seemed to be the only barrier to the full exploitation of the technological possibilities of contemporary society. In some Marxist writings there are faint traces of a fundamental distinction between the technological and the economic possibilities of expanding production, a difference which follows from the fact that even in wealthy societies the available resources never permit the utilization of all the kinds of production for which engineers can devise plans. That is the primary reason why in any society it is necessary to compare the economic importance, the value, of the output of a contemplated act of production with that of the necessary input—in other words, why profit-and-loss accounting, a system of bookkeeping, will be as important for Socialism as it is for capitalism.

During the last two decades before World War I, a number of economists tried to convince the Socialists of this truth, and the Socialist literature of the period shows a modicum of receptiveness to this criticism, although the problem was still not widely understood within the ranks of Social Democracy.[9] After the war, a new school of critics emerged, under the leadership of the Austrian economist Ludwig von Mises, who went beyond the argument that value calculation was a prerequisite of rationality by contending that values could be determined only by competition among real buyers and sellers, for producer goods as well as consumer goods. Since under Socialism there would be only one seller, the government, and at least for producer goods only one buyer, again the government, value figures could only be set arbitrarily and would not express the true economic importance of commodities. Therefore a Socialist society could not avail itself of the guidance that a rational value or pricing system alone would be able to supply; the Socialist economy would therefore be "blind."

The Communists ignored this argument. The theoreticians of Social Democracy took some time to digest it, but then a rich literature emerged in refutation. In partial resumption of the prewar line of reasoning, it was argued first, that supply-and-demand schedules, and consequently values expressing the economic importance of commodities, could be determined without actual competition, by calculating on the one hand the cost at which individual commodities could be produced, and on the other hand the prices consumers would be willing to pay in view of their needs and their purchasing power; second, that even a society in which the government held title to all the instruments of production could have actual competition, if the managers of government-owned enterprises were given a fair measure of autonomy and were instructed to strive for the greatest excess of output value over input value—in capitalist terms, for maximum profit; finally, that the practical problems involved in Socialist value calculations could be quantitatively reduced by not insisting on the nationalization of every enterprise, especially since there were many other reasons in the Social Democratic view for leaving small and medium-sized enterprises alone.

This bundle of arguments, especially the first one, forced the critics into a retreat. Friedrich von Hayek, a disciple of Mises, conceded that in principle values could be calculated in a Socialist society but maintained that in practice this would be impossible. Even in this modified form, the Mises-Hayek position has lost ground, because with the improvement of computer technology and the progress of statistics—which Hayek, to be sure, could not foresee when he wrote in the 1930's—an argument based on the non-feasibility of even very complex calculations is no longer convincing.[10]

For the Social Democratic position, this debate was of great importance. The recognition that a Socialist society not only needs and can have value calculation, but that Socialist production would have to be guided by commodity values identical with those which would emerge on a capitalist market that was purged of distorting influences (monopoly, for instance), showed the difference in the mode of operation of the two types of society to be less fundamental than previous generations of writers had assumed. Consequently, gradual, nonrevolutionary transition seemed more feasible. Another consequence was understood only after World War II. The great fear of liberals in the face of nationalization proposals had always been that the ensuing increase in governmental power could not be kept under control; even if the government were committed by law to use economic resources so as to give the consumers what they most wanted to have, rather than what the government thought they should have, many liberals doubted that in a society in which all or even many enterprises were nationalized, the economic importance of various goods for the satisfaction of consumers' wants could be recognized clearly enough to guide government planning. The new developments in economic theory tended to dispel these doubts; they gave concrete meaning to the concept of a consumer-oriented Socialism.

### *Has Social Democracy a Future?*

Although the Social Democratic parties emerged after World War II as proud bearers of a tradition that had survived fascist oppression, they soon found themselves in a new crisis. The trend toward the welfare state, which had begun in the late nineteenth century and had been much accelerated in the twentieth, mainly as a consequence of Social Democratic efforts, underwent a further acceleration. Together with the rise in productivity, which produced unheard-of living standards in all advanced countries, welfare legislation fulfilled so many of the old Social Democratic postulates that they had lost most of their urgency in the eyes of the workers. The concept of class struggle seemed pointless in a society in which the workers had finally gained access to many of the amenities previously reserved to the upper classes. Moreover, where nationalization was tried, as it was on a fairly large scale in Britain and France, it proved to be nothing better than a device that might be useful under some circumstances and harmful under others; certainly it was neither a panacea nor the fulfillment of a dream.

In this situation, the Social Democratic parties in the various countries purged themselves, with different degrees of determination and consistency, of the relics of Marxism, which now seemed just so much ideological rubble. This was a necessary sacrifice; whatever value Marxism as a unifying creed had had in the past, it had now disappeared. By ridding themselves of Marxist concepts and slogans, the Social Democrats not only satisfied urgent needs of political strategy, but also finally achieved consistency between the real beliefs of their leaders and the vocabulary they used in propaganda. As far back as 1899 Eduard Bernstein had addressed to Social Democracy an exhortation quoted from Schiller: "What she really is, she should dare to appear!" In other words, you are a party of practical social reform, striving for political and social democracy; why try to appear as a band of revolutionaries guided by the concept of an illimitable class struggle?[11] Yet well into the 1930's, the revolutionary vocabulary had persisted in much of the Social Democrats' propaganda.

The liberation from the dichotomy of vocabulary and action was dearly paid for, however, because the purging process did away not only with Marxist survivals but with the most specifically Socialist elements in the parties' programs and goals, and left a great void. Social Democracy has still retained its strong democratic and humanitarian tradition, and in a number of situations this gave it sufficient distinguishable identity to convince substantial—sometimes even increasing—numbers of voters that they should prefer the Social Democratic ticket to others. But can Social Democracy in the long run survive without a distinct economic program? And if this question must be answered in the negative, can Social Democracy develop an economic program that is both in keeping with the tradition of the movement and meaningful for the present?

The only chance for such a development appears to be offered by the concept of economic planning, in the sense not of a centralized management of the economy, but of systematic economic foresight and the use of this foresight to support desirable trends and to check undesirable trends. To be sure, to create and operate the apparatus of foresight would be a governmental function, and the state would have to manipulate the incentives (such as cheap credit, tax advantages, and in extreme cases subsidies) by which desirable tendencies would be encouraged, as well as the deterrents (such as heavier taxation and credit restrictions) by which undesirable trends would be inhibited. The economy, however, would remain free to respond or not to respond to both the inducements and the deterrents. The example of France has proved the feasibility of such a system. Yugoslavia is close to that model. In the Soviet bloc countries, the tendencies connected with the name of Yevsei Liberman seem slowly to reduce the economic powers of the central authorities, forcing them also to work with incentives and deterrents because they can no longer give direct orders, and allowing individual enterprises to be guided, as they are in strictly capitalist countries and at least in principle in France and Yugoslavia, by the profit motive, on the basis of a system of prices that reflects the importance of commodities for the satisfaction of consumers' needs.

For this development, the discussion of Socialist value calculation conducted in the interwar period was of considerable importance. Economic foresight must be exercised in value terms as well as in physical terms. It is necessary, for instance, to ascertain not only the availability of physical resources for desired investments, but also what the costs will be, and whether the incomes of consumers will be sufficient to purchase the products at prices covering these costs. Although nobody today—and certainly no Social Democrat—would think of replacing the "live" market with a "paper" or "shadow" market,* it is important to know that prices can be calculated independently of actual market operations, on the basis of known or estimated supply and demand. When the question of whether this was possible first arose, it was assumed that the state would own all production facilities, would therefore do all the selling and buying at least for producer goods, and would substitute its own price calculations for the prices resulting from the bargaining of suppliers and purchasers. Today no such substitution is contemplated in the non-Communist countries (and to a decreasing extent even in the Communist countries), but the need arises for government agencies to anticipate the prices that will conform to the expected supply and demand. Price anticipation presupposes the possibility of calculating prices independently of the market; this possibility is as essential to government agencies that must know probable prices, without waiting for them to emerge from actual market operations, as it is to a government that wants to know the rational prices in order to impose them on the economy.

The beneficent effect of organized economic foresight is, if not

* If a market is defined as a place, in a physical or a figurative sense, in which supply and demand confront each other, then the market concept can also be applied to the confrontation on paper, by drawing supply and demand curves on the basis of statistical enquiry or of estimates. For the distinction between a market in this sense and one in which real buyers and sellers meet, the terms "paper" market and "live" market seem appropriate. The term "shadow prices" has been widely adopted in economic theory for the prices formed on a "paper" market, and it would then be consistent to call the latter a "shadow" market.

beyond all controversy, at least more and more rarely questioned. Nor can it be questioned that such foresight has long been an element of the Social Democratic tradition, although it was not clearly conceived. It seems also at least conceivable that an emphasis on economic planning might establish new ties between Social Democracy, which is now largely a European movement, and the developing countries of other continents. Most of the Socialist parties in Asia and Africa are no longer in the same international organization as the West European parties; there is now a separate "Asian Socialist Conference," with a number of African associate organizations. The Japanese Social Democrats hold dual membership in this organization and in the Socialist International, which is comprised mainly of the parties of Western Europe, the British Commonwealth, and the Americas.* The separation of the Socialists in the ex-colonial nations, which weakens the position of Social Democracy, can hardly be undone, but even a rapprochement between the two international organizations would be a boon for the European Social Democrats. Economic planning in the sense of economic foresight, and action on the basis of this foresight, plays a key role in all the developing countries; it is regarded as an instrument and a symbol of their hope to attain a well-being equal to that of Europe and North America. If the Social Democrats could lead the way in advancing the principles and techniques of planning in freedom, there might emerge a community of goals between European Social Democracy, with its old traditions, and those groups in the new countries which are groping for a content to give to their Socialism.

Thus it would seem that the idea of economic planning, separated from all elements of economic despotism, could indeed become the core of a new economic program for Social Democracy. But can the concept of planning be endowed with that emotional force which is necessary for the guiding idea of a political party, as distinguished from a concept that experts might propose to audiences of scholars exploring possibilities of reform without preparing for mass action? Here doubts arise. Eliminating the capitalist's

* The Socialist International was reconstituted in 1951. The Social Democratic parties of Eastern Europe, whose representatives live in exile, are also recognized by the Socialist International.

profit, or taking away part of it to finance social amelioration, was a postulate that appealed to the self-interest of the disadvantaged and to the sense of justice of a wider audience. Schemes to improve the operation of the economic mechanism so that it might operate at full capacity had a strong appeal during periods of depression, "starvation in the midst of plenty," as in the 1930's. Proposals for economic planning, crude as they were at the time, were almost more popular in many countries than proposals for the redistribution of income, since to the suffering masses it seemed more important to get jobs than to get higher wages at the expense of profits. But we live in an age of prolonged prosperity. Can masses get interested in improving an economic machinery which, to all appearances, is working well? To be sure, economic science can point out a number of reasons why the situation is not really so satisfactory as it seems. The factors that in the past have produced recessions and depressions have not disappeared, although we have learned to mitigate the effects; even during prosperity, islands of poverty appear within affluent societies. Regional differences in well being, both between nations and between sections of the same country, are becoming more of a grievance, even if they are no greater in absolute terms. Planning is not a panacea, yet it may open the way to remedial measures for all these potential and actual maladjustments. But even if the economists can be impressed with the potentialities of planning, can the interest of masses be engaged before a new economic crisis of major dimensions occurs?

One may ask, perhaps, why it would be a disaster if Social Democracy, for want of an economic program, should decline and finally die. Is it not a natural thing for a party or a movement to cease to exist when too much of its program has been fulfilled? The answer, of course, must be yes, but what has come close to fulfillment are merely the economic postulates of Social Democracy. The Social Democratic movement as a protagonist of humanitarianism has not yet won the day, in spite of the defeat of fascism. Social Democracy can hardly live without an economic program, but its principal historical function at this time is not economic: it is the humanization of society. Social Democracy has no monopoly of this goal, but as a force working for it, the Social Democratic movement has yet to be replaced.

# The Third International

Milorad M. Drachkovitch and Branko Lazitch

# The Communist International

From the time of their success in Moscow in March 1919, the architects of the Third, or Communist, International emphasized the continuity between the new organization and its predecessors, the First and Second Internationals, and at the same time staked out broad areas of radical innovation. The official position, which was first spelled out by Lenin and reiterated thereafter by Communist historians, was that the Third International was the direct and legitimate heir of the First, and that it had taken over all that was progressive in the Second International and given continuity to the Marxist revolutionary movement. Moreover, the fact of the Third International's existence consigned to oblivion the Second International, whose Social Democratic leaders had "betrayed" the ideals and interests of the proletariat by surrendering to patriotism at the outbreak of World War I.[1] This thesis places us in the middle of one of the great historical controversies of this century, a controversy to which this essay will contribute by surveying the fundamental features of the Third International and attempting to situate it within both Marxist-Leninist and general history.

## *The Fascination of Revolutionary Power*

Two related events, World War I and the collapse of the Second International, had prepared the stage for an exceptional historical figure—Vladimir Ilyich Lenin. Without the war Lenin's road to power in Russia would have been incomparably more difficult, if not wholly barred; without Lenin the Russian Bolshevik Party would not have been what it was, nor would the events of October 1917 have unfolded as they did.[2] And without a Leninist party and a Leninist revolution, any Communist International to have seen the light of day would have been a political entity of an entirely different stamp.

The way to the Third International at first seemed long and tortuous. When Lenin declared, in the first issue of his party's journal to appear after the outbreak of war, that "the Second International has died, overwhelmed by opportunism," and then concluded with "Long live the Third International," his voice was but a whisper in the wilderness. Apart from the meager readership of his own paper, nobody took the verdict seriously. Some Bolshevik sections, like the one in Geneva, took exception to Lenin's dictum about the Second International, while the European Socialist press ignored it altogether.[3]

True, as the war progressed and the latent pacifism of some European Socialists began to make itself felt, Lenin's influence grew. But until 1917 all he could do was to broadcast his views, while he and his followers remained a minority within a minority. At the conferences of Socialist Women and Socialist Youth, held in Berne in March and April 1915, Lenin's draft resolutions were voted down, and the secretaries of the organizations, Klara Zetkin and Willi Münzenberg, rejected Lenin's ideas. Similarly in the case of the Zimmerwald movement, neither the large Italian Socialist Party, which launched the movement, nor the two most radical Socialist groups in Europe, the Dutch Socialist dissidents and the Bulgarian "Narrow" Socialists, were persuaded by Lenin's position. At the Zimmerwald conference itself, neither Giacinto Serrati, Henrietta Roland-Holst, nor Vasil Kolarov joined the Leninist "left"; nor did the German "Spartakusbund," another emerging movement of dissident leftist Socialists, or such leading Socialist figures as Angelica Balabanoff and Christian Rakovsky.

Yet after the Bolshevik victory at Petrograd, these same parties rallied to the Comintern, and all the Socialist leaders mentioned above—Münzenberg, Zetkin, Serrati, Roland-Holst, Kolarov, Balabanoff, and Rakovsky—assumed important positions within the Comintern, and in some cases within the new Soviet state. Power succeeded where Lenin's persuasiveness had failed. In this respect what Lenin wrote on the occasion of the third anniversary of the

Bolshevik Revolution has remained valid, not only for the Soviet Union but for the entire Communist International:

We in Russia committed thousands of mistakes and suffered thousands of collapses, losses, etc., as a consequence of the clumsiness of novices and incompetent people in the cooperative societies, municipalities, trade unions, etc. We have no doubt that other peoples, more civilized than we are, will commit *fewer* mistakes of this kind. But in spite of these mistakes we achieved the main thing, *viz.,* the conquest of power by the proletariat. And we have held onto this power for three years.[4]

### *A Historical Misunderstanding*

In March 1918 Lenin and his followers, some of them reluctantly, decided to abandon their original party name, the Russian Social Democratic Workers' Party, and to adopt a new one—the Russian Communist Party (Bolsheviks). The change was fateful in two respects. First, it paved the way for the proliferation of Communist parties throughout the world. Second, it was a necessary precondition for the creation of the Bolshevik-inspired Comintern.

The earliest echo of the Russian initiative by Western Communist neophytes was based on a misunderstanding. Attracted on essentially emotional rather than ideological grounds, they were hardly aware of the implications of Lenin's ideas for the organizational structure of their parties, or of the obligations they assumed in making their parties sections of the Comintern. Those who were fairly well acquainted with Lenin personally and ideologically, like the German Spartacists and the Dutch leftists, distrusted him.[5]

With respect to the German Communists, whose leaders opposed the creation of the Third International as premature, Lenin enjoyed a great stroke of political good luck in the assassination by a "class enemy" in 1919 of Rosa Luxemburg and Leo Jogiches. Their fate was shared, in a sense, by other leading Spartacists, among them Paul Levi, Ernst Meyer, Heinrich Brandler, and August Thalheimer, who were gradually eliminated from the Comintern from 1921 on. The watchful Dutch leftists clashed with Lenin as early as the beginning of 1920, at a time when other European Socialists had just begun their "journey" to Moscow.

Nearly all the newcomers were drawn to Bolshevism by the

prestige of the only successful revolution, rather than by an appreciation of the concepts underlying its success. For many survivors of the war, Socialists and non-Socialists alike, the Bolsheviks' activism was attractive because of its "curious and only seemingly contradictory insistence on both the primacy of sheer action and the overwhelming force of sheer necessity. This mixture corresponded precisely to the war experience of the 'front generation,' to the experience of constant activity within the framework of overwhelming fatality."[6] This was especially true of Socialist youth, who were for the most part hostile to the official leadership of Social Democratic parties, and who found in the Comintern an outlet for long-suppresssed revolutionary ardor and a compensation for the 1914 "betrayal" of the International, which was a particularly live issue after four years of fighting. It was no accident that the overwhelming majority of Communist leaders in the period between 1919 and 1921 were under thirty years of age, and many of them under twenty-five.

In the early years, Comintern enthusiasts were to be found in unexpected quarters. Anarchists of various shades; revolutionary trade unionists in France, Italy, and Spain; members of the Industrial Workers of the World (IWW) in the United States—all thought they had found a spiritual home in the new Russia. They were attracted not only by the successful revolution but also by Lenin's notions on the withering away of the state (set forth in his *State and Revolution*), which seemed to accord with their vision of the future social order. Wished away were those aspects of the movement which might have given them pause—the cult of organization, the genuinely military discipline of the Bolshevik Party. In much the same way, pacifists of various hues saw Lenin as an apostle of peace and the liquidator of war in Russia; they were oblivious to the fact that conflict lay at the very heart of Bolshevism, that civil and revolutionary warfare were integral parts of Bolshevist strategy. The prompt and unanimous acceptance of the Comintern by the Norwegian Labor Party, whose structure, ideology, and activities bore no resemblance to Bolshevism, is perhaps the most striking example of how contagious was the prestige of the October Revolution, and how unknown was the nature of Bolshevism, the guiding force of the Comintern.

*The Political Background*

Adherence to the Communist International in the years 1919–20 was usually the result of genuine enthusiasm and, at the same time, of political immaturity. The most enthusiastic joiners were often ignorant not only of Bolshevism but of Socialism in general. In France nearly all the partisans of the Third International at the Congress of Tours in December 1920 had belonged to the French Socialist Party (SFIO) for five or six years at most. Similarly, the newly formed sections of the SFIO, particularly those in the countryside, rallied to the Third International, whereas most of the sections in industrial areas as well as the veteran members of the Socialist Party remained faithful to the "old house," as Léon Blum called what remained of the SFIO after the Congress of Tours. In Germany, as Trotsky himself admitted after the failure of the Comintern-inspired "March action" of 1921, it was the politically underdeveloped central region of the country where the Communists were strongest in relation to the Socialists. In Yugoslavia, it was in Slovenia—the most economically advanced region, with strong trade union and Social Democratic traditions—that the Communists had the most trouble in winning over the Socialists; in the elections of November 1920, the Slovenian Communists received little more than half as many votes as the Social Democrats, and came in a poor fourth. By contrast, in the two most backward parts of the country, Montenegro and South Serbia (Macedonia), where the Socialist movement had barely existed before 1914, the Communist candidates fared well in the same elections, obtaining a relative majority in Montenegro and coming in a strong second in Macedonia.

Nevertheless, if the Communists failed to attract the older generation of Social Democrats and trade unionists, they succeeded to a considerable extent with the young. With insignificant exceptions, every Communist Party was founded by the extreme left wing of a Socialist Party, and Communist numerical strength was in direct proportion to the number of militants drawn from the Socialist camp. The Communist movement in Europe—and, apart from the Chinese adventure, the history of the Comintern is essentially European—became a political force only in those countries in which the partisans of Moscow were able to gain the support of a majority or a substantial portion of the Social Democratic Party. This was true in France, in Germany (after the Halle Congress of Independent Socialists in October 1920), in Italy, and in Czechoslovakia. Parallels were to be found in Yugoslavia, where the overwhelming majority of Serbian Socialists, in particular, went over to the Communists; in Bulgaria, where the "Narrow" Socialists prevailed over the "broad"; and in Finland, where the Communist Party was founded by several former Social Democrats. On the other hand, in those European countries where neither the leaders nor the rank and file of the Social Democrats were won over, the Communist movement was doomed to insignificance; this was the case in Great Britain, Austria, Holland, Sweden, and Belgium.

In the last analysis the strength of the different Communist parties was determined by political, not economic, factors. Economics cannot explain why Communism was an important movement in France and Germany, but not in Belgium or Austria. If economic considerations were decisive, the Communists would have been stronger in Austria than in Czechoslovakia, whereas in fact the reverse was true. The consciousness of the new Comintern recruits was determined less by their economic and social environment than by politico-psychological forces working differently in different countries.

### *The Shaping of the Comintern*

It was a supremely difficult task to forge an effective international organization from the disparate human material that came to Moscow or looked to it from afar for revolutionary inspiration and guidance. To overcome the initial difficulties, whose scope he himself did not at first realize, Lenin counted above all on two factors: first, the successful Bolshevik experience, which if applied correctly would promote the Communist cause everywhere; second, the general European, if not worldwide, revolutionary conflagration that in 1919–20 he expected at any moment.

The events of October 1917 in Russia confirmed Lenin in the correctness of his 1902 view, set forth in *What Is To Be Done?*, that spontaneity was the main enemy of the working-class movement, and that the victory of the revolution could be secured only by "the centralization of the most secret functions in an organization of professional revolutionaries."[7] Obsessed by the idea that "on some very important questions concerning the proletarian revolution, *all* countries will inevitably have to go through what Russia has gone through,"[8] Lenin warned foreign Communists that if they did not adopt Bolshevik tactics wholesale, victory would remain beyond their grasp.

Lenin's urgency stemmed from his conviction that the world revolution was around the corner: precious time should not be squandered. This is reflected in Lenin's appraisal of the international situation shortly before the founding of the Comintern:

> When we came into power in October, we were nothing more than a single spark in Europe. To be sure the sparks multiplied, and those sparks emanated from us. That was our greatest achievement, and yet those were isolated sparks. But what we see now is a conflagration that has spread to many countries: America, Germany, England. We know that after Bulgaria, the revolution spread to Serbia. We know how these workers' peasants' revolutions passed through Austria and reached Germany. The conflagration of the workers' revolution has overtaken a number of countries. In this respect our efforts and sacrifices were justified.... We were never so close to an international proletarian revolution as at this very moment.[9]

In the same optimistic vein, Grigori Zinoviev, Lenin's closest associate and the first President of the Comintern, wrote in May 1919: "At the time of writing, the Third International has as its main basis three Soviet Republics, Russia, Hungary, and Bavaria. No one will be surprised, however, if by the time these lines appear in print, we shall have not merely three, but six or more, Soviet Republics. Europe is hurrying toward the proletarian revolution at breakneck speed."[10]

The fact that only a year after the establishment of the Comintern all revolutionary efforts outside Russia had failed did not shake Lenin's belief in the imminence of the world revolution.[11] Instead it incited him to adopt even sterner measures, persuaded as he was that failure could be explained only by the shortcomings of Communist parties suffering from the prejudices and weaknesses of the Second International. As a corrective, and in anticipation of the Second Comintern Congress, which was to convene two months later, in April 1920 he wrote his celebrated booklet *"Left-Wing" Communism, An Infantile Disorder*—one of the greatest manuals on political warfare ever written.[12] The central theme of the booklet was that although the vanguard of the working class had been won over to the Comintern, the vanguard had failed to awaken the "dormant proletarian masses," and had still to "master all means of warfare" and become a "practical leader of the masses." To correct these deficiencies, two pernicious tendencies had to be combated: Menshevism, i.e., right-wing "opportunism and social chauvinism," and "left-wing sectarianism," i.e., the refusal to understand the "necessity of displaying the utmost flexibility by all Communists in all countries."[13] For the moment, however, in Lenin's opinion, "the mistake of left doctrinairism in Communism [was] a thousand times less dangerous and less significant than the mistake of right doctrinairism."[14] For that reason he put before the Second Comintern Congress Twenty-One Conditions of affiliation to the Comintern, which amounted to a projection of the Bolshevik-Menshevik split onto the international movement.

Lenin's opposition to Menshevism was absolute.* One of the Twenty-One Conditions required "a complete and absolute break" with Socialist reformists and centrists—that is, with sympathizers who balked at unconditional obedience. Another condition stressed the need for a periodical "cleansing" of party membership, to purge the halfhearted. All decisions of the Comintern's Congresses and of its Executive Committee were to be "binding on all parties belonging to the Communist International." All Comintern sections were obliged to give "unconditional support to any Soviet Republic in its struggle against counterrevolutionary forces." Two other conditions of pure Bolshevik origin demanded that each party create a "parallel illegal organization," and base its existence on the principle of "democratic centralism." "Iron discipline" was required of

* Since for Lenin the most important task was to crush the Mensheviks, he exhorted all Communist parties to do their share in the universal anti-Menshevik struggle. The postwar sufferings of the German working class were due, he said, to the failure of the German Communist Party to break with the Mensheviks. Similarly, the "eradication" of Menshevism "was the central task of Italian Socialists." See "The Italian Question," Lenin's speech to the Third Comintern Congress, June 28, 1921, in Lenin's *Selected Works,* X, 273–78.

every Comintern section "in the present epoch of acute civil war." Each party was given four months to call an extraordinary congress to examine the Twenty-One Conditions.[15]

Nothing indicates the rigidity of these conditions better than Lenin's unequivocal condemnation of Serrati's mild plea that the Twenty-One Conditions, which he accepted in principle, be applied in a way that would leave a certain measure of freedom to individual Communist parties.[16] Again, although Lenin admitted that Paul Levi was essentially right in his criticism of the Comintern-directed March 1921 uprising in Germany, he nonetheless approved Levi's exclusion from the German Communist Party for breach of discipline. The attitude that discipline was more important than truth, obedience more valuable than valid criticism, was a new, and disturbing, departure, with enormous implications for the future.

Another disturbing new practice of the Comintern was dispatching special secret emissaries to foreign countries with instructions affecting the entire future of individual Communist parties—without the knowledge of the local leaders themselves. The most important case in point was the pressure exercised by two Comintern emissaries, Khristo Kabakchiev and Mátyás Rákosi, at the Leghorn Congress of the Italian Socialist Party (January 1921), which caused a triple split in that once-unified Comintern section.* Paul Levi, who attended the Leghorn Congress, wrote a few months later, shortly before he was expelled from the German Communist Party, that the Comintern's secret emissaries "never work with the leadership of individual Communist parties, but always behind their backs and often against them. They enjoy the confidence of Moscow, but the local leaders do not. . . . The Executive Committee [of the Comintern] acts as a Chrezvychaika [i.e. Cheka, the original Soviet Secret Police] projected outside the Russian borders."[17]

The events of 1920, particularly the failure of the Red Army in

* A similar though less dramatic example of the interference of the Comintern's secret emissaries in the life of foreign Communist parties was the mission of Amadeo Bordiga and Henryk Walecki at the Second Congress of the French Communist Party, which took place in Marseille in December 1921. Of the participants in the Congress, only a handful of top leaders were aware of the presence and decisive pressure these emissaries were exercising behind the scenes.

Poland, dashed all hopes for immediate world revolution. Outside Russia the proletarian masses were in anything but a revolutionary mood, which became obvious in March 1921, when the "March action" failed in Germany. The Comintern was left in a paradoxical position. Forged as an instrument of civil war and revolution, it was bound to exist and to act, soon after its inception, in a world that was either indifferent or hostile to Communist revolution. Leninist intransigence and the mechanical imitation of everything Bolshevik by Comintern sections played into the hands of the Communists' enemies, and the most violent among them adopted Communist methods for anti-Communist ends.[18] Further, the Twenty-One Conditions of Comintern membership were largely responsible for splitting Socialist parties and weakening the common front of leftist political forces. The split in Italian Socialism caused by the Comintern in January 1921 paralyzed the workers' movement, and thus contributed to the ultimate fascist triumph.

The failure of the "March action" in Germany was perhaps only the blackest cloud on a generally darkening revolutionary horizon. Bad news from abroad was accompanied by a deterioration of conditions in Russia; together, they signaled the need for a tactical overhauling. In a significant move, Lenin combined a harsh political measure, the quelling of the Kronstadt uprising in March 1921, with substantial economic concessions in the form of the NEP, which was designed to still widespread popular discontent. A change of line was in store for the Comintern as well. Speaking as a representative of the Comintern before the Tenth Congress of the Russian Communist Party on March 16, 1921, Zinoviev explained that after the Comintern's first, preparatory phase and second, propagandistic phase, corresponding to its two first congresses, it now stood on the threshold of a third, organizational period. Comintern sections, wherever they were found, now had a new assignment that took precedence over all others, that of learning "the most elementary principles of conspiracy." This third period would pave the way for a fourth, that of direct struggle.[19] The spirit of Lenin's speech before the Third Comintern Congress, on July 1, 1921, echoed Zinoviev's description of the third, organizational phase. As if he had forgotten his admonition to the Italian Socialists in November 1920 to show a "maximum of fanaticism, loyalty to the revolution, energy, boundless audacity, and determination,"[20] Lenin now warned his listeners that "he who fails to understand that in Europe—where nearly all the proletarians are organized—we must win over the majority of the working class is lost to the Communist movement."[21]

In addressing the Third Comintern Congress, Lenin abandoned the positions and priorities he had urged upon the Second Congress. At the earlier congress right opportunism had been branded as the chief enemy; now the arrows were directed against the left, or more precisely against the "theory of offensive struggle" advocated by several Comintern sections (the German, Italian, Hungarian), as well as by the delegation of the Communist Youth International. This, in Lenin's words, was "empty phrasemongering," nothing but a "left absurdity" ("We Russians are heartily sick of these left phrases"). There were, he declared, more important things to do than "hunting centrists." What had to be done now was "to win over not only the majority of the working class to our side, but also the majority of the toiling and exploited rural population. Have you made preparations for this? Hardly anywhere."[22]

Once the Third Congress was over, for obvious political and psychological reasons Lenin insisted that the Comintern's broad goals were unchanged, and that the decisions of the Third Congress followed logically from those of the Second. The role of the Second Congress was to give the Comintern organizational coherence by purging Communist parties of Menshevik opportunism; the role of the Third Congress was to plan the training and testing of Communist parties "in all sorts of maneuvers, in a variety of engagements, of offensive operations and retreats."[23]

Clearly, Lenin had sounded a temporary tactical retreat along the entire front. The drought and catastrophic harvest in Russia in the summer of 1921 prompted the Executive Committee of the Comintern (ECCI) to abandon its intransigent line. On July 30 it made a worldwide appeal for aid to the victims of famine in Russia, and during the following months it launched an international proletarian rescue action, designed to draw on all workers, irrespective of their political or trade-union affiliation. The short step from humanitarian to political cooperation was not long in coming. In a note written on October 1, 1921, on behalf of the

Politburo of the Russian Communist Party, Lenin recommended to all the Comintern sections that they undertake "joint actions with the workers of the Second International."[24] On December 18 the ECCI issued a directive on the workers' United Front. The Comintern sections were instructed to seek limited agreements with members of the Second, Two-and-a-Half, and Amsterdam Internationals, as well as with anarcho-syndicalist sympathizers. While explaining the need for the "greatest possible unity of all workers' organizations in every practical action against the capitalist front," the directive singled out the example (as Lenin had in the note cited above) of the Bolsheviks' treatment of the Mensheviks, which won for Communism "the best Menshevik workers," using the tactic of "unity from below."[25]

The new tactics of the United Front, endorsed by the Fourth Comintern Congress in November–December 1922, did more to confuse the rank and file of the Comintern than to win over the non-Communist masses. Lenin himself, in poor health from the end of 1921 on, and overwhelmed by pressing Russian domestic problems, was unable to redeem a situation that was essentially of his own making. At the Third Comintern Congress, he had expressly approved its resolution on the organizational structure of Communist parties.[26] In his speech on November 13, 1922, to the Fourth Congress, he denounced the same resolution for being "almost thoroughly Russian; that is to say, everything is taken from Russian conditions." He warned his startled listeners that "I have the impression that we made a big mistake with this resolution, namely, that we ourselves have blocked our own road to further success." Even more disquieting was his admission that, "We have not yet discovered the form in which to present our Russian experience to the foreigners."[27]

*The Splitter*

Lenin's speech to the Fourth Comintern Congress was his last before an international Communist gathering. It rang down the curtain on an entire phase in the history of the Comintern, one that bore Lenin's indelible imprint. The failures and successes of that period must above all be attributed to him. Among the failures one must list both obsessive anti-Menshevism and the strategy of the

United Front. Anti-Menshevism was pointless because outside Russia revolutionary violence produced no yield. The United Front stratagem was simply too obvious to succeed. The widely publicized case of the Russian Mensheviks made it clear that the United Front was nothing more than an attempt to find a substitute for violence in eliminating political opposition.[28] Lenin's greatest delusion, and the basic reason for the crude export of undiluted Bolshevik doctrine to foreign parties, was his belief that what worked in Russia would work elsewhere. The idea that by splitting the Italian Socialist Party, fighting "steadily and unyieldingly against the opportunistic Serrati policy," and supporting "the proletarian masses in the trade unions, in their strikes and in the fight against the counterrevolutionary fascist movement," Communism would become a mass force in Italy was monumentally wrong, and the consequence of this error catastrophic. It was assumed that if the Bolsheviks could split the Socialist Revolutionaries in Russia and crush the Mensheviks, the Italian "Bolsheviks" could do the same.* To simultaneously both expel Serrati and win over the majority of organized workers who were loyal to him was clearly impossible in a situation in which the Communists lacked coercive power.

Leninist exclusivism had a similar self-defeating consequence in the Comintern's handling of the re-created Second International, and an even greater impact in the case of another international Socialist organization, the Two-and-a-Half International—so known because of its unwillingness, in the words of one of its leaders, Friedrich Adler, to choose between "terrorist" Moscow and "impotent" Berne (i.e., the Second International). The Comintern made no distinction between the Second and the Two-and-a-Half Internationals, both of which were led by "traitors" to the working class. Its modus operandi was to relentlessly attack and "unmask" the leadership of these organizations, and thus encourage their membership to go over to the Communists, the only genuine de-

* By the time of the Third Comintern Congress, Lenin had probably realized that a mistake had been made in Italy. This may explain why he then opposed the expulsion from the Comintern of the official heads of the French and Czechoslovakian Communist Parties, Frossard and Smeral. It was probably for the same reason that Serrati was allowed, a year later, to come to Moscow, attend the Fourth Comintern Congress, and be admitted thereafter to the Italian Communist Party.

fenders of workers' interests. In his report to the Fourth Comintern Congress, Zinoviev welcomed the fusion between the Second and the Two-and-a-Half Internationals because "the amalgamation of the two would accelerate the split in the working-class movement." "The most urgent task of the day, perhaps of the epoch," he argued, "was to defeat Social Democracy, the strongest factor in international counterrevolution."[29] As it turned out, however, the blind anti-Socialism of Lenin and his followers and their attempts to discredit the Socialist leadership with the rank and file backfired. Large numbers of workers and Socialists in general remained loyal to their Socialist parties and leaders, and instead of re-creating a strong and united proletariat, Lenin's splitting tactics were responsible for its chronic weakness in the interwar period.

The tightening of discipline from one Congress to another, and the new conciliatory line toward the Socialists, which some of the most important Comintern sections opposed,* gave rise to factions within individual Communist parties. Factions arose in two ways: either a local opposition would form to protest the Comintern's directives, or the Comintern itself would create a faction within a party in order to impose its will on a reluctant leadership. To assert its role as leader and arbiter, the ECCI regularly sent out delegates to inspect the work of its sections, and the sections were invited to assign representatives to the Comintern in Moscow. But since the "united army," in which Lenin assigned "our international comrades" a decisive role,[30] was slow to materialize, interfactional feuding became a way of life. The Executive Committee exploited the internal disputes in order to establish and maintain control.

The failure of the "first round of proletarian revolutions" (as the period 1919–20 was later designated by the Comintern) transformed what had been considered a short-term, temporary situation into an inalterable reality for the duration of the Comintern. At the time he founded the Comintern, Lenin regarded the Soviet Union as the vanguard of the European revolution. On April 15, 1919, he wrote, "For a time—it goes without saying that it is only for a short time—hegemony in the revolutionary, proletarian International has

* At the enlarged session of the ECCI (First Plenum) that convened in Moscow in February–March 1922, the French, Italian, and Spanish delegations voted against the ECCI resolution favoring United Front tactics. They were outvoted by nineteen other delegations, which supported the official Comintern line.

passed to the Russians, in the same way as at various periods in the nineteenth century it was enjoyed by the English, then by the French, and then by the Germans."[31] For a few years thereafter, variations of this theme were sounded by leading Bolsheviks. In *"Left-Wing" Communism* Lenin wrote that, "After the victory of the proletarian revolution in at least one of the advanced countries, things, in all probability, will take a sharp turn; *viz.,* soon after that, Russia will cease to be the model country and once again become a backward (in the 'Soviet' and in the Socialist sense) country."[32] Trotsky described the Soviet Union in similar terms a year later, at the Third Comintern Congress: "Our country is quite backward, indeed barbarous. It is a country that reflects a picture of misery. Still we are defending this pillar of the world revolution because there is no other one at the present moment. When there is another one in France or Germany, the Russian pillar will lose nine-tenths of its importance, and we are all ready to join you in Europe to defend another more important pillar."[33] The same idea was expressed by Zinoviev in his opening speech at the Fourth Comintern Congress: "We know quite well that in a few years several parties will overtake us, several much more industrialized countries will take our place in the front rank of the Communist International, and we, as Lenin said, will be only one Soviet country among other more advanced Soviet countries. We know that, and we are awaiting that moment as the greatest victory of those who started the revolution."[34]

Finally, Bukharin explained that in the light of Marxist logic a backward country could not remain the vanguard of an international proletarian movement:

> We must not infer that the Russian Communist Revolution is the most thoroughgoing revolution in the world; nor must we infer that the less developed capitalism is in any country, the more "revolutionary" will be that country and the nearer to Communism. The logical consequence of such a view would be that the complete realization of Socialism would first occur in China, Persia, Turkey, and other countries where practically no proletariat has as yet come into existence. Were this the case, the teaching of Marx would be completely falsified.[35]

Now, as was so often the case in the history of the Bolshevik Party, while Lenin's closest collaborators were repeating a dictum of his as if it were revealed truth, Lenin himself was already moving toward another position. He was beginning to perceive that the most favorable conditions for Communist revolutions existed in countries "where practically no proletariat has as yet come into existence." On March 2, 1923, Lenin wrote the following quasi-prophetic and certainly non-Marxist lines, in what was to be his last article:

> The final issue of the struggle depends in the last analysis on the simple fact that Russia, India, China, etc., constitute the overwhelming majority of the population of the globe. That majority is swept along during these last years, with an extraordinary rapidity, in the struggle for its liberation, and there could not exist the shadow of a doubt about the nature of the definitive result of that world struggle. For that reason the definitive victory of Socialism is assured and obtained in advance.[36]

Thus Russia remained the only center of Communist power, and Lenin, disappointed with the response in the West, was gradually turning his eyes to the East.* In both short- and long-run terms, this shift had momentous consequences, and it is to these that we now turn our attention.

*The Builder*

The preceding section probed the Comintern's failures in Western Europe. For the picture to be complete, we must also take into consideration the ways in which Lenin succeeded in giving shape to the international Communist movement. Lenin made a decisive, if unwitting, contribution to the transformation of his party from

* The gradual development of Lenin's views on this point is worth noting. The theses on the national-colonial question he presented to the Second Comintern Congress distinguished between two alternatives. The first, and, in Lenin's view, the more probable, was a speedy revolution in the West, in which case former colonial countries would immediately be transformed into Soviet Republics. On the other hand, if the West failed to go Socialist swiftly, Communist strategy would be to support the most radical elements of the backward nations' nationalist bourgeoisie. (For a detailed discussion of these points see Demetrio Boersner, *The Bolsheviks and the National and Colonial Question (1917–1928)* [Geneva, 1957], pp. 78–87.) In his speech before the Third Comintern Congress, Lenin omitted any reference to an immediate revolution in the West, stressing hopefully, however, that colonial peoples might "play a considerably greater revolutionary role than we expect." In his last article, quoted above, he maintained that the "final issue of the struggle" would depend upon the East rather than the West.

an ad-hoc revolutionary vanguard into the permanent headquarters of the entire international Communist army. The Soviet Union, established to serve the cause of world revolution, became the state to which the world proletariat owed exclusive allegiance. The Third Comintern Congress was explicit on this point: "The unconditional support of Soviet Russia," according to one of its resolutions, "remains as before the cardinal duty of the Communists of all countries."[37]

The progressive domestication of the Comintern by the Kremlin was unavoidable, not only as a consequence of the failure of revolutions outside Russia, but as an inevitable result of the existence of a central directorate to which all Comintern sections owed absolute obedience. There were, after all, only two possible solutions to the problem of international organization: either the Comintern could be an assemblage of member parties with a nominal center amounting to a "mailbox," as Lenin contemptuously designated the pre-1914 Secretariat of the Second International, or it could be a central directorate with dictatorial powers over all the sections. Only the second alternative, which amounted to a duplication on a global scale of Lenin's organization of the Bolshevik Party, would make it possible to export the techniques of Bolshevik revolution—techniques that were unknown outside the Soviet Union.

Lenin's basic concepts of organization, and of revolutionary strategy and tactics, were new—and effective if correctly implemented. His concept of organization was embodied in a centralized apparatus, staffed by professional revolutionaries, who, like secular monks, had to vow unconditional obedience to the supreme leadership, and whose material, i.e. financial, existence also depended on the center, i.e. on Moscow. Leninist strategy and tactics were both a military science and a neo-Machiavellian political game: a military science in the sense that both over-all strategy and day-to-day modes of warfare were to be modified to fit the time, place, and circumstances of the revolution; a political game in the assumption that legal and illegal actions were interchangeable, that compromises and alliances could be made in order to serve the revolution and abandoned once they lost their usefulness.

Lenin also enriched the arsenal of Communist weapons with the establishment of auxiliary organizations and political fronts. The resolutions of the Third Comintern Congress emphasized, among other things, that Communists would have to learn how to bring "unorganized and unconscious workers under lasting party influence." To this end, non-Communist workers' associations ("cooperatives, disabled veterans' organizations, educational and study groups, sports associations, theater groups, etc.") were to be used to extend Communist influence. A host of international organizations which the Comintern manipulated but which officially enjoyed an independent existence came into being during or soon after the Third Congress: the Red International of Trade Unions (Profintern); the International Workers Aid; the Red Sports International;[38] the International Cooperative Movement; the International Women's Secretariat; the Peasant International (Krestintern).

Whereas the aim of the *auxiliary organization* was to attract the masses who were unwilling to march under the Communist banner but who could be persuaded to join a larger and ostensibly non-political organization, the *front* was designed to avoid the pitfalls of political isolation.

Of three kinds of front that the Comintern established, Lenin was a direct promoter of two: the United Front, i.e. cooperation with non-Communist workers' organizations, and the broader National Front, outlined by Lenin at the Second Comintern Congress in 1920, to operate in colonial and semi-colonial countries. The third variant, the anti-fascist Popular Front, was also of Leninist inspiration, as Georgi Dimitrov, the Comintern's Secretary-General, emphasized in his report to the Seventh Comintern Congress in 1935.

All these techniques of political warfare did not bring the expected revolutionary dividends. The entire existence of the Communist International was marked by resounding failures. Still, Leninist techniques of revolution were the most valuable and enduring element of the Comintern's structure; the proof lies in their adaptation by all the Communist movements that have succeeded in seizing power—in the Balkans, in China, and, most recently, in Cuba. With remarkable intuition, Lenin perceived at the end of his life that the weapons he had forged for Communist militants in advanced Western countries could be used with much more telling effect in countries lacking an industrial proletariat.

We have emphasized Lenin's dual role as splitter and builder because later developments in the history of the Comintern—including the most excessive, which Lenin would certainly have repudiated—can be shown to have their roots in Leninist theory and practice.

*Interregnum*

There is great irony in the fact that, instead of heeding Lenin's warnings about the unsatisfactory state of affairs in the Bolshevik Party and the Comintern, his heirs chose precisely the paths he criticized along which to guide the political fortunes of Russia and the Comintern. Stalin, whom Lenin wished to remove from his post, was consolidating his power as General Secretary of the Bolshevik Party. And Zinoviev, President of the Comintern since its founding, continued to lead the organization as if Lenin had never uttered a word at the Comintern's Fourth Congress.

It is true, of course, that Lenin did not indicate any way out of a situation he himself found unpalatable, even though it was his own ideas on organizational structure that had given rise to it. To speak of the "Russification" of the Comintern, of the failure to find a form in which to present the Russian experience to foreigners, could only sharpen the foreigners' dissatisfaction. His advice to the Fourth Comintern Congress that "the most important thing in the ensuing period is study" was patently inadequate for an organization that was anything but an academic society.

Far from retiring to the study, in the fall of 1923 the Comintern was involved in the most ambitious undertaking in its history, a plan to stage a Communist uprising in Bulgaria to be followed by a Communist revolution in Germany. The attempted uprising in Bulgaria in September 1923 ended in utter failure, but this was not allowed to interfere with the Comintern's German project. A complex politico-military operation, centered on Saxony and Thuringia, was to begin with Communist participation in a coalition government with the Social Democrats in Saxony, to be followed immediately by the arming of the workers and the creation of a German Red Army. The army would march on Berlin and Munich, and in the process lend encouragement and support to other Communist groups, which were already undergoing military training throughout Germany. Scores of officers of the Soviet Red Army, mainly of Central European origin, were dispatched to instruct German Communists, while a group of top Russian military intelligence agents went to Berlin to organize the secret services of the German Communist Party.[39] "The many Russian comrades in Germany, the unlimited funds (mostly in American dollars), the professional methods of preparation, produced confidence that Russia's assistance this time was secured."[40]

All these efforts notwithstanding, the October 1923 uprising ended, like that of March 1921, in a complete fiasco. In fact, with the exception of the first, "ministerialist," episode, it never got off the ground. Ruth Fischer, a leader of the left wing of the German Communist Party, and an admittedly biased witness because of her opposition to the official leadership, which should have led the uprising, nonetheless offers a convincing explanation for the defeat of her party:

> The heirs of the militant tradition of the Spartakus uprisings, with such experienced advisers as Radek, Zinoviev, and Trotsky, should have been able to take the lead in Germany's catastrophic situation. Seen from the inside, however, the Communists were an insufficiently organized group of panic-stricken people, torn by factional quarrels, unable to come to a decision, and unclear about their own aims. Six years after the Russian Revolution, the flames had burnt so low that they could not ignite even Red Saxony.[41]

Defeat in Germany exacerbated the already strained relations among the leaders of the Bolshevik Party and the Comintern sections.* Within days of the scheduled uprising in Germany, Trotsky made his first denunciation of the dictatorial methods of the Secretariat of the Russian party, i.e. Stalin. (On October 10, two days before the German Communist leader Heinrich Brandler entered the cabinet of Saxony, Trotsky opened his attack.) The struggle for power in Russia was necessarily bound to affect all the Comintern sections. Zinoviev, as the person most responsible for the failure in Germany, was engaged in a double fight, against both

* One sentence of the Resolution of the Fifth Comintern Congress on the report of the ECCI spoke of the danger of the "crisis in the German party degenerating into a crisis of the entire Comintern as a result of the feeling of panic which could be discerned here and there among the more uncertain elements." *V^e^ congrès de l'Internationale communiste: Compte rendu analytique* (Paris, 1924), p. 364.

Trotsky and Karl Radek, the representative of the ECCI in Germany, who had been opposed to insurrectionist tactics from the beginning but who was destined to serve as the scapegoat for their failure. The German Communists quarreled bitterly over responsibility for the October disaster, and the Comintern replaced Brandler with men further to the left.

The Comintern's general situation deteriorated after the death of Lenin in January 1924; even when he was ill, he had inspired respect and restraint. Zinoviev, effective as Lenin's henchman, lost his bearings when forced both to wage a bitter struggle at home and to shore up his badly sagging prestige abroad. It is not surprising that in the circumstances he, like his rivals, found it expedient to make Leninism a state and party cult, and to increase Russian dominance of the Comintern. A man without either original ideas or any real leadership ability, Zinoviev could hardly be expected to introduce radical changes in routines established by Lenin. The safest course was to preserve, consolidate, and extend the already tested Comintern apparatus.

The conflict in the Russian Communist Party and its reverberations in the Comintern were naturally the source of great concern to Zinoviev. Trotsky was condemned in a resolution passed at the thirteenth conference of the Russian Communist Party, held in January 1924. In May, before the Thirteenth Party Congress, Bukharin, on behalf of the Russian members of the ECCI, attacked the "extreme right-wing" elements of the Comintern for supporting the Trotskyite faction in the Russian party, singling out for special opprobrium Radek, Brandler, and Boris Souvarine, formerly the representative of the French Communist Party to the Comintern.*

Although Bukharin did not say so, open dissatisfaction with the

* Souvarine, who was present at the Congress, obtained the floor to demand a personal explanation. In his speech, translated into Russian by Lunacharsky, he said that the French Communist Party was shocked by the "campaign of slanders and lies" against Trotsky, whose name was in some sense "a synonym for revolution" to the world proletariat.

The label "extreme right" had obviously become nothing more than a crude device to discredit all Trotsky's supporters. Except in these terms, it is impossible to understand how Souvarine, until 1923 a leader of the left wing of the French Communist Party, could suddenly be denounced as a rightist.

policies being followed in the Soviet Union and the Comintern extended far beyond these three men and their parties. The defeat in Germany had convinced most of the leaders of the Norwegian Labor Party that the time had come to break off their uneasy relations with the Comintern. This "cowardly desertion," as Moscow called it, resulted in a split in the party and the founding of a Norwegian Communist Party, a far cry from what originally had been one of the strongest sections of the Comintern. Social tensions in Poland in the fall of 1923, which the Communist Party did not foment and which it was unable to exploit, led to open conflicts between the "right-wing" leadership of the Polish party and the Comintern. The rift was serious because the Polish party opposed the Comintern's line on both the German and the Russian questions. The application of United Front tactics also caused difficulty, with the British and American parties being accused of "right-wing deviation" and the Italian of leaning toward the "ultra-left."

To put an end to such splits and to overcome what was termed "ideological crises within individual sections," the Fifth Comintern Congress (June–July 1924) made an important series of decisions. After denouncing the "right opportunist deviation"—that is, Trotsky and his supporters in the Polish, German, and French parties—the Congress adopted a long resolution on tactics proclaiming Bolshevization "the most important task of the Communist International." To end the confusion over United Front tactics, it was resolved that "the tactics of the United Front *from below* are necessary always and everywhere," while the United Front *from above* was condemned. Some decisions of earlier Comintern congresses or plenary meetings of the ECCI were reiterated and given new emphasis, e.g., the slogan "workers' and peasants' government," which was intended to express in popular language what was meant by dictatorship of the proletariat and which was first approved at the Third Plenum of the ECCI in June 1923.[42] Likewise, the resolution of the Fifth Congress expanding the prerogatives of the Executive Committee echoed earlier decisions. Finally, it was admitted that the Comintern had given far too much attention to the West, and that work in the East—specifically India, Japan, China, and Turkey—should be stepped up.

Stripped of its ideological façade, the decision to "Bolshevize" the Comintern served to rationalize the expulsion of all those who opposed the anti-Trotsky campaign of Zinoviev and Stalin. How else can one explain the fact that authentic Russian and foreign Bolsheviks like Radek, Souvarine, Brandler, and Thalheimer were purged in the name of Bolshevization, while former Social Democrats who sided with Stalin and Zinoviev, such as Marcel Cachin in France and the German Independent Socialists, received a clean bill of political health?

Probably the most notable contribution of Zinoviev as President of the post-Lenin Comintern was his gradual replacement of the professional revolutionaries of Lenin's day by professional bureaucrats. This transformation had a sociological effect as well as a practical one: whereas the driving force of the Bolshevik Party and of most of the first Communist parties was essentially, in Lenin's words, "the educated representatives of the propertied classes, the intellectuals," the tendency now was to replace the intellectuals by party militants of working-class origin whenever possible.* It is instructive to draw a parallel between the phenomenon deplored by the Austrian Marxist writer Max Adler, namely, the formation of the "workers' aristocracy" in capitalist countries and the emergence of a "bureaucracy" within the Comintern. In Adler's terms, one might say that just as the formation of a working-class aristocracy that was morally and materially unrelated to the workers it guided had "emptied Socialism of its soul,"[43] so had the Comintern's new workers' bureaucracy emptied Communism of its soul.

Bolshevization of the Comintern's sections, conceived as a panacea, was not even a cure. For the remainder of Zinoviev's leadership (he was replaced by Bukharin in October 1926, when Zinoviev was also removed from the Politburo of the Russian Communist Party),[44] indeed until the Sixth Comintern Congress, in July 1928, the internal affairs of the Comintern remained in a sorry state; Bukharin, too, proved unable to put them in order. Manuilsky's allusion at the Fourteenth Congress of the Russian Communist Party, in December 1925, to the "beginning of anarchy in the Comintern"[45] is proof of this. In March 1926, during the Sixth

* Since this trend became even more marked under Stalin, it is discussed in greater detail below, pp. 187–88.

Plenum of the ECCI, only the British and Chinese parties were praised for performing their duties satisfactorily. The British party was singled out for its successful implementation of United Front tactics. The May 1926 general strike in Great Britain was hailed in a manifesto of the ECCI as marking "a new era in the class war not only of the British proletariat, but of the proletariat of the whole world,"[46] while Zinoviev saw in the strike the dawn of a British October. For this reason the failure of the strike was bitterly resented. One Comintern "thesis" on the lessons of the British strike held that "the working class, demobilized by its leaders, lost the first great fight in its history."[47]

Frustration in the West was followed the next year by a major disaster in China, which in at least one essential point resembled the October 1923 debacle in Germany: like the German Communists, the Chinese had to implement remarkably inept instructions from Moscow. This time the architect of defeat was Stalin himself, with Bukharin officially in charge. The Comintern's, i.e. Stalin's, China policy from late 1926 to early 1927 must be briefly elaborated on here because it illustrates one of this essay's basic themes—the protracted influence of Lenin's ideas on the behavior of his successors. Stalin's advocacy of close cooperation with the Nationalists in the extremely complex political game the Chinese Communists were playing with the Kuomintang was based on the application of three Leninist principles. The first had been developed during Russia's 1905 revolution: the coalition of republican forces would create a "democratic dictatorship of the proletariat and peasantry," with the proletariat eventually gaining the upper hand. The cooperation of the Communists and Nationalists in China was seen as serving the same end. Second, the ideas on national and colonial questions Lenin presented at the Second Comintern Congress, and his conclusion that the best Communist strategy was to support the most radical elements in the nationalist bourgeoisies of the backward nations, seemed to apply perfectly to the Chinese situation.[48] Stalin was convinced, especially after the failures in Germany and Great Britain, that the greatest chances of revolution lay in exploiting potentially explosive situations in the East. Finally, in full harmony with Leninist neo-Machiavellianism, Stalin tried to use the provisional alliance with the Nationalists to undermine their ranks and ultimately destroy them. In a speech in Moscow on April 5,

1927, Stalin explained to high functionaries of the Russian party that it was necessary to support Chiang Kai-shek, the core of his argument being that the Rightists had to be utilized, "squeezed dry like a lemon, and then flung away."[49]

Squeezing the lemon had been approved earlier by the Seventh Extraordinary Plenum of the ECCI (November–December 1926), which voted that "the supreme necessity of winning influence over the peasantry determines... the relation of the Communist Party to the Kuomintang.... The machinery of the national-revolutionary government provides a very effective way to reach the peasantry. The Communist Party must use this machinery."[50] At the beginning of April 1927, the Chinese Communists were advised by the Comintern to hide or bury all the workers' weapons in order to prevent military conflict between the workers and the forces of Chiang Kai-shek.

Only a few days later, on April 12, Chiang Kai-shek's armed squads systematically annihilated the Communist organization in Shanghai. Thus Chiang achieved by direct means what Stalin had prepared to do more subtly. "Stalin's carefully laid plans and deceits had precipitated nothing but near-disaster for the Chinese Communists."* Lenin's central question, "Who [will destroy] whom?" was answered in the most ironical possible way.

The failures in Great Britain and particularly in China provided ammunition for the last attempt of the United Opposition (Trotsky and Zinoviev) to denounce Stalin. The battle was unequal and short. With all the command posts of the party and the state in Stalin's hands or under his control, he settled accounts with Trotsky and Zinoviev that November (1927), when both men were expelled from the party. A month later, at the Fifteenth Congress of the Russian party, Stalin announced a sharp, "leftward" turn in Soviet domestic and foreign policies, a turn that had been urged by the

* Robert C. North, *Moscow and Chinese Communists* (Stanford, Calif., 1963), p. 97. It should be noted, however, that a recent study indicates that if Stalin was the architect of the April 1927 disaster in China, he was also the guiding spirit behind the two subsequent conclaves (the Ninth Plenum of the ECCI in February 1928 and the Sixth Congress of the Chinese Communist Party in June 1928) at which a new strategy for China was worked out that foreshadowed Mao's protracted guerilla warfare based on the countryside. See the article by Richard C. Thornton in *The Comintern: Historical Highlights. Essays, Recollections, Documents,* Milorad M. Drachkovitch and Branko Lazitch, eds. (New York, 1966).

defeated United Opposition.[51] The new line was also a warning to Bukharin. By the summer of 1928 he had been removed in fact, if not in name, from leadership of the Comintern; at the Sixth Comintern Congress he was left with the thankless task of defending a new line that went against his own convictions. With the downfall of Bukharin—"the most valuable and important theoretician of the party, ... the favorite of the whole party," in Lenin's words—no human obstacle remained on Stalin's path to total personal power. Bukharin's aid in purging the Comintern apparatus of Trotskyites and Zinovievists did not save him. The time had come for the Bukharinists to either leave the stage or make their peace with Stalin.

After a lengthy interregnum in Comintern affairs, a new phase in its history had begun. But now it was a far different organization from the one Lenin had founded. The "historical misunderstanding" that was so helpful to Lenin at the outset was by now largely dispelled. In the words of a knowledgeable insider:

> The history of the Communist International was ... a history of schisms, a history of intrigues and of arrogance on the part of the directing Russian group toward every independent expression of opinion by the other affiliated parties. One after another, they were forced to break with the Communist International: the currents most attached to democratic and parliamentary forms (Frossard), the groups most attached to legality and most opposed to attempts at coups d'état (Paul Levi), the libertarian elements who deluded themselves about Soviet democracy (Roland-Holst), the revolutionary trade unionists who opposed the bureaucratic submission of the trade unions to the Communist Party (Pierre Monatte, Andres Nin), the groups most reluctant to break off all collaboration with Social Democracy (Brandler, Bringolf, Tasca), and the extreme left wing, which was intolerant of any opportunist move (Bordiga, Ruth Fischer, Boris Souvarine).[52]

It should be added, however, that the disaffection of these men and their followers did not lead to the disintegration of the movement they had helped establish. Their places in the Communist ranks were taken by others who for a variety of reasons were better suited to follow the meandering stream of Comintern history.

*The Comintern under Stalin*

In its fourteen years under Stalin's unofficial but complete command, the Comintern was transformed into the simple tool of one man's will, an unprecedented fate for an international organization. With the same ruthless determination with which he had eliminated all political rivals, Stalin launched his gigantic enterprise of building "Socialism in one country" by means of intensive industrialization and rapid agricultural collectivization. At the same time, he imposed on foreign Communist parties a tighter straitjacket than they had ever known.

It was assumed at the Sixth Comintern Congress that a so-called "third period" in the development of the international labor movement was beginning; the expected "radicalization of the masses" and "severe intensification of the general capitalist crisis," indicated a sharp leftward turn in Comintern tactics, which was closely related to the over-all tightening of domestic policies in the Soviet Union. The long Comintern Program adopted by the Sixth Congress, the first detailed Program in the Comintern history, spelled out the requirements necessary for establishing a dictatorship of the proletariat throughout the world. The vehemence with which it was worded recalled the early Comintern documents drafted by Lenin:

> The development of the contradictions within the world economy today, the accentuation of the general capitalist crisis, and the armed attack of imperialism on the Soviet Union [will] lead with iron necessity to a tremendous revolutionary explosion. The explosion will bury capitalism under its ruins in a number of so-called civilized countries; in the colonies it will unleash the victorious revolution, immensely expanding the base of the proletarian dictatorship, and so mark a gigantic step forward to the final victory of Socialism throughout the world.

The Program went on to score the "bourgeois degeneration" of "Socialist reformism," accusing it of borrowing "all its principal theories from the code of imperialist politics," and branding it as the "chief enemy of revolutionary Communism." The attack on left-wing Social Democracy was no gentler. "Austro-Marxism" was described as "a particularly dangerous enemy of the proletariat, more dangerous than the avowed adherents of predatory social imperialism."

In contrast to capitalist (and Socialist) gloom and decay, a radiant picture of the future under Communism was painted by the Program:

The abolition of private property, the withering away of classes, will put an end to the exploitation of man by man. To work will no longer mean to work for the class enemy. From being nothing more than making a living, it will become the first necessity of life. Poverty will vanish, economic inequality among men will vanish along with the poverty of the oppressed classes and the wretchedness of material life in general; the hierarchy established by the division of labor will disappear and with it the antagonism between intellectual and manual labor; finally, all traces of social inequality between the sexes will disappear. Together with all these, the agencies of class rule will disappear, above all the state. As the embodiment of class rule, it will wither away as classes themselves disappear. Gradually every kind of coercion will die out.[53]

The utopianism of these predictions is all the more extravagant for being based on a prophecy of "tremendous revolutionary explosion," an explosion for which the Comintern was utterly unprepared. The Comintern Program was actually an exercise in the "empty phrasemongering" Lenin had deplored at the Third Congress. Proclaiming "the radicalization of the masses" abroad was well suited to Stalin's leftward turn at home, but its consequences for the most important Comintern sections, and indirectly for world history, were less fortuitous.

The decisions of the Sixth Congress ended the vacillation of the previous years over United Front tactics. A single voice spoke from the Kremlin, and the systematic and continuous purge of the other Communist parties alleviated, at least on the surface, the chronic condition of crisis. The new leaderships learned to follow whatever order came from Moscow. But the price for this monolithic unity was exorbitant. The "class-against-class" tactics imposed on the French Communist Party reduced it from a strong party with 131,000 members in 1921 to an isolated fringe movement, subject to state persecution, with 28,000 members in 1932. Similar directives given the German Communist Party, which was obliged to consider the "social fascism" of the German Socialists the main enemy, were a boon to Hitler and his quest for power, and later to his destruction of what had been the most promising Comintern section.[54] The same irrational orders drove the Communist Party of Yugoslavia into sporadic but disastrous terrorism and insurrection in 1929, which reduced the party to a few hundred disheartened members, deprived of the support of their exiled leaders (who were soon to be murdered in the Soviet Union). Stalin seemed unperturbed by the fact that the Italian Communists, 70,000 strong in 1921, were a decade later no more than a scattered handful of clandestine militants, while the once-powerful Czechoslovakian Communist Party lost nine-tenths of its membership within ten years, its 350,000 members in 1921 melting to 35,000 by the end of 1931.

A by-product of the "revolutionary purity" of "class against class" was a systematic cult of the proletariat at the expense of the intellectuals in all the Communist parties.* "Comrade Ercoli" (Palmiro Togliatti), speaking as the Comintern's representative to the Fourth Congress of the Communist Party of Yugoslavia (held in Dresden in October 1928), defended the new "Proletkult" in the following terms:

> The intellectuals are not the same as workers. They are easily influenced by the petty-bourgeois and bourgeois milieus from which they come. For that reason they waver easily, especially when difficult decisions must be made. In our movement the intellectuals cannot be allowed to oppose the workers and their leaders. In the central committees of all the other parties, including the Russian, the German, and others, most of the members are workers. These central committees function very well. The intellectuals should not be cast aside, but they should understand what their role is. They should adapt themselves to the working class, they should yield to it, but they should not lead the working class and allow the influence of other classes to permeate its ranks.[55]

After the Fifth Congress of the Comintern, there was a marked change in the social composition of the parties' executive organs. In the first Central Committee of the French Communist Party, elected at Tours in 1920, only four of the 32 members were workers;

* "We [intellectuals] were in the Movement on sufferance, not by right; this was rubbed into our consciousness night and day. We had to be tolerated, because Lenin had said so, and because Russia could not do without the doctors, engineers and scientists of the prerevolutionary intelligentsia, and without the hated foreign specialists. But we were no more trusted or respected than the category of 'Useful Jews' in the Third Reich.... The 'Aryans' in the Party were the Proletarians, and the social origin of parents and grandparents was as weighty a factor both when applying for membership and during the biannual routine purges as Aryan descent was with the Nazis." Arthur Koestler, in Richard Crossman, ed., *The God That Failed* (New York, 1949), pp. 48–49.

at the Marseille Congress the next year, the ratio was three out of 27. By 1926, 39 of the 80 Central Committee members were workers; in 1929 the proportion rose to 48 out of 69, and in 1932 it was 49 out of 64. The core of the French Party's Politburo—Maurice Thorez, Jacques Duclos, François Billoux, Raymond Guyot, and Benoît Frachon—were all non-intellectuals. In the Central Committee of the American Communist Party in 1919, seven of the 22 members were workers; in 1935, 25 of the 35 members were workers. The first *Zentrale* of the German Communist Party, formed in 1919, was composed of 12 members, 10 of whom were intellectuals—six of them with doctorates in law or philosophy. The only political survivor of the original German party leadership was Wilhelm Pieck, a worker. Another worker, Ernst Thälmann, was the only survivor of Stalin's later purge of the party's left wing. The Italian, Yugoslav, Bulgarian, Czechoslovakian, Chinese, and Japanese parties, all of which had had very few working-class leaders, underwent a similar transformation. So did the Comintern itself. Between the Second and Third Congresses, all the Secretaries of the Comintern—Radek, Otto Kuusinen, Jules Humbert-Droz, Rákosi, and Souvarine—were intellectuals. The nominal head of the Comintern under Stalin—Georgi Dimitrov—was a worker.

The inevitable result of this trend was the increasing intellectual sterility of the Comintern. The all-inclusive discipline of the Comintern, particularly once the early, revolutionary phase had ended, was incompatible with any attempt at original thought, even by convinced Communists who also happened to be intellectuals of great stature. The philosopher Georg Lukács and the economist Eugen Varga had to choose between silence and conformity; either option was detrimental to the quality of their thinking and to the Comintern's doctrinal development. At the Fourteenth Congress of the Russian Communist Party in December 1925, the Director of the Moscow Marx-Engels Institute, D. B. Riazanov, made a sad and witty speech, concluding with the ominous remark that "the theoretical level of our party has become extremely low."[56] His interjection at the Sixteenth Party Conference, in April 1929, "They don't need any Marxists in the Politburo,"[57] remained the literal truth throughout Stalin's rule of the Comintern.

The image of the Soviet Union as the homeland of all the workers of the world was another by-product of Stalin's "proletarization" of the Comintern. Dimitrov wrote in the Comintern's official organ:

The Soviet Union is not an ordinary country. It is the cause of the world proletariat, of the world revolution. Its real boundaries pass through the whole world and embrace all those who live for the working class and fight for its cause. The Soviet Union, the country where Socialism is being built, where the ideals of the world proletariat are being fulfilled, is the Socialist fatherland of the toilers of all countries.[58]

Promoting the Soviet Union to the position of fatherland of the world proletariat permitted Stalin to make support of his policy—even when he was delivering supplies to Mussolini and Hitler—a matter of loyalty to the working class. The principle of "unconditional support of the Soviet Union," devised by Lenin as a protective measure, became a matter of dogma under Stalin.

The decrease in the Comintern's combat strength that followed the Sixth Comintern Congress did not seem to preoccupy Stalin until events in Germany—especially the assassination of Ernst Roehm on June 30, 1934, and the Nazi victory in the Saar referendum of January 1935—showed that Hitler was ruthless and popular enough not only to exterminate the German Communist Party but also to endanger the Soviet Union itself. Stalin's belated realization that both the USSR and the Comintern had to change their line was symbolized by the Franco-Soviet Treaty of mutual assistance, signed on May 2, 1935, and solemnly announced at the Seventh and last Comintern Congress, which took place in Moscow in July–August 1935 amidst a display of total unanimity. Dimitrov presented the key report to the Congress. In essence it was a series of long variations on the main themes from Lenin's *"Left-Wing" Communism,* combined with a critique of the "narrow sectarian attitude" of many Comintern sections that was reminiscent of Lenin's speech at the Third Comintern Congress.[59] After condemning the Social Democrats for their "class collaboration with the bourgeoisie," to which he attributed the victory of German fascism, Dimitrov launched an all-out attack on fascism, which he called "the most vicious enemy of the working class and of all working people." Such an enemy made it imperative to establish "unity of action by all sections of the working class, irrespective of the party or organization to which they belong." Anti-fascism, Dimitrov emphasized, was the Comintern's only condition for such unity of action.

The new formula of anti-fascist unity was in fact an extension of the concept of the United Front, adopted at the Fourth Comintern Congress. This time, in Dimitrov's words, "the formation of a *wide anti-fascist People's Front on the basis of the proletarian united front* [was] a particularly important task."[60] And, as if to remind every Communist that the new line did not mean the abandonment of the Comintern's perennial goals, the main resolution of the Congress stated: *"The establishment of the united front of the working class is the decisive link in the preparation of the working people for the forthcoming battles of the second round of proletarian revolution."*[61]

The Popular Front, as the People's Front was usually called, enjoyed only a short and limited life on the international scene. Still, it represented a second period of ascending fortunes in the history of the Comintern. As a defensive anti-fascist alliance, it permitted the French Communist Party to break out of its isolation and to score a significant success at the polls in May 1936, increasing its parliamentary representation sixfold (from 12 deputies to 72), and nearly doubling its percentage of the votes cast (from 8.4 per cent in 1932 to 15.4 per cent); the Popular Front majority put the SFIO in power for the first time in history. In Spain, the February 1936 elections also brought victory to the Popular Front, opening a large field of operations to a small but well-organized Communist Party. In other countries, too, including Great Britain and the United States, a Popular Front mystique revived the long-dead unity of the left. The experiment, however, soon fell apart. In France, the same parliament which in 1936 convened in an atmosphere dominated by the impressive victory of the Popular Front, in September 1939 voted to ban the Communist Party, and in June 1940, granted full powers to Marshal Pétain. In Spain, the Communists and their Soviet advisers devoted more energy to undermining and destroying their non-Communist partners in the Popular Front than to fighting General Franco. The Non-Aggression Pact between the Soviet Union and Germany, signed on August 23, 1939, completely shattered the already faltering anti-fascist alliance. As in the past, the Comintern took second place to what seemed to Stalin a supremely adroit move.

Thus the history of the first decade of the Comintern under Stalin must be understood in terms of its relation to him. Stalin's attitude toward the Comintern was one of barely concealed contempt.* Convinced very early that the Western Communist parties were incapable of staging a successful revolution (he had been skeptical about the 1923 uprising in Germany), and burned by the Chinese adventure, Stalin regarded foreign Communists as pawns of his foreign policy at best. He obviously preferred a weak but docile Communist Party to a strong and influential one that showed any inclination to disobey. He was unable to eliminate all factionalism within the Comintern's sections, but his ruthlessness in purging, expelling, and liquidating one faction and replacing it with another at least gave the Comintern a monolithic façade.

Two aspects of Stalin's relationship with the Comintern are so extraordinary, indeed unique, that they must be discussed briefly. Both derive from the totalitarian essence of his regime. The socioeconomic transformation of the Soviet Union, which began with the first Five-Year Plan, and which was accompanied by the creation of the personal cult of Stalin in Russia and abroad, had a power of fascination comparable to that which the Bolshevik revolution had originally exercised in many, albeit different, quarters in the West. In contrast to the capitalist world, gripped by economic depression and political atony, the Soviet Union offered solutions—a centrally directed economy and the reshaping of an entire society—that seemed to many both rational and engaging. Capitalist weaknesses and Stalinist promises combined to generate a quasi-religious, fanatical devotion to the cause that the USSR and Stalin symbolized. Many intellectuals and non-intellectuals alike espoused the New Faith, ignoring anything that might shake their commitment and tolerating humiliations that under other circumstances they would have found intolerable. Two cases illustrate this phenomenon. Bertolt Brecht, a former anarchist and libertarian poet, "was not attracted by the workers' movement—with which he was never acquainted—but by a profound need of total authority, of total submission to a total power, the immutable, hierarchical

* "'*The Communist International represents nothing and only exists by our support,*' Stalin said one day before witnesses, and Lominadze took note of the remark." Boris Souvarine, *Stalin: A Critical Survey of Bolshevism* (London, n.d.), p. 586. Italics in the text.

Church of the new Byzantine state, based on the infallibility of its chief."[62] Milovan Djilas, a professional revolutionary with an ethnic, social, and cultural background wholly different from Brecht's, felt the same craving for the absolute. In his own words, "Stalin was something more than a leader in battle. He was the incarnation of an idea, transfigured in Communist minds into pure idea, and thereby into something infallible and sinless."[63]

Only a readiness to believe in Stalin's "infallibility and sinlessness" can explain the strange process that molded new Comintern cadres whose "brains had been reconditioned to accept any absurd line of action ordered from above as [their] innermost wish and conviction."[64] Moreover, in many non-Communist circles in the West, particularly after the completion of the first Five-Year Plan and the adoption of the 1936 Constitution, the Soviet Union was regarded as a country that was giving birth to a new and superior civilization. The strangest aspect of Western Stalinophilia was the readiness of many to treat as nonexistent demonstrable facts and known events: famine, genocide, staged trials and spectacular purges, and subordination of the Comintern to Stalin's domestic needs.

In this context, consideration should be given to a matter that is generally neglected: the fate of foreign Comintern cadres who had been forced by a variety of circumstances to take up residence in the USSR. Many of them served as Comintern functionaries; others lived in the Soviet Union as political refugees. Among the former were practically all the executives of a number of European Communist parties—Polish, Yugoslav, Hungarian, Baltic, Finnish, Rumanian, etc.—who were liquidated by Stalin's police during the great purges of the mid-1930's, without public trial or notice of execution. Soviet police put to death more Comintern leaders than all the European police forces, including the Gestapo, taken together. One cannot understand Stalin's campaign of terror against the Comintern cadres (to paraphrase Nikita Khrushchev's 1956 denunciation of Stalin's crimes against the Russian Communist cadres), in strictly political terms, for among the victims were more "Stalinists" than "Trotskyites" or "Bukharinists." Political considerations fade before those rooted in what Boris Nicolaevsky has called Stalin's "paranoid tyranny."[65]

Some foreign leaders of the Comintern survived the purges and remained at their posts until the end. The large majority of them lived in bourgeois democracies, very few in the Soviet Union. Whatever their original revolutionary idealism and zeal might have been, they all became "aparatchiks," and in the process sacrificed their personalities to the machinery that had crushed so many of their comrades. Duplicity and demoralization, cynicism and corruption, became second nature to these servants of an absolute despotism. How else can one explain Eugen Varga's asking Zinoviev, before the Fifth Comintern Congress, whether he should report on the temporary stabilization of capitalism or on its imminent collapse? In a similar vein, we have Jacques Doriot's simultaneously circulated versions of the events in China in 1927: one for the ECCI, the other, which contradicted the first, to be used only in private conversation.

The conditions of totalitarian monocracy, established by Lenin and carried to their logical extreme by Stalin, made the Comintern a glittering citadel for outsiders and a death trap for those within its walls. It is not difficult to understand why all the Communist parties (though not all Communists) endorsed the Nazi-Soviet Pact without reservations, and why, when the Soviet Union was attacked by its treacherous ally in June 1941, their defeatism was transformed overnight into fervent anti-fascism. The Comintern's last official act, its disbanding of itself in May 1943, illustrates perhaps better than anything else Stalin's contempt for the Communist International.[66] It also illustrates Stalin's ability to gain something without sacrificing anything in return. Calculating, correctly, that a spectacular announcement of the Comintern's dissolution might reap great diplomatic and psychological dividends, he simply terminated the official life of an organization that he had never allowed to have a life of its own.*

### *From Lenin to Stalin: A Balance Sheet*

Lenin and Stalin, two men who were not officially in charge of the Comintern, left their indelible stamp on its history: Lenin, in

* A typical example of the kind of wishful thinking that Stalin undoubtedly wanted to encourage in the West is the following statement by Harold Laski, quoted in a Reuters dispatch: "Dissolution of the Communist International by Moscow is one of the most hopeful events in political developments since 1919 and opens perspectives for unification of working class interests in Europe and Asia which offer the most real prospects so far opened for gathering the fruits of victory." *New York Times,* May 23, 1943.

the hopeful expectation that the Comintern would become the vehicle of world revolution; Stalin, in the contemptuous realization that at best it would be the instrument of his personal rule. In the shadows, the two nominal heads of the Comintern, Zinoviev and Bukharin, unwittingly aided the process by which the Communist International was gradually robbed of an independent existence.

It is certainly true that Lenin's personal approach to both Russian and non-Russian Communists was basically different from Stalin's. Lenin's inclination was to argue and convince; his readiness to forgive and forget the repentant's mistakes was not shared, to put it mildly, by Stalin. At the four congresses of the Comintern that were held during Lenin's lifetime, important issues were discussed freely, and though the factionalism within foreign Communist parties was officially condemned, in practice it was tolerated. Such expulsions as occurred were the outgrowth of genuine differences of opinion, and not of one man's determination to rule out the possibility of such differences.

Still, making all possible allowances for the personal differences between Lenin and Stalin, the Comintern must be seen as the impersonal organization that Lenin founded, with the ideology, tactics, and goals that he had given it. "In the end, the obsession with power which dominated Lenin's outlook since the days of *What Is To Be Done?* had proved the only durable element in his thought."[67] An unwillingness to compromise on doctrine, coupled with the acceptance of any stratagem that would make it possible to seize power and hold on to it; a concept of organization more appropriate to a monastic order or military unit than to a political party; "Bolshevikocentrism," a deeply rooted belief that the path of his party was the *only* right one; the isolation of Russia in order to prevent its contamination by infidels—these were Lenin's legacy to the Comintern. Stalin simply exploited the full potential for evil of practices that were well-established in Lenin's lifetime.

Though Lenin would no doubt have disapproved of the way in which his heirs, particularly Stalin, administered the Comintern, it remained perceptibly his creation. Even at the height of Stalin's excesses, certain elements of continuity were preserved. Although nearly all the founders of individual Communist parties were eliminated in one way or another, at least one of them continued at the head of each of the Comintern sections throughout the section's life—Marcel Cachin in France, Wilhelm Pieck in Germany, Umberto Terracini in Italy, Otto Kuusinen in Finland, Bohumir Smeral in Czechoslovakia, Mátyás Rákosi in Hungary.

Because the Comintern had a continuous history, Lenin and Stalin must share the blame for its failures and the credit for its successes. The first and most conspicuous failure was the Comintern's inability to bring off a single successful Communist revolution. All the really important revolutions or attempted revolutions took place either before the Comintern was founded (the Bolshevik Revolution, the Finnish Revolution of 1918, the German uprising in 1919), or after it was disbanded (the successful revolutions in Yugoslavia, Albania, and China, and the near-miss in Greece). In Louis Fischer's words, "The new non-Soviet Communist parties needed the money, the facilities, and above all the prestige of the first Communist state, and they paid for these in the coin of serfdom and everything that came in its train: loss of identity, death of revolutionary spirit, and aid to the advent of fascism in Italy and Germany. Moscow was a matriarchate which practiced infanticide."[68]

It is a mistake, however, to take Fischer's judgment literally, or to conclude with Franz Borkenau that the Comintern was "simply a failure."[69] For if Moscow failed to make a world revolution, it succeeded in building a world Communist Party. The Comintern was the first organization in modern history to have both worldwide ends, namely world revolution, and the worldwide means to pursue them—a single control center with detachments on five continents.

The Soviet Union alone can be credited with this achievement. It was the existence of a Soviet state and the image it projected abroad that attracted Communists-to-be in the interwar period, under Lenin and Stalin alike. Their subsequent readings of the works of Marx and Engels convinced broad categories of non-Russians that the ideals of Communism's founding fathers were becoming a reality in the Soviet Union.

The identification of the cause of Communism with the cause of the Soviet Union during the life of the Comintern explains why only those Communist parties which accepted Russian direction survived as a significant political force. Many of the original founders of national Communist parties—Paul Levi in Germany, Louis-Oscar Frossard in France, Giacinto Serrati in Italy, and Ch'en Tu-hsiu in China—proved unable to build Communist parties outside the framework of the Comintern once they had split with Moscow. This was equally true of the various Trotskyite groups, which later failed to draw members from the regular Communist parties. The history of dissident Communist groups between 1919 and 1939 was an exercise in political frustration. Fifteen years were to pass after the disbanding of the Comintern before the authority of the Soviet Union was seriously challenged—by the Chinese Communists—on a worldwide scale.

The Soviet Union's ambivalent role in the Comintern's destiny ("infanticide" on the one hand, essential sustenance on the other) was reflected in the dual mission of the Comintern's emissaries and instructors. They brought to the foreign Communist parties a knowledge of Leninist techniques that was of utmost importance in the building of a disciplined organization prepared for revolution. But at the same time they imposed a system of control that became an obstacle to revolution whenever the interests of the local party and those of Moscow conflicted. It was no accident that Communist revolutions succeeded only where Bolshevik revolutionary techniques were assimilated, but on-the-spot control by the Kremlin was circumvented—in China after 1935 for example, and in Yugoslavia after 1941.* By contrast, where technical assistance and Kremlin control went hand-in-hand, as they did in Republican Spain, the chances of a successful revolution were lessened.

Two other special characteristics of the Comintern deserve mention in this study: its reliance on secrecy and its unpredictability. Throughout its history, the Comintern operated largely in secret; like the visible portion of an iceberg, its surface appearance belied

* The Communists could not have seized power in Yugoslavia without the convergence of the following three factors: the assimilation of Leninist precepts on political warfare; fanatical devotion to the Soviet Union and Stalin; and Stalin's inability, because of the war, to supervise Tito's partisans directly. For a detailed discussion of this topic, see Milorad M. Drachkovitch, "The Comintern and the Insurrectional Activity of the Communist Party of Yugoslavia in 1941–1942," in Drachkovitch and Lazitch, eds., *The Comintern: Historical Highlights*.

the extent of what lay beneath. In this respect as in so many others, the Comintern drew on the experience not of the Second International, but of the Russian Bolsheviks. The Bolshevik legacy included the dual secret apparatus—one branch concealed from the eyes of the enemy, the other from most of the Comintern's sections.

The historian with access only to the Comintern's official statements and publications sees only a fraction of the whole, and not the most important fraction. Three examples will illustrate this point. The first is taken from the Leninist period of the Comintern. The Third World Congress was preoccupied above all else with the "March action" in Germany and Paul Levi's break with Moscow. In the thousand pages of official minutes of the Congress, hardly a word is mentioned about the central role in the German affair of Béla Kun and his two lieutenants. The second example has to do with the OMS (Otdelenie Mezhdunarodnoi Sviazi, or International Communications Section), the organization responsible for all the secret activities of the Comintern, including assistance to foreign Communist parties, throughout the world. According to W. G. Krivitsky, the OMS was "a worldwide network of permanently stationed agents" who served as liaison officers between Moscow and the supposedly autonomous Communist parties. "Neither the rank and file, nor even the majority of the leaders of the Communist parties, know the identity of the OMS representative, who is responsible to Moscow and who does not participate directly in party discussions."[70] Despite the key role of the OMS, it is rarely mentioned in the literature of the Comintern, and then only casually.

The last example is the case of the famous "Stepanov," who between 1919 and 1939 was entrusted with secret missions of the greatest importance and who filled a number of high positions in Moscow. "Stepanov" began working in the central apparatus of the Comintern soon after its formation. Under the pseudonyms "Lorenzo Vanini" and "Chavaroche," he was an active figure in Western Europe, and later turned up in Stalin's secretariat, bearing the name "Lebedev." He next emerged as "Stepanov," in his role as head of the Comintern's Latin Secretariat, where he replaced Humbert-Droz. Later "Stepanov" served as one of the Comintern's chief agents in Spain, returning to Moscow after the victory of

Franco. His name is never mentioned in the official lists of Comintern personnel.*

The secrecy characterizing so much of the Comintern's activity is equalled by its unpredictability. Many of the most important Communist victories were utterly unforeseen. Several apparently hopeless situations were saved at the last minute. Virtually nobody in Russia, not even many of the Bolsheviks themselves, anticipated the events of October 1917; it was only after the fact that Lenin's victory was seen in Russia and the West as a "historical necessity." Only a few weeks before the establishment of Béla Kun's revolutionary government in Hungary, no rational person seriously expected to see a Communist regime in power. For several years after the Communist collapse in China in 1927, the Communist cause was considered doomed; the partisans of Mao Tse-tung and Chu Teh, numbering barely two thousand men in 1928–29, seemed a force with no significance for the future. Nobody could have predicted that the Yugoslav Communist Party, reduced to a few hundred members in 1933, and considered one of the weakest Comintern sections in 1937, would be able to launch an armed insurrection in 1941 and seize full power three years later. The case of Albania was even more spectacular. The Albanian Communist Party was established only in November 1941; it was recognized by the Comintern in March 1943, and captured the reins of power the very next year.

When everything is taken into account, then, the Comintern's record is at once meager and impressive. It is meager if we emphasize the number of revolutions that failed. It is impressive if we consider that without the influence of Lenin and Stalin, the red flag would not today be flying over one-third of mankind.

### *The Comintern's Place in History*

We return to a problem touched on at the beginning of this essay: Lenin's thesis that the Third International was the only legitimate heir of the First, and the redeemer of the sins of the Second. The problem is of course complex, but it can be reduced to a relatively

* Stepanov was in fact a Bulgarian with the family name Mineff. Before joining the Bolsheviks, he was a left-wing Socialist and lived in Switzerland.

simple proposition. Inasmuch as Marxism in theory and practice was both deterministic and voluntarist, revolutionary and reformist, it was easy for Lenin, and even for Stalin, to select one facet of the Marxist heritage, represent it as the whole, and appoint themselves as the only guardians of orthodoxy. Marx himself was at various times (and within short intervals) a Blanquist and an anti-Blanquist, a supporter of the bourgeois republic in France and the inflamed avenger of the Paris Commune, a believer in the possibility of peaceful transition to Socialism and the author of the most inflammatory manifesto of the nineteenth century.[71] When Lenin, therefore, extolled "the living soul of Marxism . . . its revolutionary content,"[72] he was selecting a side of the real Marx, the passionate and impatient revolutionary who, as his private correspondence shows, expected social upheavals from every complication in the life of nations, and whose hatred of the bourgeoisie and contempt for political rivals matched Lenin's in intensity. In the name of this Marx, Lenin launched the Third International. Henri de Man has graphically described the link between voluntarist Marxism and the militancy of the Third International:

> The Communist movement is the only mass movement in which Marxism survives as a vigorous faith. The Communists have drawn all the energy that can be drawn from the emotional impetus of Marxist phraseology. . . . The sap of the Marxist trunk has all flowed into the Communist branch. The "pure" Marxists, the Socialists who repudiate modern Communism, make books; the Communists, the "vulgar" Marxists, guide parties. The ruminant Marxism of the Socialists is powerless against the carnivorous Marxism of the Communists.[73]

By founding his International *in the name of* Marx, Lenin did not necessarily make it *according to* Marx. In fact, the concept of the International held by Marx and Engels was basically different from Lenin's. Marx's strictures against "sects and amateur dabblers who seek to assert themselves within the International against the genuine movement of the working class,"[74] and Engels' insistence on a program for the International that would include all shades of Socialist thinking and be the rallying point for all Socialist groups,[75] were both at the furthest remove from Lenin's organizational sectarianism and ideological exclusivism.

Another fundamental point of difference between the founders of the First International and Lenin concerned the choice of the road, and the vehicle, by which the revolution was to be achieved. In this respect the distinctive political physiognomy of the Communist movement, formed under the aegis of the Comintern, owed more to Lenin's revolutionary techniques than to Marxist ideology. Marx's legacy to the proletariat of the industrialized countries of the West was essentially doctrinal and inspirational; he gave virtually no consideration to the problems of organization and revolutionary tactics. Engels, impressed at the end of his life by the progress of European Social Democracy, believed that the strongest weapon in the hands of the proletariat was universal suffrage, and that "the time of surprise attacks, of revolutions carried through by small, conscious minorities at the head of unconscious masses, is past."[76] In his wake, practically all Western Europeans who were revolutionary Marxists before 1914 adopted the view that the victory of the proletariat would come as the inevitable result of the maturing of the working class, and as an end product of the genuine democratization of industrialized society. What distinguished Lenin from these men, and at the same time constituted his most striking revision of established Marxist tenets, was his advocacy of "surprise attacks," of "revolutions carried through by small, conscious minorities," and his complete distrust of spontaneous mass movements. His obsessive concentration on a professional revolutionary elite was closer to the views of Marx's arch-enemy in the First International, Bakunin, and to the actions of the Russian non-Marxist revolutionary populists, than it was to Marx's ideas. This helps explain why many anarchists and other advocates of violent revolution with political roots in anti-Marxist nineteenth-century movements at first welcomed Bolshevik violence, particularly when it was directed against Social Democracy. In the words of Pavel Axelrod, "The fact that the Bolshevik attack on Social Democracy is waged in the name of Marxism and under its banner makes it a particularly sweet revenge for Bakuninism, which has taken on new life—revenge for the defeats Marxism once administered to the revered memory of the federalist [Bakuninist] International."[77]

The dual nature of Leninism—continuance of the Marxist revolutionary tradition while breaking with Marxist organizational and political practice—lies at the root of the confusion attending the creation of the Third International. Jules Guesde, before 1914 the most orthodox of the French Marxists and a dedicated Socialist all his life, expressed his bewilderment before the strange new entity in these terms: "Communism is at once what I have fought for all my life and what I have fought against all my life."

Guesde's perplexity derived in part from the radical stance of the Second International on many occasions prior to 1914. Like Guesde, Karl Kautsky, the most prominent Marxist theoretician after the death of Engels, was so concerned over the rise of reformism and revisionism within the Second International that in 1902 he expressed the hope that the Russian revolutionary movement would prove to be "the most potent means for driving out that spirit of flabby philistinism and sober politics which is beginning to spread in our ranks; it will cause the lust for battle and passionate devotion to our great ideals to flare up in bright flames again." In the same article, Kautsky also stated his opinion that "the revolutionary center is shifting from the West to the East . . . The new century opens with events that induce us to think that we are approaching a further shifting of the revolutionary center, namely to Russia."[78] Kautsky's prophecy, much to his dismay in his later anti-Communist days, came true, but not in the way he had hoped. The fire that Lenin lit was intended not to purify and illuminate the house of European Social Democracy, but to burn it. And there was a large share of truth in Lenin's claim that the Second International had betrayed its solemn pledges and resolutions, and that someone had to take action as Kautsky had advocated at the beginning of the century.[79]

Lenin's criticism of the Second International, justifiable though it may have been, was not so much a political critique as a theological excommunication. Blind to nuance and deaf to rational argument, Lenin saw in Western Social Democracy nothing but an even more hypocritical version of Menshevism. He was unwilling to take into account the complex historical, psychological, and sociological forces that had molded the ideas and influenced the behavior of leading Western Marxists. Unless they did penance for their sins, they were beyond redemption. Lenin cut the cord that had previously tied him to them in the vain hope that by denouncing their leaders, he could persuade the masses to follow him. He succeeded in splitting Western Socialism, but revolution in the West proved unattainable. With some disappointment, he turned his eyes to the East. There, at least, the industrial proletariat did not exist, and therefore it could not spoil his game.

The shifting of the revolutionary center to Russia and the transformation of Russia into the only bastion of Communism was in effect the repetition of the victory of Bolshevism over Menshevism in a major key. Whereas Bolshevism, in Nicholas Berdyaev's words, represented the "russification and orientalizing of Marxism," the creation of the Comintern meant the "russification and orientalizing" of the international Communist movement. Thus the Comintern, whose original mission was to bring revolution to the capitalist countries of the West, became an instrument and a technique for the conquest of power in the backward countries and continents. In this sense, the Comintern, officially disbanded twenty-three years ago, continues to live and to make history.

Stefan T. Possony

# The Comintern as an Instrument of Soviet Strategy

At the founding of the Communist International in 1919, the survival of Lenin's government seemed most uncertain. The International was founded, among other reasons, to facilitate that survival, by building up much-needed support throughout Europe and America. "Everywhere there are proletarian armies, though sometimes they are badly organized and in need of reorganization," said Lenin on July 17, 1920, concluding his first speech to the Second Congress of the Communist International. "If our international comrades help us to create a single army, then no mistake will be bad enough to ruin our plans."[1]

Hopes were high that the Red Army would defeat the Polish Army, that Poland would become a Communist state, and that the revolution would be carried into Germany and beyond. On July 23, 1920, Zinoviev asserted that large-scale uprisings in many countries could occur from one day to the next. He believed, however, that revolutionary situations could not develop into full-fledged revolutions in countries without a Communist Party. And indeed, except for two short-lived revolutions in Bavaria and Hungary, the revolutionary situations that had arisen all over central and southeastern Europe were nowhere exploited effectively. The Red Army was beaten, Poland rejected Communism, and the world revolution came to a grinding halt.

Nevertheless, the revolutions of 1917 could not have succeeded in Russia without direct and indirect assistance from abroad, and the existence elsewhere of conditions favorable to it. The October Revolution could not have occurred at all without World War I and the political and economic disruption it caused. It is worth mentioning that the Red Army fought the initial phase of the civil war as an international force, with many of its units recruited from non-Russian national groups (e. g. the Letts) and prisoners of war.[2] More important, the combination of internationalism and ideological commitment enabled the Communists to foment mutiny in the French fleet, and forced the subsequent withdrawal of French "interventionists" from the Black Sea. The Red Army, as the Italian delegate Giacinto Serrati explained to the Second Comintern Congress, was supported in the conflict with Poland by English workers and German and Italian sailors. In many European countries Communists interfered with the flow of supplies to Poland.

In his speech of July 17, 1920, Lenin expressed the hope that the "mechanism of the capitalist world economy" would soon collapse completely. The war had caused an "immense sharpening of all capitalist contradictions," and the revolutionary movement was growing tremendously. By 1928, however, the world seemed to have shaken off the economic and political ills of the war. The world depression was still a whole year away, and the world looked more peaceful than it had for a long while. Yet in an address to the Fifteenth Congress of the CPSU, on December 3, 1927, Stalin warned that the situation of capitalism "is becoming more and more putrid and unstable." There was good ground "for asserting that Europe is obviously entering a period of new revolutionary upsurge; to say nothing of the colonies and dependent countries, where the position of the imperialists is becoming more and more catastrophic." Stalin was presumably giving these pro-forma assurances to comfort the party faithful. But he was probably expressing his real convictions when he added that one or two years earlier, "it was possible and necessary" to speak about "peaceful coexistence" between the USSR and the capitalist countries, but now "the period of 'peaceful coexistence' is giving place to a period of imperialist assaults and preparations for intervention against the USSR."[3]

On July 13, 1928, a few days before the Sixth Comintern Congress convened, Stalin asserted before the CPSU's Central Committee that at the time of the Fifth World Congress (June–July 1924, before the French evacuated the Ruhr) "a certain equilibrium, unstable, it is true, but more or less prolonged, had been established between . . . the world of soviets and the world of capitalists." Now, he argued, "the days of this equilibrium are drawing to a close." There was a danger of "new imperialist wars and interventions." "It is to be presumed that the Sixth World Congress will take this circumstance . . . into consideration."[4]

Why this fresh concern over "new imperialist wars and interventions?" Not because, as Stalin asserted, the situation "of capitalism is becoming more and more putrid and unstable," but because exactly the opposite seemed true. The French had occupied the Ruhr in 1923 but withdrew the following year, with the adoption of the Dawes Plan for reparations payments. In October 1925 the Locarno Treaties were initialed, and it was generally expected that the "spirit of Locarno" would usher in a new era of peace and goodwill. In September 1926 Germany joined the League of Nations; during the same year the Preparatory Commission for the World Disarmament Conference began its work at Geneva. And in 1927 diplomatic exchanges began that developed a year later into the Kellogg-Briand Pact outlawing war. By 1927, instead of an impoverished, war-weary Europe, paralyzed by mutual fears and hatreds, the Soviet government faced a prosperous Europe, which was to all appearances more united than it had ever been before.

And this united Europe showed signs of turning against the Soviet Union. The general strike had failed in Britain in 1926; the following year, after a police raid on Soviet trade offices in London produced evidence of subversive activities, the British government broke off diplomatic relations with Moscow. During the same year, 1927, Poincaré demanded the recall of the Soviet Ambassador to France, and the Soviet representative in Warsaw was assassinated. In Asia, Chiang Kai-shek turned on the Chinese Communists.

The Sixth World Congress of the Communist International, which was held in Moscow from July 17 to September 1, 1928, defined the tasks of the Communist parties outside the Soviet Union during a war with the "imperialists." Speaking for the German, Czech, Polish, Austrian, Hungarian, Lithuanian, Latvian, Swedish, Norwegian, Finnish, and Danish delegations, and for the Communist Youth International, the German Communist

Ernst Thälmann issued a declaration emphasizing the inevitability and imminence of a "gigantic class war" against the USSR. Hence the foremost Communist task was "to mobilize the world proletariat and all the subjugated peoples for the defense of the Soviet Union," and, subsequently, to transform the war of the exploiters "into the civil war of the oppressed."[5]

The military tasks of the "political army" had been discussed repeatedly since the Second Congress, both during the major congresses themselves and during plenary sessions of the Executive Committee of the Communist International (ECCI), e.g. in 1921, 1926, and 1927. At the Sixth Congress, the Communist leadership had at its disposal extensive studies on the whole spectrum of military strategy and tactics, revolutionary operations, and nonmilitary warfare, as well as the provisional field service regulations of the Red Army, which the Comintern resolutions were supposed to supplement.

According to the doctrine that had grown out of these studies, the main task of revolutionary organizations in target countries was to disarm the bourgeoisie by means of such techniques as antimilitarism, revolutionary pacifism, and defeatism.[6] Bourgeois armies should be "disintegrated" from within, for the double objective of making effective resistance impossible and of switching fragments of the bourgeois armies to the side of the revolutionaries. Such switches would transform the international war into a civil war.

Anti-war activities must be the work of the entire party, and constitute part of the over-all activity of the masses.

To accomplish the various "tasks" posed by the struggle, three basic techniques were recommended. The first, of course, was to organize for each specific undertaking by setting up a "legal" and an "illegal" apparatus and combining functional groups (e.g. reserve units) with mass and front organizations. The second technique was that of linking the undermining of bourgeois armies to other "causes." Legislation should be sought that would facilitate the penetration of the armed forces. Punishment of rebellious officers and soldiers should be exploited for political campaigns. Soldiers' relatives and munition workers should be bombarded with propaganda. And the Communist Party should favor any reorganization of the armed forces that would reduce their effectiveness. In multi-national states, the "struggle" against national oppression should be linked to other types of struggle. The third technique was that of the practical and plausible "partial demand" to attain an interim objective. Once one partial demand had been met, the next one would be presented. Partial demands should be used to mobilize the masses against imperialism. The ultimate demand should be approached by a chain of partial demands.

During the Sixth Congress, to illustrate concrete tasks, a Pole called for the organizing of railroad personnel, for action committees in the metal and munitions industries, for agreements between the unions involved in war work, and for anti-war work among miners.[7] A Norwegian asserted that his country's fishing and canning industries would play a great role in a war against the USSR. An ECCI representative talked about factory cells and stressed Communist strength in the chemical industry. An Indonesian Communist discussed the strategic significance of the rubber and oil industries, and linked the "energetic defense" of the Soviet Union with the liberation of Indonesia from Holland.

Thomas Bell, a British Communist, extolled the anti-colonial struggles in India, Egypt, China, Morocco, and the Middle East during World War I.[8] The next war, whether it was between two imperialist blocs or a war of the imperialists against the Soviet Union, was "bound to release this repressed colonial mood." The Frenchman André Ferrat stated that anti-militarist work must be performed among colonial troops as well as the troops of the mother country.[9]

Li Kuan urged Communists to infiltrate imperialist armies and navies, and to create cells among transport workers and seamen.[10] The American Bertram Wolfe recalled the work of the Pacific longshoremen who prevented the sending of munitions to Kolchak. "We have the tradition of the American soldiers who mutinied in Archangel and compelled the government to withdraw them."[11]

Bell stressed the importance of the Young Communist League and of pacifist organizations. Housewives, underpaid women workers, and pacifistically inclined women were "one of the most fertile fields for our Communist propaganda." Attention should be given to the peasantry, the unemployed, minority groups, and new recruits; organizers and propagandists should concentrate on seaport towns, harbors and industrial centers.[12]

The Pole Krulikovski emphasized the role of the peasantry in war,[13] and an Irish Communist named Carney that of the unskilled Irish workers in the British chemical industry and on the Liverpool and London docks.[14] The Austrian Fiala stressed that anti-militarist work could "neutralize" professional armies as easily as conscript armies. According to Mehring, representing the Communist Youth International, mercenary armies were vulnerable because they were recruited from unemployed proletarians. Anti-militarist techniques could be used against the volunteer armies of Germany, Britain, and the United States, as well as against navies and air forces, which were not made up of conscripts.[15] Too, revolutionaries who entered the military forces would receive military training and weapons. Hence the really revolutionary slogan was to join the army as one step in the process of "arming the proletariat." Infiltrated units might fraternize with and even join the Red Army. But if they would be more useful in fomenting revolt and disintegration in their own imperialist army, they should not cross the line.[16]

Defeatism was defined as "the desire for and the furtherance of the defeat of one's own government."[17] Active defeatism should serve to create a revolutionary fighting spirit and to arouse the workers' hatred of the bourgeoisie. Revolutionary defeatism should shake "the foundations of the imperialist army" and lead to mass action. (Although it did not lead to mass action, Communist defeatist propaganda during the "phony war"—September 1939 to May 1940—certainly helped undermine the foundations of the French Army.)

Ferrat criticized the view of the mass strike as a means for transforming the imperialist war into a civil war, i.e., a "means that is applied after and not before the declaration of war." Similarly, fraternization is falsely "looked upon as an act that takes place only at the front." Fraternization begins with collective demonstrations, and must be developed through the technique of partial demands. It results in desertion to the Red Army, the forming of partisan groups and of Red Guards, and the initial steps toward setting up a workers' militia. When fraternization occurs at the front, the whole operation has reached its "apex."

In brief, the struggle against war must form part of the general struggle to overthrow the bourgeoisie.[18] Slogans for the "struggle against war" include rejection of national defense, defeatism, internationalism, and transformation of war into civil war.[19] According to the resolutions of the congress, Communists must fight against imperialist war before its outbreak. Illegal organizations must be created to continue the work after the outbreak of war. The central slogan must not be peace, but proletarian revolution. The main task in war is to render the class struggle increasingly acute.

Addressing the secretaries of the Moscow organization of the party on November 26, 1920, Lenin had stressed "a fundamental rule with us, namely, that we must take advantage of the antagonisms and contradictions between two capitalisms, between two systems of capitalist states, inciting one against the other."

> As long as we have not conquered the whole world, as long as, from the economic and military standpoint, we are weaker than the capitalist world, . . . we must know how to take advantage of the antagonisms and contradictions existing among the imperialists. . . . We are at present between two foes. If we are unable to defeat them both, we must know how to dispose our forces in such a way that they fall out among themselves.[20]

"The main front in the policy of all imperialist powers," a Comintern resolution of 1928 stated, "is directed more and more openly against the Soviet Union and the Chinese revolution. But in view of the sharpening antagonisms between the imperialist powers themselves, a clash between the imperialist groups of power in the struggle for world supremacy is possible even before this war breaks out."[21] But what could be done to transform this possibility into reality? Which antagonisms could be incited or exploited?

In 1927 Stalin had mentioned the "so-called Pacific problem (the America-Japan-Britain antagonism)" and "the Mediterranean problem (the Britain-France-Italy antagonism)."[22] These antagonisms were widely discussed, but no major war seemed in the offing. Nevertheless, according to Stalin, of the "contradictions in the capitalist camp, that between American capitalism and British capitalism has become the principal one." This was a great change from the days of the Fifth Congress, when an Anglo-American alliance appeared in the making. The antagonisms between the United States and Japan, Britain and France, France and Italy, Germany and France, still existed. However, "these contradictions are linked . . . with the principal contradiction, that between capitalist Britain, whose star is declining, and capitalist America, whose star is rising."[23] But alas!—no Anglo-American war seemed likely.

By 1928 Moscow feared that the League of Nations would succeed in overcoming the antagonisms between the capitalist states. In this fashion, a united "imperialist" front would emerge against the Soviet Union. This "war policy" of the imperialists could be carried out only "thanks to the cooperation of international Social Democracy." The Social Democrats "have developed their greatest activity in support of the imperialist war preparations against the Soviet Union."[24] These ravings against the Social Democrats, dubbed "open social imperialists," struck many contemporary observers as bordering on persecution mania.[25] But the Communists seem to have really feared that the Social Democrats would succeed in bringing about a genuine rapprochement between Germany and France.

At the time of the Sixth Congress, the German Socialists had just formed a government, although foreign policy remained in the hands of Gustav Stresemann, a non-Socialist. Thälmann alleged that just as the Social Democrats had signed the Versailles Peace Treaty, they "will carry out at present the rapprochement with France." According to Thälmann, Social Democratic Finance Minister Rudolf Hilferding had insisted that no more credits be given to Soviet Russia. The Socialists would not hesitate to apply "measures directed against the Soviet Union . . . ruthlessly." In Thälmann's interpretation, the German Social Democratic Party not only opposed the proletarian revolution, it was joining the bourgeoisie for the purpose of preparing war against the Soviet Union.[26]

By 1929 the German Communist Party, according to Walter Ulbricht, saw its most important task in the "unmasking of the imperialist, social-fascist character of the policy of the Social Democratic Party."[27] A German Communist Party resolution of June 4, 1930, alleged that "fascization" was being brought about by the "fascist battle organization"—the "bourgeois state apparatus and its social-fascist agents." "The struggle against fascism is, accordingly, unthinkable without the fiercest struggle against the Social Democratic Party."[28] After the elections of September 1930, the Communist Party alleged that a fascist dictatorship already existed in Germany. The party was directed "to prepare for the overthrow of *this* dictatorship," a directive that remained in force until the bitter end.[29]

There were two methods of dealing with this threat. The first method was that of the "United Front from below," i.e. take-over of the Social Democratic Party from within; this approach had proved impractical. The other method was to bring about the destruction of Social Democracy. Since the Communists were unable to achieve this goal by their own means, their objective could be achieved *only* with the help of the enemies of their enemy, i.e. the activists from the right. The theoretical justification for such a policy was that the Social Democratic parties, while retaining strong proletarian membership and still attracting proletarian votes, were transforming themselves into bourgeois parties.[30]

The cooperation between Communists and German nationalists had a long history dating from Imperial Germany's aid to Lenin during World War I.[31] It included Communist readiness to enter into an alliance with Germany against the Entente powers in the summer of 1918; the sparing of Karl Radek's life in January 1919; Radek's mission to Germany in 1919; overtures for a military alliance during the Russo-Polish war in 1920; industrial collaboration in the field of armaments after 1921; the Treaty of Rapallo in 1922; and support for German moves against the French occupation of the Ruhr and for negotiations on mutual defense during 1923. The Berlin Treaty of April 24, 1926, came close to being a formal alliance.[32] There were, moreover, numerous instances of military cooperation between the Soviet Union and Germany (training, the development and testing of new weapons, etc.). This collaboration, despite difficulties created by both sides, was of great importance to the two countries.[33]

In 1928 the Nazis polled about one-fourth the contemporary Communist vote, and, together with other rightist groups, numbered well over a million members. The leader of the S.A., then the main Nazi paramilitary organization, asserted that the Communist movement provided a model for the National Socialist struggle.[34] *Der Angriff,* the Nazi organ in Berlin, was constantly harping on the theme that the Nazi fighters for German freedom had to break the chains of capitalist slavery. On January 30, 1928, the paper applauded the "mounting anti-Semitic wave in Soviet Russia." On February 6, 1928, Joseph Goebbels asserted that it was now "beyond any doubt that the peasant wing, under the leadership of Stalin and Rykov, definitely won over the wing of the urban proletariat, led by Trotsky and Zinoviev." "Jewry in Soviet Russia is beginning to lose its decisive influence." On August 6, 1928, in the midst of the deliberations of the Sixth World Congress, *Der Angriff* published a front-page cartoon showing a Nazi and a Communist "fighter" holding hands across the body of a lifeless Jew. The picture merged the symbolism of the swastika with the hammer and sickle. The caption read: "Brothers of one people."

Within a year after the Comintern Congress, the world depression hit with full force, and unemployment became the foremost reality of German politics. The German masses were indeed being revolutionized, and the Communists were making gains. The radicals of the right, however, made far more impressive progress. By mid-1930 it was clear that the National Socialists were developing into a genuine mass party, and that they were attracting a large portion of the activist elements within German society.

In August 1930, in a programmatic declaration on the national and social liberation of the German people, the German Communist Party (KPD) protested against the enslavement of Germany by the Versailles Treaty, declared the obligations imposed by that treaty to be null and void, and objected strongly to the territorial "dismemberment" of Germany. Former German areas should be allowed the right of self-determination and be able to join a future Soviet Germany. The Communists called upon the masses to establish Soviet power in order to tear up the Versailles Peace Treaty.[35]

This declaration was issued in the midst of a violent election campaign and closely paralleled the main line of the nationalist opposition. When the election was over, the world was stunned to learn that the Nazi vote had increased twelve-fold, and that, with more than a hundred seats in the Reichstag, they were suddenly the second-strongest party in Germany. By October 1930, the Nazis supported a Communist-led strike of the Berlin metal workers. Ulbricht characterized this strike as "the first great battle" against the "dictatorship" of Germany's democratic government, and expected this joint Communist-Nazi assault to aggravate "the economic and political crisis."[36]

Evaluating the elections of 1930, Radek asserted that the "victory of the fascists" proved "the indignation against the capitalist order in Germany, even outside the ranks of the class-conscious workers." The capitalists, he added, preferred the Social Democrats to the fascists as the "watch dogs of the capitalist order."[37] During its Eleventh Plenum, the ECCI criticized the Communist parties "of the dominant nations" for their "weak participation... in the revolutionary movements for liberation of the oppressed nations in Europe." D. Z. Manuilsky called on the Communists to exert "greater activity in the mobilization of the masses for the struggle against national oppression."[38] One of his contentions was that the policy of France and the Communists' weakness throughout Europe were hindering "the development of the revolutionary crisis in Germany."[39]

By June 1931, Thälmann was characterizing fascism as a "mass movement" and as a "mass party." On July 31, 1931, the KPD announced its support of a Nazi-sponsored referendum for dissolution of the Prussian Diet. This policy had been opposed by the leaders of the KPD, but these were overruled by the Comintern.[40] Thälmann explained that the "struggle against fascism does not mean resistance only to the Nazis, but above all struggle against finance capital itself, against the Brüning cabinet as the government for the institution of the fascist dictatorship." The Prussian government of the Social Democrat Carl Severing, he alleged, was the strongest bulwark of Heinrich Brüning's rule.[41] Therefore, the Communists must direct their "most vigorous offense" against the government of Prussia.

It is interesting to analyze this logic. The need for a struggle against fascism is asserted as a premise, but fascism is deemed less important than finance capital. To fight fascism, the Communists were arguing, one must fight the Brüning government because it was instituting a fascist dictatorship (or had already instituted one). But since the Brüning government in turn was dependent on Prussian support—Prussia was the largest German state—the Social Democratic government of Prussia must be destroyed. (Note that the Social Democrats did not participate in Brüning's government.) This logic really said that to fight the Nazis, the Communists must ally themselves with the Nazis against the Socialists.

Cooperation with the Nazis on the referendum was by no means an isolated incident. On May 24, 1932, Wilhelm Pieck introduced a motion in the Prussian Diet to overturn the Social Democratic cabinet. This motion was backed by the National Socialists and passed. On June 24, 1932, the Nazi-Communist majority in the Prussian Diet adopted a bill to expropriate the properties of East European Jews who had taken up residence in Germany since August 1914.[42] The Nazis who had initiated this bill accepted a Communist amendment to close the stock exchanges.[43]

The Twelfth Plenum of the ECCI, which convened at the end of August 1932, concluded that "capitalist stabilization had ended." "A new phase in the preparation of intervention against the USSR" was beginning. This was an allusion to renewed German attempts for a rapprochement with France. The Comintern insisted that decisions concerning the struggle against imperialist war and intervention be put into effect with the greatest urgency. Waldemar Knorin, who handled KPD affairs in the ECCI, called for "partial opposition" to the Nazis and the elimination of Social Democracy. Otto Kuusinen said that the struggle against the National Socialist movement would have to be strengthened, but he emphasized that the "main offensive" must be directed against the Social Democrats.[44]

On November 2, 1932, the Communists and Nazis supported a transport workers' strike in Berlin. Materially of little importance, the strike had considerable political impact, since it demonstrated the impotence of the Social Democrats, who opposed it. This event also exhibited the power of the Nazi-Communist alliance. Though deemed temporary, the alliance was not expected to break up before the overthrow of the Weimar Republic. This well-founded expectation contributed to the demoralization of the democratic elements in Germany. Just twelve days before Hitler's assumption of power, *Inprecorr* printed a speech by Ulbricht in which he explained that the "main blow" still must be struck against the Social Democrats, and that any modification of the general line leading to the weakening of the struggle against the Socialists would have to be rejected.

During the first part of October 1932, Soviet Foreign Minister Maxim Litvinov briefed Ivan Maisky, who was about to take up his new duties as Soviet Ambassador to London. He was not setting forth his personal views, Litvinov explained, but the directives of higher authorities. Among other points, he imparted this information. "If not today, then tomorrow, Hitler will come to power." He added, so Maisky reports, that in this case "Germany will be transformed from our friend into our enemy."[45]

But if a hostile Germany was in prospect, and if, as Litvinov also explained, the chances of an alliance with the West were dubious, surely something could have been done about this danger. There was absolutely no reason to accept fatalistically the demise of the Weimar Republic. In fact, the Communists could have saved German democracy simply by breaking the voting alliance with the Nazis in the Reichstag. After the elections of July 1932, when the Nazis polled their largest vote, as well as after the election of November 1932, the combined votes of the middle parties and of the KPD exceeded those of the right and the Nazi party.[46] Depending on the attitude of non-Nazi rightist parties, simple Communist abstention from voting in the Reichstag might have been sufficient to maintain a stable government; and in this case, the Communists could have bargained for a chancellor of their preference.[47]

At the very least, since the elections of November 1932 showed that the Nazis were beginning to lose votes, even a temporary change in Communist voting behavior could have prevented the immediate collapse of the German republic. Moreover, it might have led to the replacement of Hitler by Gregor Strasser as the primary Nazi leader. From the Soviet point of view, Strasser, who considered himself a genuine socialist, should have appeared safer than the erratic Hitler. Thus, there still were real options for alternate Communist policies. That there was no deviation from the course, nor even an attempt at modification, would seem to indicate that no changes were desired.

Documents from the German Foreign Office throw some light on the debates that were raging in Moscow during the summer and fall of 1931.[48] According to German intelligence reports, there was a considerable difference of opinion between the Comintern and the Foreign Commissariat. Molotov reportedly read an ECCI evaluation to the Politburo on August 15: "The Communist revolution in Germany is a question of six months at most." This assertion, it was reported, made no impression on the Politburo, which showed more interest in the possibility of French credits.[49]

The Politburo allegedly considered the German question again on August 17. This debate was based on a report by Krumin, Soviet Consul General in Hamburg. The German intelligence services apparently secured a copy of this report in the original Russian and quoted from it liberally in a document that was submitted to Brüning. The Krumin paper is not just another agent's report, but a Soviet document that the Germans presumably obtained from within the Consulate General. We do not know the full text, but there are several pages of actual quotations. It seems safe to consider it authentic.[50] In somewhat literal translation, for the sake of accuracy, the sentences of obvious political interest read as follows:

> Money from the "economic leaders" and from heavy industry has been flowing in big waves to support Hitler's storm troopers. This circumstance provided the Comintern with a big trump card, inasmuch as the Comintern, which for tactical reasons has been supporting nationalism, was able in its financial preparation of the German revolution to make certain economies; for the preparation of the German revolution considerable resources were available in the country itself (through Hitler).

As a result of the financial crisis gripping Germany, Krumin continued, the situation had changed. The industrial corporations were close to bankruptcy, and the impoverishment of the industrial leaders meant the impoverishment of Hitler. "For the Communist Party this means a fundamental change in tactics." The new tactic must be based "on the necessity of gaining immediate mass support and of leaving out the interim phase of National

Socialism." Krumin ended his report with two questions: Will the Brüning government have enough money to continue paying unemployment compensation? Will the KPD get enough money to strike a decisive and last blow against German capitalism?

According to the "most modest calculations" by the Presidium of the ECCI, the German revolution required sixty million gold marks.[51] But Andrei A. Andreyev, a member of the Politburo, reportedly disclosed that the special funds were almost exhausted. Thereupon the Politburo decided to instruct a working group of the party, the ECCI Presidium, and the "financial organs of the Soviet government" to figure out how sixty million marks could be procured. On September 5, we learn from a third report,[52] the question was debated again by the Politburo. At this time, it would seem, no way had been found to finance the German revolution. And other sources confirm the hand-to-mouth position of the Soviet government with regard to foreign exchange; the first Five-Year Plan required much expensive machinery from abroad.[53]

The Comintern took the line that the situation might soon permit a "dress rehearsal" for the revolution, and that the KPD should be helped in preparing the upheaval. By contrast, the Foreign Commissariat expected no favorable developments. Hence putsches would only hurt the KPD and tend to isolate the Soviet Union. The main task was to obtain technical and financial help to complete the Five-Year Plan: this was the way to improve the chances of the world revolution. The Politburo (i.e. Stalin) resolved, so the German report related, that the Foreign Commissariat should try to get French and American credits, and that the Comintern should "temporarily" abandon the policy of preparing putsches.

Krumin had proposed large-scale financial support for the KPD and by implication less reliance or none at all on the activities of the German nationalists. He clearly recommended "a fundamental change in tactics." Moscow had three alternatives: (1) more money for the KPD; (2) continued reliance on the National Socialists as the "icebreaker of the revolution"; or (3) Communist cooperation with the Social Democrats. The first alternative was too expensive; we have no evidence that the third was ever seriously contemplated.

The Communist policy of holding the stirrup so the Nazis could climb into the saddle has occasionally been explained by the theory that the Kremlin really wanted a civil war, which, it anticipated, the Communists would ultimately win. Naturally the Communists did not help the Nazis merely because they wanted Hitler to win. The question was: Would civil war come prior to an international war, or would it, in line with orthodox Leninism, arise out of international conflict? Since according to the ECCI Plenum there was no "directly revolutionary situation,"[54] obviously revolution could only result from war. In 1932 Manuilsky had predicted that the bourgeoisie would not allow the Nazis to take over the government because "Hitler's accession to power would ... speed up the growing revolutionary crisis" in Germany. But in this forecast he stated his conviction that a National Socialist government would "mean a sharpening of the contradictions of the Versailles Treaty and unprecedentedly strained relations in Europe."[55] Since the Soviet government had never signed, had indeed repeatedly denounced the 1919 "Diktat," it presumably did not fear "a sharpening of the contradictions of the Versailles Treaty." In a conversation with Gustav Hilger, of the German Embassy in Moscow, in July 1932, the manager of Tass, the Soviet news agency, expressed the conviction that even a National Socialist government would maintain good relations with the USSR. "All he feared was that the accession of Hitler might be followed by a rather disturbing period of transition before normal relations could again be achieved."[56]

But the accession of a revanchist government in Berlin was hardly calculated to improve Franco-German relations; it might in fact lead to a second Ruhr, perhaps even to war. In the event of a war between Germany and one or more Western powers, the USSR would be in an ideal position to follow the policy Stalin had elucidated secretly on January 19, 1925. War would come, he said, "not tomorrow or the day after, of course, but in a few years' time." When it comes, "We shall not be able to sit with folded arms. We shall have to take action, but we shall be the last to do so. And we shall do so in order to throw the decisive weight in the scales, the weight that can turn the scales."[57]

After Hitler came to power and military cooperation between the Soviet Union and Germany ended, Stalin probably realized that he had embarked upon an overly hazardous course of action.[58]

But the fact remains that even after Hitler's initial steps had demonstrated the hazards of Communist strategy, Stalin was in no hurry to alter course. On July 1, 1934, Georgi Dimitrov—who after his appearance in a Nazi court was allowed to speak his mind relatively freely—questioned the necessity to equate Social Democracy and social fascism.[59] The next day he suggested the adoption of new tactics to the Preparatory Commission for the Seventh Congress. Dimitrov's proposal, which was supported by Togliatti, Manuilsky, and Kuusinen, was strongly opposed by Béla Kun, Lozovsky, Knorin, and Varga.[60] The Seventh Congress was postponed.[61] In the end, however, it was agreed that the appellation "social fascist" could be applied only to some of the Social Democratic leaders.

By October 1934, the Comintern at last changed its line; the Seventh Congress was convoked for the following summer. The French party already had veered strongly toward a united "antifascist" front. Yet a strong faction of the German party, which in all likelihood was reflecting Stalin's thinking, insisted on pursuing the old course. The struggle continued till January 1935, when the two KPD factions, during a conference sponsored by the Comintern, came to physical blows over the party line on Nazism.[62] The issue was finally resolved by the Seventh Congress and the adoption of "Trojan Horse" tactics. At the Sixth Congress of the Socialist Unity Party of Germany, in 1963, entirely forgetting that in earlier years he himself had opposed the policy of "primitive anti-fascism," Ulbricht made a partial disclosure of the truth. He averred that together with Georgi Dimitrov, Maurice Thorez, Palmiro Togliatti, Klement Gottwald, Harry Pollitt, and Wilhelm Pieck, he had worked for a policy of a United Front against Hitler, but that he had encountered the resistance of prominent Communist leaders. No doubt, the main resistance came from Stalin.

Contrary to Stalin's hopes and expectations, the Nazi accession produced no immediate conflict between Germany and the Western powers. Instead it resulted in Hitler's reintroduction of conscription, occupation of the Rhineland, annexation of Austria and the Sudetenland—all without effective Anglo-French opposition. Even more ominous, ties between Berlin and Warsaw seemed to be growing ever tighter, especially at the time of Munich.

Since no other policy was feasible, Stalin turned to the "United Front from above"—cooperation with Western democrats and some Socialist parties. The Soviet Union had joined the League of Nations and at Geneva Maxim Litvinov preached eloquent sermons on the indivisibility of peace and the necessity of resisting aggression. The Communist parties of Europe assisted in this campaign to encourage resistance to Germany. The Comintern played a major role in temporary Soviet support of the Loyalists during the Spanish Civil War.

Finally, on March 31, 1939, the British government gave a guarantee to Poland and on April 13 a similar guarantee to Rumania. This meant that Hitler could no longer attack the USSR through these countries without becoming involved in a major war with Britain and France. Stalin immediately returned to his policy of 1932 and early in 1939 made the first feelers that were to result in the Nazi-Soviet Pact of August 23. On May 3 he sacked Litvinov, the champion of collective security—peace was no longer indivisible.

There was initially no concept, let alone a plan, that would have tied together the hopes of the early twenties with the realizations of the late forties. The concepts that did exist had to be modified and sometimes abandoned. In the face of failures and successes, the Communists learned that strategy requires more than concepts and plans, and that success is predicated upon undogmatic improvisations to exploit unexpected opportunities. A strategic maneuver, including its underlying concepts, evolves as it is being executed. It results from intent and singleness of purpose, which, over a long period of time, are applied to reality through frequently changing plans and flexible operations. Nevertheless central ideas inherited from Lenin dominated Stalin's strategic thinking:

(1) The defense of the Soviet Union is the paramount task, and an attack against the still-weak "Socialist Fatherland" must be avoided.

(2) For this reason one must exacerbate or create "contradictions" between the enemies of Communism, and instigate wars among the main "imperialist" powers.

(3) The many different forces serving Communism, directly or indirectly, must be controlled from a central command post, which necessarily will be located in Moscow.

(4) Communist parties must be organized in as many countries as possible, and each party should be given specific tasks.

(5) In time of war, the main tasks of the Communist parties in enemy countries are to weaken the existing state structure, to obtain alliances with one or another of the "imperialist" blocs, to facilitate the military victory of Communist forces, and ultimately to seize power from the "capitalists."[63]

In a word, Communist strategy was on the one hand to stabilize the Communist regime inside the Soviet Union, and on the other to unsettle the international situation and incite war between the non-Communist great powers. In this strategy, which displayed "contradictions" of its own and which should not be misconstrued as a simple linear development of a central concept, the Comintern, after an initial phase of relative independence, served as a tool of Soviet statecraft.

The Sixth Congress, convoked after Trotsky's final defeat, marked a major turning point in the history of world Communism. It was then that the predominance of the Russian party over the world movement was definitely established by Stalin. The necessity for unity of command doomed the autonomy of individual Communist parties. The obvious drawback of this change was that henceforth national parties found it difficult to operate successfully because, to paraphrase Khrushchev, their clocks had to be synchronized with Moscow and could but rarely be synchronized with the political environment in which they were functioning.

But even the highly disciplined, "Bolshevized" Communist movement could not be switched and zigzagged as easily from thesis to antithesis as the laws of dialectics demand. There is an ideological time lag, and there is "friction" that precludes utter disregard of the political formula. The dialectics of revolution are *not* restricted to strategy and tactics, but also embrace ideas and traditions. Their preconceptions disposed the idealistic Communists to support the Social Democrats rather than the Nazis. But one of the essential points of dialectics, as Lenin commented on Hegel, is to recognize the necessity of "the jump," and of the interruption of gradual processes. Without the Comintern and without its ability to suppress the "spontaneity" of the KPD, the "jump" needed to implement Soviet strategy never could have been performed. It is easy to see how the contradictions between ideology, reality, strategy, and power ultimately eliminated ideology as an independent force, and led to the mass homicide of Communists at the hands of Stalin. These contradictions also paved the way for the Nazi attack on the USSR.

If Stalin had foreseen his predicament of 1941 and 1942, he might have changed his policy in 1932. But he weathered the storm, partly because of Soviet military strength, partly because of his alliance with Britain and the United States, and partly because the foreign Communist parties had been psychologically effective and had carried out some of the practical tasks assigned them by the Sixth Congress. Communist rear warfare was far from being as potent as the planners had hoped. But in a considerable number of countries, the Communists were able to mount successful operations, and they were far better prepared for guerrilla warfare than other resistance groups.

The Comintern served the world revolution well. Never before had the world experienced strategy so astute and complex, and never were operational concepts executed with greater skill and more cynicism. There was defeat in victory, and the Comintern did not survive the war. But Communist power arose from the ashes of Communist parties. It was all in line with the insight which Lenin drew from Hegel's philosophy of history: "Dialectics equals the destroying of oneself."

# Notes

# Notes

## The Rise and Fall of the First International

1. The most important published collections of documents relating to the First International are the following: (1) *Répertoire international des sources pour l'étude des mouvements sociaux aux XIXe et XXe siècles: La Première Internationale.* 3 vols. (Paris, 1958–63). Hereafter cited as *Répertoire*; (2) *La Première Internationale.* Documents published under the direction of Jacques Freymond, with text presented by Henri Burgelin, Knut Langfeldt, and Miklós Molnár. 2 vols. (Geneva, 1962). Hereafter cited as Freymond, *La Première Internationale*; (3) *The General Council of the First International, 1864–1866, The London Conference, 1865: Minutes,* Vol. I. (Moscow, 1962). Hereafter cited as *Minutes*; and (4) *Archives Bakounine:* I, *Michel Bakounine et l'Italie.* Edited and with an introduction by Arthur Lehning. 2 vols. (Leiden, 1961–63).

2. See E. E. Fribourg, *L'Association internationale des travailleurs* (Paris, 1871).

3. Howell's letter to Morrisson, undated, but in answer to a letter of April 29, 1872. Howell Collection, Bishopsgate Institute, London.

4. See *Dokumente des Sozialismus* Vol. V (Berlin, 1905), No. 7, pp. 324–29, and No. 8, pp. 373–77.

5. Pierre Vésinier, "Histoire de l'Association internationale des travailleurs" (London, 1872), incomplete ms., 233 pp., plus fragments. Amsterdam, International Institute for Social History.

6. See p. 161 of David Riazanov's study, "Zur Geschichte der ersten Internationale: Die Entstehung der Internationalen Arbeiterassoziation," *Marx-Engels-Archiv,* Band I, pp. 119–202.

7. Edmund Silberner, "Neues Material zur Geschichte der Genfer Espérance," *International Review of Social History,* Vol. VIII (1963), Part 3, p. 447.

8. Jacques Freymond, "Etude sur la formation de la Première Internationale," *Revue d'histoire suisse,* Vol. XXX (1950), No. 1, pp. 1–45.

9. See Bordage's letter to Vésinier, in the archives of the Amsterdam International Institute for Social History.

10. Theodor Rothstein, "Aus der Vorgeschichte der Internationale." Supplements to *Die Neue Zeit,* No. 17 (October 31, 1913), 44 pp.; Arthur Mueller-Lehning, "The International Association (1855–1859): A Contribution to the Preliminary History of the First International," *International Review for Social History,* III (1938), 185–284; and Riazanov, "Zur Geschichte der Ersten Internationale."

11. Riazanov, "Zur Geschichte," p. 120.

12. Rothstein, "Aus der Vorgeschichte," pp. 4–5. At a session of the General Council of the IWA on July 12, 1870, where the question of moving the Council headquarters from London to Brussels was aired, Marx made a remark that supports Rothstein's thesis that "the first International Association had been established at Brussels, and the *Fraternal Democrats* of London had been a branch of it." Unpublished minutes, July 12, 1870.

13. Mueller-Lehning, "The International Association," p. 185.

14. Freymond, *Etude,* p. 40.

15. Georges Duveau, *La Vie ouvrière en France sous le Second Empire* (Paris, 1946), p. 550.

16. Fribourg, *L'Association internationale,* pp. 29–30.

17. *Ibid.,* p. 30.

18. *Ibid.*

19. An excellent analysis of this period is given in Richard Hostetter, *The Italian Socialist Movement, Vol. I: Origins (1860–1882)* (Princeton, N.J., 1958).

20. *The General Council of the First International, 1864–1866: Minutes,* p. 263.

21. *Ibid.,* pp. 251–60.

22. Procès-verbaux de l'Association Internationale des Travailleurs, Section de La Chaux-de-Fonds (17 avril 1866–13 juin 1868). Ms. For excerpts from this document, see Jules Humbert-Droz's study in *Etudes et documents sur la Première Internationale en Suisse* (Geneva, 1964).

23. The unpublished minutes of the Brussels section are in the archives of the International Institute for Social History. Boris I. Nicolaevsky kindly allowed us to consult his personal copy.

24. *Minutes,* p. 127. An analogous incident arose at the beginning of 1865 between the Paris office, headed by Tolain and Fribourg, and the General Council, with Le Lubez venting his hostility to Tolain. See Fribourg, pp. 25–26, and *Minutes,* pp. 71ff. This affair was not settled as quickly and clearly as Fribourg alleged.

25. Louis Bertrand, *Histoire de la démocratie et du socialisme en Belgique depuis 1830.* 2 vols. Brussels, 1906–7; Hélène Collin-Dajch, *Contribution à l'étude de la Première Internationale à Bruxelles (1865–1873).* Extract from *Cahiers bruxellois,* Vol. I, fasc. II (1956), pp. 109–46; and Jan Dhondt, "De Socialistische beweging 1865–1875," in *Geschiedenis van de socialistische arbeidersbeweging in Belgie* (Antwerp, n.d.), No. 8, pp. 227–46.

26. An interesting analysis of the origin of the factions in the Spanish labor

movement is given in Salvador de Madariaga, *Spain: A Modern History* (New York, 1958), pp. 143–55 (chapter on labor).

27. *Minutes,* p. 50, session of November 22, 1864.

28. *Minutes,* p. 164, session of February 6, 1866.

29. Excerpts from these minutes have been published in *La Première Internationale en Suisse* (Geneva, 1964). *Der Vorbote,* organ of the central section to which all the German-speaking sections belonged, reported, upon Fanelli's return to Geneva, the fact that "at the initiative of the international Social Democratic Alliance strong central sections were founded in Madrid and Naples, whose most immediate task is to establish new sections everywhere in Spain and Italy" (February 1869, p. 26).

30. W. Tcherkessov, *Les Précurseurs de l'Internationale* (Brussels, 1899).

31. Letter of June 20, 1873, to Bebel; Marx and Engels, *Ausgewählte Briefe* (Berlin, 1953), p. 337.

32. See Miklós Molnár, *Le Déclin de la Première Internationale,* Publications de l'Institut universitaire de hautes études internationales No. 42 (Geneva, 1963), 258 pp.

33. *Briefe und Auszuege aus Briefen von Joh.-Phil. Becker, Jos. Dietzgen, Friedrich Engels, Karl Marx, u.A. an F.A. Sorge und Andere* (Stuttgart, 1921), pp. 138–41.

34. See Marx and Engels, *Briefwechsel* (Berlin, 1950), IV, 233–39, letter of November 4, 1864.

35. Karl Marx and Friedrich Engels, *Letters to Americans, 1848–1895: A Selection* (New York, 1953), p. 65.

36. The influence Marx assigns to Lincoln's policies on world developments is brought out by the sequel of the letter cited above: "If you consider, dear uncle, how at the time of Lincoln's election the only issue was *not to make any further concessions to the slave owners,* whereas now the *abolition of slavery* is the avowed and partly already realized aim, it must be admitted that such a gigantic revolution was *never* carried out so fast. It will have the most beneficial influence on the whole world." Werner Blumenberg, "Ein unbekanntes Kapitel aus Marx' Leben," *International Review of Social History,* Vol. I (1956), letter No. 23, p. 107.

37. "The local French branch ... will have to be expelled from the International. The ranters of all nations cannot be allowed to endanger the International Association just when it is beginning to gain real power as a result of events on the Continent." Marx to Engels, July 7, 1868.

38. Resolution of the General Council of March 9, 1869. Freymond, *La Première Internationale,* II, 271.

39. Letter of November 28, 1871, to Friedrich Bolte, quoted in *ibid.,* Introduction, p. xx.

40. *Ibid.,* II, 236.

41. *Briefe und Auszuege aus Briefen von Joh.-Phil. Becker, et al.,* p. 119.

42. Reproduced by Ernst Schräpfer, "Der Zerfall der Ersten Internationale

im Spiegel des 'Neuen Social-Demokrat,'" in *Archiv fuer Sozialgeschichte, Jahrbuch der Friedrich-Ebert Stiftung,* III (1963), 509–59.

43. *Ibid.*, p. 523.

44. Letter from Engels to Liebknecht of December 15, 1871, in *Wilhelm Liebknecht, Briefwechsel mit Karl Marx und Friedrich Engels,* herausgegeben u. bearbeitet v. G. Eckert (The Hague, 1963), p. 146.

45. *Ibid.*, p. 167. The letter is dated May 15, 1872, but was probably written May 22.

*Secret Societies and the First International*

1. Typical examples of their attitudes toward masonry are cited by Gustave Lefrançais, in his *Souvenirs d'un révolutionnaire* (Brussels, 1902). Several examples of how revolutionaries (especially the Blanquists) manipulated masonic lodges toward the end of the 1860's are given by Maurice Dommanget in *Blanqui et l'opposition révolutionnaire à la fin du Second Empire* (Paris, 1960), pp. 141–43.

2. See Nettlau's article "Zur Vorgeschichte der Internationale" in *Dokumente des Sozialismus* (Berlin, 1905), Vol. V.

3. The most important recent publication on the subject is the article by Professor Jean Bossu, "Une loge de proscrits à Londres sous le Second Empire et après la Commune" in the January–October 1958 issues of *L'Idée libre,* a now-defunct monthly magazine published in Herblay (Seine-et-Oise), distributed only to members of French masonic lodges. I am deeply grateful to Professor Bossu for having graciously provided me with photocopies of his article.

4. The name was altered several times. In 1857 the documents of the Lodge of the Philadelphians bore the heading "L'Ordre Maçonnique Réformé de Memphis." Toward the end of the 1860's the documents speak of "le rite universel."

5. Bossu, pp. 22, 301. A number of general works on masonry provide information on Marconi and the early history of the Philadelphians. See, for example, Albert Lantoine, *Histoire de la Franc-maçonnerie française: La Franc-maçonnerie chez-elle* (Paris, 1925), pp. 294–97 and *passim.*

6. See *Freemasons' Magazine and Masonic Mirror* (London), August 27, 1859, pp. 150–51.

7. These data were supplied by the Lodge itself in its polemic with England's conservative Masons. *Ibid.*, pp. 103–34.

8. His list is far from exhaustive.

9. We must consider the meeting it organized on June 13, 1852, as the first appearance of the Commune; see Edouard Renard's *Louis Blanc* (Paris, 1922), p. 186. The first leaflets of La Commune Révolutionnaire were dated August 1852; see reports on the Paris trial of La Commune Révolutionnaire in July 1853, in Charles de Bussy, *Les Conspirateurs en Angleterre, 1848–1858* (Paris, 1858), p. 341.

10. The name "La Grande Loge des Philadelphes" appeared on the letter-

head of the certificate the Lodge issued on September 9, 1857, to its member Melchior Volksmuth. I am citing a photocopy of the original.

11. Louis Blanc's *Histoire de dix ans* indicates that he was well informed about the affairs of the secret societies of the 1830's, and that his information could not have stemmed solely from knowledge of published sources. In particular, it indicates that he was familiar with the relations between these societies and "regular" masonry. The appropriate passages in Louis Blanc's work have been used more than once against the masons in the literature on the subject; see Paul Fesch and Joseph Denais, *Bibliographie de la Franc-maçonnerie et des sociétés secrètes* (Paris, 1912), I, 153.

12. These papers were used extensively in Edouard Renard's *Louis Blanc* (Paris, 1922).

13. See, for example, Emmanuel Rebold, *Histoire des trois Grandes Loges* (Paris, 1864), p. 597.

14. Bossu, pp. 180, 301. The official name of this Supreme Council was "Le Conseil des Sublimes Maîtres du Grand Oeuvre," according to Albert Lantoine, p. 297; in England it became "Le Grand Conseil de l'Ordre Maçonnique Réformé de Memphis" (according to the certificate of the Philadelphians cited in Note 10 above).

15. Arthur Mueller-Lehning, "The International Association (1855–59)" in the *International Review for Social History* (Leiden, 1938), III, 185–286. The citation is from p. 285.

16. A. Luzio, *Carlo Alberto e Giuseppe Mazzini* (Turin, 1923), p. 246. Luzio gives special attention to Mazzini's terrorist activities.

17. *Procès et Biographie du Dr. S. Bernard avec la défense complète de son avocat, Mr. Edwin James, Q.C.*, ed. Henry Bender (London, 1858), 30 pp.

18. "L'Attentat du 14 janvier," in *Bulletin de l'Association Internationale*, No. 10 (March 1, 1958), p. 1. A facsimile of this page is given in the appendices to the Mueller-Lehning article cited in Note 15 above.

19. Hypathie Bradlaugh-Bronner, *Biography of Bradlaugh*, 7th ed. (London, 1908), I, 204. This biography also reveals that Bernard was a prominent member of the Lodge of the Philadelphians, and that it was under his sponsorship that Bradlaugh was admitted to the Lodge. Bernard's obituary can also be found in *National Reformer*, December 6 and 13, 1862.

20. Bossu, p. 180.

21. Mueller-Lehning, p. 280.

22. Edmund Silberner, *Moses Hess Briefwechsel* (The Hague, 1959), p. 363.

23. Data on the Legion are taken from the article by Johann-Philipp Becker, "Polen, die Diplomatie und die Revolution" in *Nordstern* (Hamburg, Nos. 219–23, July 1863). Becker himself took part in Garibaldi's movement, made trips to Italy, etc. He, too, was undoubtedly a mason: how else can one explain the fact that Mazzini addressed him as "Dear Brother"? See letter of June 1861, published by Rheingold Ruegg in *Neue Zeit*, VI (1888), 458.

24. Bossu, p. 181.

25. Bradlaugh-Bronner, I, 204.

26. At that time, personal relations between Garibaldi and Mazzini were far from good, but of course I cannot go into this here.

27. This information is found in the editorial note commenting on Pierre Coullery's letter in *La Rive Gauche,* November 26, 1865. The note is signed "L. F.," which undoubtedly stands for Léon Fontaine, who was directly involved in the organization of the Brussels Congress; Garibaldi's letter gave Fontaine's home address to arriving delegates.

28. Data on the congress are taken primarily from documents in the Vienna Staatsarchiv, Informationsbureau 9191/B.M.

29. See Marx's letter to Engels of April 19, 1864. Marx was informed about this congress by Joseph Valentin Weber, who was there as a delegate of the Deutscher Arbeiter Bildungs Verein of London.

30. *La France Libre et Garibaldi* (London, 1864), 18 pp.

31. At the September 25, 1865, conference of the International in London, César De Paepe said, "Two years ago an International Association was formed, but it had too much of the middle-class element in it. It broke up." *The General Council of the First International* (Moscow, 1961), p. 238. Even more explicit was Johann-Philipp Becker, who May 30, 1867, wrote to Friedrich Albert Sorge: "In 1862 I was among the initiators of the international democratic congress, from which in 1864 emerged the International Workingmen's Association." *Pis'ma K. Marksa, Fr. Engel' sa i dr. k' F. Zorge i dr.* (St. Petersburg, 1908), p. 5.

32. I must note here that I have at my disposal only the draft of the Alliance's Statutes, which accompanied Garibaldi's letter of invitation to the congress of September 7, 1863, in the copy in the Vienna Staatsarchiv. The actual text of the statutes adopted by the congress is unknown, and I have not chanced on it in any archival deposit.

33. Brussels, so far as I know, was the only city where a Belgian section of the Alliance was organized, in the winter of 1863–64. On April 6, 1864, it sent an address to Garibaldi; a note on this appeared in the Brussels *Tribune du Peuple* of April 17, 1864, p. 2.

34. We know that Joseph Goffin, author of *Histoire populaire de la Franc-maçonnerie* (Spa, 1862), in 1857 founded in Vervier, Belgium, the lodge "Les Libres Penseurs," which was under the supervision of the Lodge of the Philadelphians in London (letters of Georges de Froidcourt of Liège, historian of Belgian Freemasonry, to the present author). Subsequently Goffin lived for some time in London, and was secretary of the Grand Lodge of the Philadelphians.

35. In the Circular Letter "Rundschreiben der deutschen Abteilung des Zentralkommitees der Internationalen Arbeiter Association für die Schweiz an die Arbeiter" (Geneva, November 1865, printed in *Nordstern,* Hamburg, January 13, 1866), Johann-Philipp Becker defined the International Workingmen's Association as "in its form and its effect, an up-to-date, rejuvenated, vigorous Freemasonry of the working class."

36. Sometime later Pierre Vésinier wrote that Le Lubez "selected and proposed" to the meeting September 28, 1864, a list of members of the General Council, which was approved. (See the article "Congrès de Genève," in the Brussels newspaper *L'Espiègle,* January 13, 1867.) A confederate and personal friend of Le Lubez, Vésinier undoubtedly based this assertion on what Le Lubez himself had told him.

37. Biographical data are especially sparse for the English members, who were a majority (75 per cent) of the General Council. We have almost no information on the connections of these members with the so-called Freethinkers, who formed the radical wing of English Freemasonry and were connected with the French Philadelphians. Victor Le Lubez was himself active in the Freethinkers, and undoubtedly induced some of them to take part in the International.

38. The list is derived from an address to President Abraham Lincoln signed by all the members of the General Council on November 29, 1864. (At that time nearly all the Italians were Mazzinists.) For more detail on Holtorp, see Note 46 below.

39. For example, the German Heinrich Bolleter was among them.

40. Marx to Engels, November 4, 1864.

41. Le Lubez's note is quoted by Nettlau, in *Dokumente des Sozialismus,* V, 326.

42. Marx and Engels, *Sochinyeniya,* 2d ed., Vol. XVI (Moscow, 1960), p. 644, Note 14.

43. The protocols state that nine were elected, but several lines later they mention the supplementary inclusion in the subcommittee of Constantin Bobczyńsky as a representative of the Poles. Moreover, the list does not mention the Council's Secretary-General, William Randal Cremer, who was a member of the subcommittee by virtue of his secretarial office.

44. Marx informed Engels about this committee in a letter dated May 17, 1866. On Holtorp and Langewicz, see Note 46 below.

45. See, for example, the account of the trial of Trabucco, Greco, and others in *Complot des Italiens: Attentat contre la vie de l'Empereur* (Paris, 1864), 137 pp.

46. The question of the participation of Polish groups in the International in its first phase, i.e. before the September 1865 London conference, is one of the most important unstudied questions in the history of the International. Emile Holtorp, who throughout this period was the Corresponding Secretary of the General Council for Poland, remains a mysterious figure. Apart from Marx's report of Holtorp's adherence to Mazzini's International Republican Committee (see Note 44), the only other place his name appears is in the minutes of the General Council. It is not even known precisely which group he represented in the International. His name was not mentioned in the press, not even in the Polish *Glos Wolny* (published in London from 1863 to 1866), which devoted much space to the Polish émigré colony in London. But *Glos Wolny* does enable us to establish which group Holtorp represented in the General Council.

Garibaldi's arrival in London in April 1864 set off intense struggle within the Polish colony. The two main older groups of Polish émigrés—the "aristocrats," supporters of Count Czartoryski, and the "democrats," headed by Ludwig Oborski, Antoni Zabicki, and others—drafted a joint address to Garibaldi, which was approved by a large majority at a meeting on April 7 and presented to Garibaldi at the April 18 meeting in the Crystal Palace. This address, of course, spoke of support for the Polish uprising, but passed over in complete silence the question of the slogans for the uprising; at this moment the conflict between the "white" and the "red" insurrectionaries, principally over their relationship to the peasantry, was particularly acute.

This struggle found its reflection in London, where a small group, identified by *Glos Wolny* (No. 39, April 21, 1864) as "the self-appointed delegation from Vistula," demanded the adoption of its text of the address to Garibaldi. This address was rejected (only five of the 125–130 participants voted for it) on the ground that it was then necessary "not to write international manifestos" and not "to create small international committees," but to organize a movement supporting "the fight that Poland is leading." Nevertheless, the authors of the second address went ahead on their own, and were received separately by Garibaldi.

I have been unable to find the text of this second address. In 1962, however, the "Manifesto of the Polish Revolutionary Center in London" was published in Moscow (*Slavianskii Arkhiv,* pp. 244–46). This "Manifesto" undoubtedly reflects the disputes around the reception of Garibaldi and originated with the group that formulated the second address. Dated April 19, 1864, it sets down the conditions under which the "Center" will cooperate with other Polish émigré groups, and names Stanislaw Frankowski and Ludwig Bulewski as the persons authorized by it to carry on negotiations with these groups. These names make it clear that the "Center" was actually connected with the Warsaw Revolutionary Government (Frankowski was a delegate of that government), and that at the same time this "Center" was the erstwhile Polish nucleus of the "Alliance Républicaine Universelle," which Bulewski formed later. Holtorp entered the International through the "Center," and his joining Mazzini's International Republican Committee followed from his connection with that group.

The question of Marian Langewicz is more complicated. The Institute of Marxism-Leninism in Moscow describes him as "one of the leaders of the conservative landowner wing" in the Polish 1863 insurrection, which makes his joining Mazzini's committee seem completely absurd. But, though we know very little about Langewicz, we do know that he was never a conservative or a representative of the landowners. Langewicz, who was a prominent figure in the military school founded by Garibaldi in Genoa in 1860 for the training of military cadres to lead revolutionary national uprisings, gave every indication of being a "technician," who judged this kind of movement by its chances of success, and for whom the program was only secondary. Furthermore, he had been incorrectly informed that the Warsaw Government would welcome him as a dictator. Langewicz spent only eight days as dictator;

having learned the truth about Warsaw's attitude toward him, he left the country and almost deserted the Revolutionary Government. Once abroad, however, he joined the "reds," in whose camp he had previously enlisted, rather than the "whites," and established contact with Garibaldi and close ties with Bulewski's organizations. His joining Mazzini's International Republican Committee was thus a completely natural step.

47. At the time, the Blanquists spoke about this openly. The first Russian group of Blanquists plainly wrote that the real reason for transferring the General Council to New York was the concern of the Marxists "that the Blanquists should not achieve a dominating influence, that they should not turn the International from that legal ground on which they were trying to keep it." [From the introduction to the Russian edition of the brochure *Internatsional i revolutsiya* (Geneva, 1876).] This brochure (*Internationale et révolution: A propos du Congrès de la Haye par des réfugiés de la Commune, ex-membres du Conseil général de l'Internationale,* London, 1872) is a protest by the London group of Blanquists, adopted September 15, 1872, of the decision of the Hague Congress of the International. This group included Antoine Arnaud, F. Cournet, Margueritte, Constant Martin, Gabriel Ranvier, and Edouard Vaillant; its author, so far as we were able to determine, was Ranvier. At the time, this group actually headed the French section of the International in London, the same one that was organized in 1865 and was headed by Le Lubez. Ranvier was not only a member of that group, he was also connected with the Philadelphians (Pierre Vésinier was married to his daughter).

*The Anarchist Tradition*

1. George Plechanoff (Plekhanov), *Anarchism and Socialism* (Chicago, 1907), p. 52.
2. Pierre Joseph Proudhon, *Correspondance,* XIV (Paris, 1875), 218–19 (April 4, 1862).
3. Proudhon, *De la capacité politique des classes ouvrières* (Paris, 1924), p. 386 (original 1865 edition, p. 421).
4. *Ibid.,* p. 398.
5. Max Nettlau, *Der Anarchismus von Proudhon zu Kropotkin* (Berlin, 1927), p. 130.
6. Bakunin, *Gesammelte Werke* (Berlin, 1921–24), III, pp. 123–25.
7. Bakunin, III, 8–63.
8. Bakunin, III, 88. "The revolution, as we understand it, must on its very first day completely and fundamentally destroy the state and all state institutions." See also Nettlau, *Der Anarchismus,* p. 199, where the author quotes a resolution of the Congress of St.-Imier which contains the sentence, "The destruction of all political power is the first duty of the proletariat." That resolution was, according to Nettlau, written by Bakunin.
9. Bakunin, III, 97.
10. Nettlau, p. 112.
11. *Ibid.,* p. 108.
12. Bakunin, III, 84–90.

13. Nettlau, p. 129.

14. *Ibid.*, pp. 107–8, 148.

15. Marx and Engels, *Lés Prétendues Scissions dans l'Internationale* (Geneva, 1872). Private circular of the General Council of the IWA.

16. The equivalent of the expression used in *L'Alliance de la Démocratie Socialiste et L'Association Internationale des Travailleurs,* published anonymously but written by Engels, Lafargue, and Marx (London, 1873).

17. E. Belfort Bax, *Reminiscences and Reflections of Mid and Late Victorian* (London, 1918), pp. 32, 151.

18. Franz Mehring, *Karl Marx: Geschichte seines Lebens* (Leipzig, 1918), p. 491. See also Belfort Bax, *Reminiscences,* p. 151.

19. Nettlau, p. 212.

20. Carlo Cafiero had placed his entire fortune at Bakunin's disposal, to be used for revolutionary purposes.

21. Bakunin, III, 95–97. In this passage Bakunin extols the discipline characterizing the Jesuit order.

22. See Note 14.

23. Max Nettlau, *Anarchisten und Sozialrevolutionäre* (Berlin, 1931), pp. 202–31.

24. *Ibid.*, p. 208.

25. Rudolf Rocker, *Johann Most: Das Leben eines Rebellen* (Berlin, 1924), p. 128.

26. Nettlau, p. 221.

27. *Ibid.*

28. *Ibid.*, p. 227.

29. *Ibid.*

30. Milorad M. Drachkovitch, *Les Socialismes français et allemand et le problème de la guerre* (Geneva, 1953), p. 321.

31. *Résolutions approuvées par le Congrès Anarchiste tenu à Amsterdam, Août 24–31, 1907.* Publiées par le Bureau International (London), p. 7.

32. *Congrès anarchiste, tenu à Amsterdam, Août 1907* (Paris, 1908), p. 82.

33. *Ibid.*, p. 85.

34. Peter Kropotkin, *The Conquest of Bread* (New York, 1927), p. 64.

35. Lewis L. Lorwin, *Labor and Internationalism* (New York, 1929), p. 573.

36. Yuri Steklov, *Mikhail Bakunin* (Moscow, 1926), I, 343.

*The Second International: 1889–1914*

---

1. "Liebknecht was, inevitably, the moving spirit of the Congress." James Joll, *The Second International: 1889–1914* (New York, 1956), p. 37.

2. Quoted in Joll, *The Second International,* p. 56.

3. For the concept of potestas see Bertrand de Jouvenel, *The Pure Theory of Politics* (New Haven, Conn., 1963).

4. This was the argument of Eugène Guérard in 1896. Cf. J. Braunthal, *Geschichte der Internationale,* I (Hanover, 1961), 297.

5. Sorel, *La Décomposition du marxisme,* as quoted in I. L. Horowitz, *Radicalism and the Revolt Against Reason* (New York, 1961), p. 251.

6. On the concept of the "people in insurrection," see Gerhart Niemeyer, "Babeuf and the Total Critique of Society," in *Politische Ordnung und Menschliche Existenz,* Aloys Dempf, Hannah Arendt, and Friedrich Engel-Jánosi, eds. (Munich, 1962), pp. 439f.

7. Quoted in Victor Adler, *Aufsätze, Reden und Briefe,* VII (1929), 114.

8. Quoted in Karl Kautsky, *Der politische Massenstreik* (1914), p. 161.

9. Guenther Roth, *The Social Democrats in Imperial Germany* (Totowa, N.J., 1963). Roth prefers the term "subculture" to Yinger's "contraculture," rightly, in my view.

10. *Ibid.,* p. 124.

11. *Ibid.,* p. 125.

12. Carl E. Schorske, *German Social Democracy* (Cambridge, Mass., 1955), p. 127.

13. *Ibid.,* p. 109. Schorske lists a number of situations created by actions of the ruling circles against the Social Democrats, and the reformist adjustment to these situations as it was determined by the influence of the unions.

14. Joseph Buttinger, *In the Twilight of Socialism* (1956), pp. 56f. Quoted in Roth, *The Social Democrats,* p. 210.

15. *Autobiography of a Working Woman* (1912), p. 120. Quoted in Roth, pp. 207f.

16. Karl Bröger, *Der Held im Schatten* (1930), pp. 135f. Quoted in Roth, pp. 204f.

17. Quoted in Braunthal, *Geschichte,* p. 278.

18. *Ibid.,* p. 204. Cf. also Gustav Mayer, *Friedrich Engels* (New York, 1936), p. 256.

19. For the concept of ersatz religion, see Eric Voegelin, "Religionsersatz," in *Wort und Wahrheit,* XV (January 1960), 5–18; also "Ersatz Religion," in *Politeia,* I, No. 2 (Spring 1964), pp. 2–13.

20. Max Weber, "Parlament und Regierung im neugeordneten Deutschland," in *Gesammelte politische Schriften* (Tübingen, 1958), p. 354.

21. Quoted in Adler, *Aufsätze,* VII, 32.

22. G. D. H. Cole, *History of Socialist Thought,* III (New York, 1956), 55.

23. Quoted in Kautsky, *Sozialisten und Krieg* (Prague, 1937), p. 299.

24. *Ibid.*

25. *Ibid.,* p. 307.

26. *Ibid.,* p. 307.

27. *Ibid.,* p. 306.

28. Mayer, *Friedrich Engels,* p. 311.

29. Carl Landauer, *European Socialism* (Berkeley, Calif., 1959), I, 541.

30. Cf. Cole, *Socialist Thought,* III, 84f.

31. For the concept of the "ideal state" (a parallel to the "ideal," i.e. reasonable, man), see Walter Schiffer, *The Legal Community of Mankind* (New York, 1954), esp. Chapter 7.

32. Landauer, *European Socialism,* I, 540.

33. Mayer, *Friedrich Engels,* p. 277.

34. Landauer, *European Socialism,* I, 491.

35. Adler, *Aufsätze,* VII, 61.

36. Quoted by Milorad M. Drachkovitch, *De Karl Marx à Léon Blum* (Geneva, 1954), p. 25.

37. Cole, *Socialist Thought,* III, 29.

38. Kautsky, *Sozialisten,* p. 317.

39. *Ibid.,* p. 325.

40. Quoted by Drachkovitch, *De Karl Marx,* p. 28.

41. Schorske, *German Social Democracy,* p. 94.

42. Van der Esch, *La Deuxième Internationale* (Paris, 1957), p. 84.

43. Kautsky, *Sozialisten,* p. 361.

44. For the concept of autonomous community, which was created by Joachim of Flora, see Eric Voegelin, *The New Science of Politics* (Chicago, 1952), Chapter 4.

45. Adler, *Aufsätze,* VII, 9.

46. Cole, *Socialist Thought,* III, 9.

47. *Ibid.,* p. 32.

48. Adler, *Aufsätze,* VII, 21ff.

49. Mayer, *Engels,* p. 265.

50. Kautsky, *Sozialisten,* p. 442.

51. Adler, *Aufsätze,* VII, 30.

52. Braunthal, *Geschichte,* I, 337.

53. Drachkovitch, *De Karl Marx,* p. 39, calls Socialism "a protest and not a force."

54. Cole, *Socialist Thought,* III, 379.

55. *Ibid.,* p. 58.

56. Schorske, *German Social Democracy,* pp. 108f.

57. See, for an example, Kautsky, *Sozialisten,* p. 439. Kautsky claimed that he was spared a surprise because of his *"Erkenntnis der Volksseele."*

*Social Democracy*

---

1. See Rudolf Meyer, *Der Emanzipationskampf des Vierten Standes,* I (Berlin, 1874), 159–60. Since no fully reliable primary sources on this address are available, it is important that Friedrich Engels expressed the same thought in his criticism of the Erfurt Program of German Social Democracy. The criticism was posthumously published in *Die neue Zeit* (1901–2), XX, 1; see also Karl Marx, *Kritik des Gothaer Programms* (Berlin, 1946), p. 75 (Appendix: "Engels ueber das Erfurter Programm). Engels, of course, was fully aware of Marx's motives, and in his critique of the Erfurt Program spoke not only in his own name but as the intellectual heir of Karl Marx; therefore his statement precludes the otherwise plausible assumption that Marx spoke as he did at Amsterdam with a tactical purpose in mind, i.e. to relieve government pressure on various sections of the International in the post-Commune atmosphere of persecution.

2. "Blanqui puts his faith (*fait fond*) primarily in the revolutionary minority, although he has always sought, appealed for, and expected the support of the great mass of people. He puts his faith in the minority to conquer power and to keep it after the victorious insurrection. But the work of education (*lumières*) which he expects of the revolutionary dictatorship, and without which he cannot imagine the advent of Communism, implies,

nevertheless, a desire to win the support of the masses." Maurice Dommanget, *Les Idées politiques et sociales d'Auguste Blanqui* (Paris, 1957), p. 402. It is Dommanget's belief that the differences between Marxism and Blanquism are not as great as some authors assume; he therefore was certainly not inclined to overstate the emphasis placed by Blanqui on the role of the revolutionary minority.

3. Karl Marx and Friedrich Engels, *Communist Manifesto* (New York, 1933), p. 73.

4. *Ibid.*, p. 92.

5. Karl Marx, *The Class Struggles in France* (New York, 1924), p. 24.

6. *Communist Manifesto*, p. 93.

7. The classical study of the influence of the Russian Revolution of 1905 on German Social Democracy is Carl Schorske, *German Social Democracy: 1905–1917* (Cambridge, Mass., 1955). Aside from the existence of the Prussian problem, to which the Russian method of a mass strike seemed to offer a solution, the presence of Russian leftist émigrés in Germany might have been to some extent responsible for that influence. Since Russian émigrés also lived in Paris in large numbers, it might be worth investigating their influence upon French Social Democracy; to the best of my knowledge, no such investigation exists.

8. The term was first used in this context by Günther Roth, in his book *The Social Democrats in Imperial Germany* (Totowa, N.J., 1963), pp. 159ff.

9. See especially Jean Jaurès, "Organisation socialiste," *La Revue socialiste*, XXI–XXII (1895); and Karl Kautsky, *Am Tage nach der Sozialen Revolution* (Berlin, 1902).

10. For a survey of this debate, with references to the most important literature on the subject, see Carl Landauer, *European Socialism* (Berkeley, Calif., 1959), II, 1602ff.

11. See Eduard Bernstein, *Evolutionary Socialism*, trans. by Edith C. Harvey (New York, 1909), p. 165; or better—because the translation of the quote from Schiller is inadequate—the German original: *Die Voraussetzungen des Sozialismus und die Aufgaben der Sozialdemokratie* (Stuttgart, 1906), p. 140.

*The Third International*

1. "The First International laid the foundation of the proletarian, international struggle for Socialism. The Second International marked the epoch in which the soil was prepared for a broad, mass, widespread movement in a number of countries. The Third International gathered the fruits of the work of the Second International, purged it of its opportunist, social-chauvinist, bourgeois and petty-bourgeois dross, and *has begun to effect* the dictatorship of the proletariat." Lenin, "The Third International and Its Place in History," an article written on April 15, 1919, and published in Lenin's *Selected Works* (New York, 1938), X, 31. Italics in the text.

2. In his *Diary in Exile, 1935* (Cambridge, Mass., 1958), p. 46, Trotsky in-

sisted that without Lenin "there would have been no October Revolution." For an illuminating discussion of the same subject, see Sidney Hook, *The Hero in History* (Boston, 1943), particularly Chapter X, "The Russian Revolution: A Test Case," pp. 184–228.

3. In a letter to Lenin dated September 27, 1914, Karpinsky disagreed with Lenin in the name of the Geneva section of the Bolsheviks: "The International has not perished, and cannot perish. There is no treason in the base sense of the word, merely a temporary preponderance of opportunism." Quoted in Olga Hess Gankin and H. H. Fisher, *The Bolsheviks and the World War* (Stanford, Calif., 1940), p. 149.

4. From Lenin's article "False Speeches About Freedom," written between November 4 and December 11, 1920, and published in the December 1920 issue of the journal *Kommunisticheskii Internatsional,* No. 15; also in Lenin's *Selected Works,* X, 257.

5. How greatly the Spartacists differed from Lenin on a central issue may be seen in the following quote from a pamphlet published by the Second District (Pomerania) of the German Communist Party, *Was will der Spartakusbund?* (n.d.), p. 17: "The Spartakusbund will never assume governmental power except through the clear and unequivocal will of the large majority of proletarian masses in Germany, in no other way but through their conscious adherence to the views, aims, and methods of struggle of the Spartakusbund."

6. Hannah Arendt, *The Origins of Totalitarianism* (New York, 1958), p. 331.

7. Lenin, *Selected Works,* I, 338–39.

8. From *"Left-Wing" Communism, An Infantile Disorder,* in *ibid.,* X, 68. Italics in the text.

9. "O mezhdunarodnoi revolutsii," speech made at the Sixth All-Russian Congress of Soviets, session of November 8, 1918. *Sobranie sochinenii* (Moscow, 1922), XV, 550, 555.

10. "Perspektivy proletarskoi revolutsii," *Kommunisticheskii Internatsional,* I (May 1, 1919), 38.

11. In April 1920, for example, Lenin wrote that "conditions for the successful proletarian revolution are obviously maturing [in England]," and stated that "the Third International has already scored a decisive victory in the short space of one year; it has defeated the Second, yellow, social-chauvinist International." *"Left-Wing" Communism, Selected Works,* X, 127, 134.

12. Zinoviev called this work of Lenin's "the gospel of the proletariat," adding that "for the tactics of Communist parties this work is no less important than Karl Marx's *Kapital* for the theory of Marxism." According to Franz Borkenau, *"Left-Wing" Communism* . . . is perhaps the most powerful thing Lenin has ever written. . . . It is a handbook of revolutionary tactics and as such can sometimes be compared, for force of arguments, realism, directness, and convincing power, with Machiavelli's *Il Principe.*" *The Communist International* (London, 1938), p. 191.

13. *"Left-Wing" Communism, Selected Works,* X, 145.

14. *Ibid.,* p. 146.

15. The excerpts quoted from the Twenty-One Conditions are taken from *ibid.,* pp. 200–206.

16. On the floor of the Second Comintern Congress, on July 30, 1920, Serrati pleaded with the ECCI not to force an ill-timed split in Italian Socialist forces: "Esteemed comrades, leave the Italian Socialist Party the possibility of choosing the appropriate moment to purge its own ranks. We all assure you—and I don't believe that anyone can say we have ever broken our word—that the purge will be thorough, but please leave us the possibility of carrying it out in a way that will be helpful to the masses of the workers, to the party, and to the revolution that we are preparing in Italy." *Der Zweite Kongress der kommunistischen Internationale.* Protokoll der Verhandlungen (Hamburg, 1921), p. 346. When on October 14, 1920, Serrati defended the same viewpoint in a letter published in *L'Humanité,* Lenin assailed his stand as "utterly wrong." "False Speeches About Freedom," *Selected Works,* X, 255.

17. *Unser Weg Wider den Putschismus* (Berlin, 1921), pp. 55–56.

18. "Fascism in its Italian, German, or Spanish form was a sort of anti-Communist dictatorship, applying . . . against [Communism] the methods of propaganda, intimidation and repression in which Communism previously claimed a monopoly." Thierry Maulnier, *La face de méduse du communisme* (Paris, 1951), p. 56.

19. *Desiatyi sezd RKP(b)* (Moscow, 1933), pp. 519–20.

20. Lenin, "False Speeches About Freedom," *Selected Works,* X, 259.

21. "In Support of the Tactics of the Communist International," *ibid.,* p. 281. On another occasion Lenin warned that "exaggeration, if it is not corrected, would kill the Communist International for certain." "A Letter to German Communists," written on August 14, 1921, in *ibid.,* p. 297.

22. *Ibid.,* p. 288.

23. "A Letter to German Communists," *ibid.,* p. 297.

24. "Proekt postanovleniya Politburo TsK RKP(b) o taktike Edinogo Fronta," in V. I. Lenin, *Polnoe sobranie sochinenii,* 5th ed. (Moscow, 1964), XLIV, 262.

25. *Protokoll des Vierten Kongresses der Kommunistischen Internationale* (Hamburg, 1923), p. 1026.

26. In a letter of July 9, 1921, to Otto Kuusinen and Wilhelm Koenen, Lenin wrote: "I read with great satisfaction your draft theses on the organizational question. In my opinion you have done a good job." *Polnoe sobranie sochinenii,* 5th ed., XLIV, 56.

27. "Five Years of the Russian Revolution and the Prospects of the World Revolution," *Selected Works,* X, 332–33.

28. In *"Left-Wing" Communism,* Lenin explained why British Communists should vote for the Labour candidate in all constituencies where the Communists did not have their own candidate: "I wanted to support Henderson [British Labour leader] with my vote in the same way as a rope supports the hanged." The establishment of a Labour government would "bring

the masses over to my side, and will accelerate the political death of the Hendersons." *Ibid.*, pp. 130–31.

29. *IV vsemirnyi kongress Kommunisticheskogo Internatsionala* (Moscow and Leningrad, 1923), p. 372.

30. "International Situation and Fundamental Tasks," Lenin's report to the Second Comintern Congress, July 19, 1920. *Selected Works,* X, 199.

31. "The Third International and Its Place in History," *ibid.*, p. 34. In his speech of November 8, 1918, before the Sixth All-Russian Congress of Soviets, Lenin reiterated: "The complete victory of Socialist revolution is unthinkable in one country. It requires the most active collaboration of at least several leading countries, among which we cannot count Russia." *Sobranie sochinenii,* XV, 546.

32. *Selected Works,* X, 57.

33. *III vsemirnyi kongress Kommunisticheskogo Internatsionala* (Leningrad, 1922), pp. 186–87.

34. *Protokoll des Vierten Kongresses,* p. 12.

35. Nikolai Bukharin and E. Preobrazhensky, *The ABC of Communism* (London, 1922), pp. 131–32.

36. "Better Fewer, But Better," reproduced in *The Essentials of Lenin* (London, 1947), II, 854.

37. *Thèses et résolutions adoptées au III^me^ congrès de l'Internationale Communiste* (Moscow, 1921), p. 42.

38. In his report on the Comintern submitted to the Fourteenth Congress of the Russian Communist Party, Zinoviev declared that "friends and enemies know that this [Sportintern] contains the future cells of the Red Guards, particularly in Czechoslovakia and Germany."

39. "Our Intelligence Department . . . had given us very definite instructions. We were sent to Germany to reconnoiter, to mobilize elements of unrest in the Ruhr area, and to forge the weapons for an uprising when the proper moment arrived. We at once created three types of organizations in the German Communist Party: the Party Intelligence Service working under the guidance of the Fourth Department of the Red Army; military formations as the nucleus of the future German Red Army; and *Zersetzungsdienst,* small units of men whose function was to shatter the morale of the Reichswehr and the police." W. G. Krivitsky, *In Stalin's Secret Service* (New York and London, 1939), p. 39.

40. Ruth Fischer, *Stalin and German Communism* (Cambridge, Mass., 1948), p. 327.

41. *Ibid.*, p. 338.

42. Including the peasants in the forefront of the revolutionary struggle served the purpose of finding new allies at a time when the Comintern's non-Communist allies were in short supply. The short-lived cooperation between the Krestintern and the Croatian agrarian leader Stjepan Radić is another example of a Comintern maneuver destined to fail.

43. Max Adler, *Métamorphoses de la classe ouvrière* (Paris, 1935), p. 30.

44. "In view of the anti-Leninist line of the Opposition Bloc in the CPSU; in view of the leading role Comrade Zinoviev played as chairman of the Communist International in the carrying out of this false line; in view of the monstrous anti-organizational and factional activities of the Opposition Bloc, unprecedented in the history of the Bolshevik Party; and in view of Comrade Zinoviev's extension of these factional activities to the ranks of the Communist International—the Delegation of the ECCI, meeting in the combined Plenum of the Central Committee and of the Central Control Commission of the CPSU, and acting in accordance with the decisions of the most important sections of the Comintern, has decided it is impossible for Comrade Zinoviev to continue his work at the head of the Comintern." *International Press Correspondence,* Vol. VI, No. 70 (October 28, 1926), p. 1221. Minor stylistic changes have been made here in the official English text.

45. *XIV sezd RKP(b)* (Moscow, 1926), p. 695.

46. *International Press Correspondence,* Vol. VI, No. 41 (May 13, 1926), p. 654.

47. *Ibid.,* Vol. VI, No. 47 (June 17, 1926), p. 768.

48. For a detailed discussion of these points see Conrad Brandt, *Stalin's Failure in China, 1924–1927* (Cambridge, Mass., 1958), Chap. I. Brandt's book offers a particularly interesting discussion of the quarrel between Stalin and Trotsky over China, which shows how both men used "Leninist myths" against their opponent.

49. Quoted by Robert C. North, *Moscow and Chinese Communists* (Stanford, Calif., 1963), p. 96. Stalin's methods of combating political enemies were consistent. He advised Tito in September 1944 to use and "squeeze" King Peter: "You need not restore him forever. Take him back temporarily, and then you can slip a knife into his back at a suitable moment." Vladimir Dedijer, *Tito Speaks* (London, 1953), p. 234.

50. Quoted in Robert C. North and Xenia J. Eudin, *M. N. Roy's Mission to China. The Communist-Kuomintang Split of 1927* (Berkeley and Los Angeles, Calif., 1963), pp. 140–41.

51. See Leonard Schapiro, *The Communist Party of the Soviet Union* (New York, 1959), p. 303.

52. Ignazio Silone, in Richard Crossman, ed., *The God That Failed* (New York, 1949), p. 100.

53. *Protokoll des 6. Weltkongresses der Kommunistischen Internationale* (Berlin, 1929), p. 61.

54. In his report to the so-called "Brussels Conference" of the German Communist Party (which was actually held in Moscow in October 1935), Wilhelm Pieck admitted what he qualified as the "strategic mistake" of the German party in the period before Hitler's coming to power: "We directed our main attack against the Social Democracy at a time when the main attack should have been directed against the fascist movement." *Der neue Weg zum gemeinsamen Kampf für den Sturz der Hitlerdiktatur* (Strasburg, n.d.), pp. 13–14.

55. *Istorijski Arhiv Komunističke Partije Jugoslavije* (Belgrade, 1950), II, 467–68.
56. *XIV sezd RKP(b),* p. 691.
57. Quoted by Schapiro, p. 394.
58. *International Press Correspondence,* Vol. XIV, No. 60 (December 1, 1934), p. 1621.
59. As Lenin fourteen years earlier asked the Communists to "go to the masses," so Dimitrov pleaded now for an "active Bolshevik mass policy," and criticized the existing "isolation of the revolutionary vanguard."
60. *VII Congress of the Communist International* (Moscow, 1939), p. 149. Italics in the text.
61. *Ibid*., p. 586. Italics in the text.
62. Herbert Luethy, "Du pauvre Brecht," *Preuves,* March 1953.
63. Djilas, *Conversations with Stalin* (New York, 1962), p. 57.
64. Arthur Koestler, in *The God That Failed,* p. 44.
65. For a detailed discussion of this problem see Branko Lazitch, "Stalin's Massacre of Foreign Communist Leaders," and Boris Souvarine, "Comments on the Massacre," in Drachkovitch and Lazitch, eds., *The Comintern: Historical Highlights.*
66. It is worth quoting here an excerpt from Stalin's speech at the Second Congress of the Soviets of the Union, on the eve of Lenin's funeral: "In leaving us, Comrade Lenin enjoined on us fidelity to the Communist International. We swear to thee, Comrade Lenin, to devote our lives to the enlargement and strengthening of the union of the workers of the whole world, the Communist International." Quoted in Souvarine, *Stalin,* p. 352.
67. Quoted by Schapiro, pp. 229–30.
68. Louis Fischer, *The Life of Lenin* (New York, Evanston, and London, 1964), p. 527.
69. Borkenau, p. 9.
70. Krivitsky, p. 52.
71. Nobody, in our judgment, has explored the ambiguous legacy of nineteenth-century Marxism with greater clarity than Bertram D. Wolfe in his *Marxism: 100 Years in the Life of a Doctrine* (New York, 1965).
72. Lenin, "The Collapse of the Second International," *Selected Works,* V, 183.
73. Henri DeMan, *The Psychology of Socialism* (London, 1928), p. 418.
74. From Marx's letter to Bolte, written on November 23, 1871. Marx and Engels, *Ausgewaehlte Briefe* (Zurich, 1934), p. 259.
75. From Engels' preface to the 1890 German edition of the Communist Manifesto. *Karl Marx and Frederick Engels: Selected Works* (Moscow, 1962), I, 30–31.
76. From Engels' introduction, written in March 1895, to a reissue of Marx's *The Class Struggles in France: 1848 to 1850.* Marx's and Engels' *Selected Works,* I, 134.
77. *Perezhitoe i peredumannoe* (Berlin, 1923), pp. 221–22.

78. Quoted in Lenin's *"Left-Wing" Communism, Selected Works,* X, 58–59.

79. Lenin's strongest case against the Second International was certainly the discrepancy between the resolution of the Stuttgart Congress (1907) that in the case of war the task of all the Socialist parties was "to make use of the violent economic and political crisis brought about by the war to rouse the people, and thereby to hasten the abolition of capitalist class rule," and the total disregard of that pledge when World War I broke out.

## *The Comintern as an Instrument of Soviet Strategy*

1. *Der Zweite Kongress der Kommunistischen Internationale* (Vienna, 1920), p. 52.

2. According to *Pravda,* February 11, 1928, between 1918 and 1921 the international units included five infantry divisions, three infantry brigades, one cavalry brigade, 55 infantry regiments, four cavalry regiments, 40 separate infantry battalions, and many special units. Czechs, Germans, Rumanians, Serbs, Belgians, Bulgarians, Englishmen, Frenchmen, Swedes, Estonians, Italians, Slovaks, Americans, and, above all, 60,000 Latvians, 50,000 Poles, 80,000 Hungarians, and 50,000 Chinese were serving under the Red banner. Foreign Socialist officers, in addition to commanding occasionally small units, helped to train the Red Army. On later thinking concerning "national" (i.e. non-Russian) troops within the Red Army, see M. W. Frunze, *Ausgewählte Schriften* (Berlin, 1956), pp. 274f.

3. Stalin, *Works,* X (Moscow, 1954), 292–95.

4. Stalin, XI, 209.

5. *International Press Correspondence,* English edition, 1928, p. 1137. Hereafter cited as *Inprecorr.*

6. See, for example, Thomas Bell, *Inprecorr,* pp. 1006 and 1535f; also p. 1590. On pp. 1151f, Yaroslavsky talks about anti-militarist experiences and intelligence activities during the Russian revolution of 1905.

7. *Inprecorr,* p. 1061.

8. *Ibid.,* p. 1008.

9. *Ibid.,* p. 1010.

10. *Ibid.,* p. 1094.

11. *Ibid.,* p. 1096.

12. *Ibid.,* p. 1010.

13. *Ibid.,* p. 1063.

14. *Ibid.,* p. 1064.

15. The concept of infiltration was elaborated during the Seventh World Congress, when it was extended to hostile class warfare organizations in general, including "fascist" groups.

16. Bell in *Inprecorr,* p. 1153.

17. *Ibid.,* p. 1146.

18. *Ibid.,* p. 1586.

19. *Ibid.,* pp. 1588f., 1763. Since the USSR is "the international driving force of proletarian revolution that impels the proletariat of all countries to seize power," national defense in the proletarian countries "is an unfailing

revolutionary duty." Outside the USSR the concept of national defense must be destroyed in favor of slogans for the defense of the proletarian state.

20. Lenin, *Selected Works,* VIII (New York, 1937), 279–80, 282. The full text of this speech was published in the earlier Russian editions of Lenin's works, appearing for the first time in the 1924 edition. In the Second Edition—*Sochineniya,* XXV (Moscow-Leningrad, 1932), 498–513—the text filled 16 large pages (the passages I have quoted are on pp. 498 and 500). In the Fifth Edition, however—*Sochineniya,* XLII (Moscow, 1963), 43–46—the text fills only three much smaller pages. The passages quoted here have been omitted. A note at the end of the Fifth Edition version says that the speech was "printed according to the text of the newspaper *Pravda*" of November 30, 1920, and collated with the stenographic report.

21. *Inprecorr,* p. 1584.

22. Stalin, *Works,* X, 283f.

23. *Ibid.,* XI, 207f.

24. *Inprecorr,* p. 1584.

25. The antecedents of this policy reached back to 1903, of course, and to 1914. On September 20, 1924, Stalin described fascism "as a combat organization of the bourgeoisie which is basing itself on the active support of Social Democracy" (*Works,* VI 252f.). Fascism and Social Democracy were not "antipodes" but "twins." The Kremlin's fury against the Socialists became uncontrollable when, in 1926, the German Social Democrats revealed the arms cooperation between the Red Army and the Reichswehr, and Philip Scheidemann, in the Reichstag, congratulated the Communists: when they were being suppressed by the Reichswehr, they would have the pleasure of knowing that they died under Soviet grenades. The Kremlin was also scornful of the British Labour Party, which had prevented the nine-month strike of British miners from developing into a revolutionary situation. (Remember that Britain was considered the main enemy of the USSR).

26. *Inprecorr,* pp. 878ff. On March 17, 1929, Hermann Matern, a district leader of the KPD, alleged that the Social Democratic parties were preparing "war against the shield of the world revolution." "German social democracy stands in first place in the agitation against proletarian Russia. It has assumed the role of the active organizer and instigator of the imperialist war." *Im Kampf für Frieden, Demokratie und Sozialismus* ([East] Berlin, 1963), I, 42.

27. Carola Stern, *Ulbricht, eine politische Biographie* (Cologne, 1964), p. 59.

28. Marx-Engels-Lenin-Stalin Institute, Berlin, *Zur Geschichte der Kommunistischen Partei Deutschlands* (Berlin, 1955), p. 277.

29. Herbert Wehner, *Erinnerungen* (Bonn, 1957), p. 8 (italics added).

30. Still, within most Communist parties and notably within the German party, there was reluctance to go all-out against the Social Democrats; and influential factions recommended a united front against the right. The Bolshevization of the Communist parties, which at that time was pursued with great ruthlessness (in part through the ECCI), was aimed at those elements who did not agree that the "central thrust" should be directed against the

Social Democrats. "Bolshevization" served to transform each party into an obedient tool of Soviet strategy. Indeed, if the various parties had been given the green light to adopt courses of action to exploit local opportunities, the Comintern would have rapidly slipped from Moscow's control. See Ruth Fischer, *Stalin and German Communism* (Cambridge, Mass., 1948), pp. 396–400, 543. The struggle for the Bolshevization of the foreign parties was closely linked to Stalin's struggle for power inside the Soviet Union.

31. See my *Lenin, the Compulsive Revolutionary* (Chicago, 1964), pp. 262–76.

32. The Rapallo Treaty was approved by German Social Democrats, while the Communists were shocked. The Berlin Treaty was opposed in the Reichstag by only three votes—of dissident Communists (Fischer, pp. 192 and 527).

33. Certainly there had been discontinuities in this continuity. Radek, for example, in 1918 initially advocated revolutionary war against Germany and from time to time (mostly between 1921 and 1923) pleaded for a united front with the German Social Democrats. Late in 1923, when they feared Germany would negotiate successfully with France and Britain, Zinoviev and other Comintern leaders executed a zigzag and ordered an uprising (which almost coincided with Hitler's putsch).

34. Ernst Roehm, *Die Geschichte eines Hochverräters* (Munich, 1928), p. 288. The Nazis were operating on the principle, as stated by Goebbels, that they "will not shrink joining forces with Marxism at times," rather than collaborate with "bourgeois parties" (*Berliner Lokal-Anzeiger,* November 19, 1929). Goebbels is reported to have said, sometime after 1933: "There was once a time, before coming to power, when we cooperated with the Communists. And I must say . . . that it was not the worst period. . . . In several respects we were striving for the same things." (Friedrich Christian, Prinz zu Schaumburg-Lippe, *Dr. G., Ein Porträt des Propagandaministers*—Wiesbaden, 1963, p. 122). Prince Schaumburg-Lippe was a youthful admirer of Hitler and Goebbels; in his earlier writings he held back this sort of information.

35. Hermann Weber, ed., *Der Deutsche Kommunismus, Dokumente* (Cologne, 1963), pp. 58–65. The Bolsheviks had wrestled with the national problem in the intraparty disputes before the "split" in 1903 and during the revolution of 1905–6. Before 1914, Lenin and Stalin wrote about the subject and developed their version of the concept of national self-determination. Lenin was preoccupied with national questions during the war, and in 1917 used self-determination slogans, among others, in overthrowing the democratic regime. The quasi-federal concepts underlying the establishment of the Soviet Union and notably the notion that any of the Union Republics could secede from the USSR reflect theoretical concepts frequently and clearly expressed by Lenin and Stalin. This is not the place to investigate the "contradictions" between Communist theory and practice; the point is that Lenin and Stalin attached great significance to the question of national self-determination, and that Stalin did not suddenly discover the national factor.

36. Walter Ulbricht, *Zur Geschichte der deutschen Arbeiterbewegung,* 5th ed., I (Berlin, 1955), 498.

37. *Inprecorr,* October 2, 1930, p. 948f.

38. *XI. Plenum of the Executive Committee of the Communist International: Theses, Resolutions and Decisions* (New York, 1931), p. 18; D. Z. Manuilsky, *The Communist Parties and the Crisis of Capitalism* (New York, 1931), p. 35.

39. Manuilsky, pp. 102f. In 1930 the struggle against Versailles was by no means a particular fight by the German party. On the contrary, this struggle was emphasized by virtually all Communist parties in eastern and central Europe. Even the French Communist Party announced its "full and complete" support of the KPD program (*Die Rote Fahne,* September 4, 1930). Upon seizing power, the proletariat has the duty "immediately to declare the imperialist treaties null and void and refuse to honor their clauses." Hence the French Communists supported "every effort by the national minorities who seek to attach themselves to Soviet Germany." This meant willingness to cede Alsace, which needless to say did not help the Comintern in France. (The various declarations upholding German claims were not printed in the English edition of *Inprecorr.* They do appear in the German-language edition.)

The Italian Communist Party (then in exile) announced that it favored the "complete national liberation" of the "suppressed German and Slavic populations including their secession from the Italian state" (*Die Rote Fahne,* September 10, 1930). The Czechs averred that "millions of German working people" were being oppressed in Czechoslovakia. (*Die Rote Fahne,* September 11, 1930). The Polish Communist Party stated its "complete agreement" with the KPD program, and explicitly favored the return of the Polish parts of Upper Silesia and the so-called "corridor" to Germany (*Die Rote Fahne,* September 9, 1930). In this context the PCP did not mention the plebiscite in Upper Silesia nor that the ethnic composition in the corridor was mixed. In due time, the PCP also promised to liberate Danzig "from the claws of Polish and international imperialism in fraternal alliance with the German proletariat" (*Die Rote Fahne,* May 5, 1932). In brief, the territorial objectives of aggressive German nationalism were approved by the international Communist movement. In fact, this was about the only effective assistance that the radical German nationalists received from abroad.

40. The KPD switched its line within a few days. See Ossip Piatnitzky, *The Work of the Communist Parties of France and Germany and the Tasks of the Communists in the Trade Union Movement* (New York, 1932), pp. 24f.

41. Severing was Minister of the Interior and Social Democrat Otto Braun Prime Minister of Prussia.

42. A shocking incident but not without precedent. As early as 1893 the line had been taken that anti-Semitism was "the last phase of the dying capitalist society." Wilhelm Liebknecht stated at that time: "Yes, Mssrs. anti-Semites, plough and sow, and we Social Democrats will reap. Their successes

are by no means unwelcome to us." Quoted from Edmund Silberner, *Sozialisten zur Judenfrage* (Berlin, 1962), p. 205.

43. *Sammlung der Drucksachen des Preussischen Landtages,* IV. Wahlperiode, Band 764, pp. 204–6; *Sitzungsberichte des Preussischen Landtages,* IV. Wahlperiode, Band 1, cols. 805ff.

44. *Die Kommunistische Internationale,* November 15, 1932, pp. 1195f, and 1208; Otto Kuusinen, *The International Situation and the Tasks of the Sections of the Comintern* (London, 1932), pp. 101–6; *Capitalist Stabilization Has Ended: Theses and Resolutions of the XII Plenum of the Executive Committee of the Communist International* (New York, 1932), p. 21.

45. Ivan Maisky, *Who Helped Hitler?* (London, 1962), p. 15f.

46. Statistisches Reichsamt, *Statistik des Deutschen Reiches,* 434 (Berlin, 1935), 13 and 81.

47. For example, Kurt von Schleicher or another general might have been relied upon to strengthen Germany's military-industrial cooperation with the Soviet Union.

48. National Archives, German Auswärtiges Amt, Büro des Reichministers, Akten betreffend Russland, Serial 2860, reel 1417.

49. Report to Chancellor Brüning on October 20, 1931. Reel 1417, No. D 562237–40.

50. Reel 1417, No. D 562241–46. For an evaluation of this report and further interpretation, see Joseph Korbel, *Poland Between East and West* (Princeton, N. J., 1963), pp. 269–71.

51. About 15 million dollars—reel 1417, No. D 562245f; this document contains intelligence data in addition to the Krumin quotes.

52. Reel 1417, No. D 562233–36.

53. See Walter G. Krivitsky, *In Stalin's Secret Service* (New York, 1939).

54. *Capitalist Stabilization Has Ended,* pp. 7f.

55. *Communist International,* October 1, 1932, pp. 607f.

56. Gustav Hilger and Alfred G. Meyer, *The Incompatible Allies* (New York, 1953), p. 253.

57. Stalin, VII, 13–14. This speech, to the Central Committee of the Party, was first disclosed in 1947.

58. Apparently Stalin expected that his collaboration with the Reichswehr as the foremost "ally" of the Soviet Union would continue regardless of political change in Germany.

59. *Voprosy istorii KPSS,* 1965, No. 7, pp. 83ff.

60. *Probleme des Friedens und des Sozialismus,* 1965, No. 8, as quoted in *Ost-Probleme,* December 3, 1965, p. 747.

61. *Ibid.,* p. 748.

62. Stern, pp. 83 and 317. The KPD was at that time practically defunct, and the French party was the most important non-Russian member of the Comintern.

63. I have been able to discuss in this essay only some aspects of the Soviet alliance with Germany. The second prong of this strategy consisted of attempts to conclude alliances with the West whenever Germany was hostile.

# Index